FANDOM AS CONSUMER COLLECTIVE

BOOK 3 IN THE FRAMES OF FANDOM SERIES

ROBERT V. KOZINETS

HENRY JENKINS

GATEWAY
PLANET PRESS

FRAMES OF FANDOM: THE BOOK SERIES

—

Founded in 2024, Gateway Planet Press is committed to publishing innovative and useful knowledge that reaches beyond the confines of traditional academic presses. Our mission is to deliver accessible, affordable, and high-quality research and teaching resources to scholars, professionals, and curious readers worldwide. By embracing new technologies and fresh perspectives, we seek to foster understanding, inspire critical thought, and spark meaningful change. Many such journeys are possible—let us be your gateway.

First Published 2025 by Gateway Planet Press

Gateway Planet Press, Los Angeles, California

Fandom as Consumer Collective: Book 3 in the Frames of Fandom Series was

Edited by Samuel Boyce Miles

Formatted by Robert V. Kozinets

Indexed by Henry Jenkins and Robert V. Kozinets

Front and Back Covers Designed by Robert V. Kozinets using Google Gemini AI

Final Cover Art by Robert V. Kozinets

ISBN: 979-8-9992083-1-6

PRAISE FOR FANDOM AS CONSUMER COLLECTIVE

"This series is a riotously interdisciplinary inquiry marked most memorably by deep introspection and historically inflected cultural analysis.It explores the engines and pillars of contemporary consumption in a delightfully conversational style.Can't wait for the next installment from the Fantastic Fandom Tandem. Collect 'em all!"

–John F. Sherry, Jr., Faculty Emeritus, Concurrent Anthropology, Professor, Raymond W. & Kenneth G. Herrick Professor of Marketing, University of Notre Dame.

"I love this book series! It uses ethnography to make the "collective effervescence" of contemporary fandom come alive and make brilliant sense theoretically. But I also love it because both authors share their personal stories as lifelong ardent fans. Truly engaging and insightful!"

–Russell Belk, Distinguished Research Professor and Kraft Foods Canada Chair in Marketing, Schulich School of Business at York University. Fellow of the Royal Society of Canada.

"Eminently readable, accessible, with a clear historical timeline building the substrate of fandom studies in consumer research. I like the way it pulls two fields together. Well done."

–Melanie Wallendorf, Professor Emerita, Eller College of Management at the University of Arizona.

"Everyone is a fan of someone or something. More often than not, of many things. As fans, we share common ground with like-minded others. Collectively, we support the things we most appreciate, with our money, our attention, and our energy. This book by Rob Kozinets and Henry Jenkins, third in the series Frames of Fandom, is the definitive work on fans as consumer collectives. Within its scope it is thorough, well-researched, and highly entertaining. Whether you are a practitioner looking to better understand and connect with your fans, a scholar studying fandom, or a fan looking for insight into your own participation, this book will delight you. It is incisive in its depth of analysis, and yet it remains, in every paragraph, utterly approachable and readable. What can I say? I'm a big fan."

–John W. Schouten, Professor of Social Enterprise, Memorial University.

"Jenkins and Kozinets bring their genius to the baroque splendor of 21st century consumer culture via the lens of fandom. Fame, once a matter of local renown to the select few has become global, digitally driven, tumultuous, explosive fandom. The book Fandom as Consumer Collective is kaleidoscopic, telescopic, multi-perspectival, sophisticated. The oracles have spoken. I am a fan."

–Eric J. Arnould, Emeritus Professor, Aalto University Business School

"Fandom as Consumer Collective is an indispensable guide to understanding how passion, commerce, and community intersect in today's cultural landscape. Blending the depth of fan studies with the insights of consumer culture theory, Henry Jenkins and Robert Kozinets reveal how fandoms operate as creative, critical, and connected marketplaces of meaning. Rich with case studies, theoretical clarity, and decades of lived expertise, this book is both a scholarly achievement and a practical toolkit for anyone who wants to understand—or work with —the cultural power of consumer collectives. An insightful look at how fandom turns buying into belonging and consumption into culture."

–Markus Giesler, Professor of Marketing, Schulich School of Business at York University

TABLE OF CONTENTS

ACKNOWLEDGMENTS

———

🙏First and foremost, we want to thank our students—those in the class we teach together on fan relations through the USC strategic communication program, those Rob has taught in PhD and master's seminars on Consumer Culture Theory and those whom Henry has taught through the years in his PhD seminar on Fandom, Participatory Culture and Web 2.0. Many of Rob and Henry's advanced students have gone on to publish in consumer culture theory and fandom studies and are cited where appropriate throughout the *Frames of Fandom* series. The students' engagement with this material, the presentations they made, and the questions and comments they offered have shaped these books more than they may ever realize. Rob has also brought these books back into his classes, run these exercises, and tested the approaches to customize them for future students.

We thank in particular Celeste Oon and Alice Shu, who were our research assistants at the start of this project and helped us to identify a broad range of core resources that shaped our coverage in these books. Also big thanks to Teresa Ning who helped us to think through the marketing challenges for a self-published book in this space.

We thank our colleagues and friends who have given comments and helped us improve the manuscript—in particular, Eric Arnould, Russ Belk, John Deighton, Fuat Firat, Markus Giesler, Beth Hirschman, Diane Martin, Tom O'Guinn, Daiane Scaraboto, John Schouten, Suzanne Scott, John Sherry, Sangita Shresthova, Sarah MacFarland Taylor, Melanie Wallendorf, Henri Weijo, Diane Winston, and Sebastian Wurzrainer. Ross Gambetti has been an especially devoted, supportive, and incisive reader.

We especially want to thank Ulrike Gretzel and Cynthia Jenkins, our partners, our first readers, our harshest critics, and our most loving supporters. This book emerged from many decades of conversations together on these topics.

And we want to thank Amanda Ford for keeping the trains running on time with the softest of touches and the warmest of hearts.

We dedicate this book to fans everywhere, living your best life, creating your own culture, telling your own stories, asking your own questions, and reshaping our relationship with popular media.

PREFACE

Welcome to Book Three

Gone are the days when fandoms were relegated to the fringes of pop culture. Nowadays, fandoms are thriving, woven into the webwork of our collective conversation and experiences, profoundly interlinked with our identities, and influencing our decision-making. They encompass not only sports and entertainment franchises but also a full spectrum of activities and interests that engage diverse, passionate audiences.

Dear Gentle Reader, we welcome you to this book, **Fandom as Consumer Collective**, the third in a series exploring the multifarious world of fandom. Throughout these books, we examine, explain, and find delight in these diverse and varied manifestations of fans and fandoms. To understand them, we adopt a series of different conceptual perspectives, viewpoints, or frames.

This book is one volume in a 15-book series called Frames of Fandom. Each book is self-contained; they can be read separately or in any order. If you choose to read them in sequence, you will find there is an intentional logic and flow, which makes it the optimal experience. We briefly considered releasing them as an episodic book series reminiscent of the serial formats of the original fan tales, like Sherlock Holmes or

Batman. However, this notion was disregarded in favor of a series that presented a collection of stories and conceptual connections that try to bring to life the captivating world of fandoms that would then be explained using the most sophisticated frameworks currently available. Bringing this complex world to life is done by using a series of frames (ways of understanding) that each represents a lens through which to consider what kind of community a fandom is and how it relates to the popular culture it consumes. We celebrate the collectives that have emerged, the impact they wield, and the potential they hold for business and society.

Each book focuses attention on a particular paradigm scholars have used to understand some dimension of fandom. These frames may be overlapping, as in the case of, for example, **Fandom as Co-Creation** and **Fandom as Participatory Culture**. Both explain fandom as a site of cultural production, the first from the perspective of industry and within the field of consumer research, the second from the perspective of the fan and within the theoretical traditions of cultural studies. Sometimes, one frame—say, **Fandom as Public**—provides the preconditions for the second—**Fandom as Activism**. And in some cases, the relationship between the two is harder to nail down as in the relationship between the focus on affect in **Fandom as Desire** and on religion in **Fandom as Devotion**. However encyclopedic the scope of this project may seem, the range of frames here is not exhaustive. We do, however, try to capture most of the dominant paradigms in the field.

Fandom as Consumer Collective is the third book in the *Frames of Fandom* series. In it, we look at the historical, theoretical, and cultural dimensions that shape these collectives and their interrelation with consumer culture and the material world. What does it mean to say that you are "a consumer"? Back in **Defining Fandom**, we discussed how consumer culture refers to cultural resources that come from the industrial marketplace, which has been a conspicuous part of Western global society since the 1940s. People are consumers when they interact with the various types of resources—cultural, capital, and material—of industrial marketplaces. As this emphasis on industry would suggest, the moment we start talking about consumers, we unerringly set up an implicit dichotomy and must begin talking about producers, production, and labor. When we focus on our lives as consumers, we are explicitly highlighting the aspects of life that exist outside of our work lives and our roles as economic laborers. When we focus on our consumption, we are drawn to think about our relationships with the physical, with things that have materiality like branded products.

For decades, consumer researchers have challenged simplistic dichotomies, such as the assumption that production is inherently value-creating while consumption is value-destructive. A noteworthy example is the way Fuat Firat and Alladi Venkatesh (1995) highlighted how such distinctions mirror other binaries, such as culture versus economy or communities versus markets, often leading to the stigmatization of consumers as passive and isolated. In fandom studies, Matt Hills (2002) has similarly critiqued binaries that see active or creative fans as good while those who merely consume as bad. Both fans and fan scholars have sought to rescue fandom from what Hills calls 'the tainted and devalued term of 'consumption'" (Hills, 2002, p. 6). Others in fandom studies—such as Janice Radway (1986) and Alan McKee (2004)—have questioned the arbitrary distinctions between the amateur fan and the professional producer, describing complex interminglings of the two identities within actual conditions of cultural production.

Consumer collectives overlap with, include, and also transcend subcultures and audiences to form a new type of social grouping, simultaneously engaged with and critical of consumer culture. The book explores this tension—between individual consumer and social collective, participation and resistance, community and market, consumer and producer—unpacking how consumer collectives challenge existing commercial norms while also embracing the cultural opportunities they offer. It demonstrates a bridging of unhelpful disciplinary divides and calls for an enhanced appreciation of the creative, critical, and transformative potential of consumer collectives. Furthermore, it builds and then demonstrates an integrated conceptual toolkit for better understanding a world where passionate consumers participate in collectives that provide them with a deep sense of fulfillment. For scholars, practitioners, and fans alike, this book explores fandom as a critical engine of cultural production, a source of creative collective effervescence, and a force for cultural expression in an increasingly fragmented world.

When you see a bolded title, such as **Fandom as Audience**, **Fandom as Subculture**, or **Locations of Fandom**, it is meant to signify the title of another volume in the series. Throughout this book and the others, we will be referring to these titles as if they are all already published. Not all of the books we refer to may yet be available, but they have all been drafted (if not finalized) at the time of this release. Eventually, we will have all of the books we mentioned available for you, and this book will be an accurate reflection of the entire series.

Goals of this Book Series

As we embark on our journey through the frames of fandom, please remember that we have three specific purposes in mind. The first is intellectual. The book series seeks to develop the synergies between Henry's world of fandom studies and Rob's world of marketing and consumer research. Both fields draw on tools and models from cultural anthropology to explain how everyday people operate within a consumer economy and in relation to the media industries. These approaches would seem to provide common ground for us to learn from each other. In fact, we have been exchanging ideas with each other for almost 30 years.

The second purpose, interrelated with the first, is to inform various practices. Marketers, brand managers, and industry professionals increasingly need to understand and work with fandoms. Understanding the passionate engagement behind fandom makes amazingly good sense from a business perspective. Yet managers who dive for treasure in the shark-infested social media backwaters of brand-fan interactions know that working with fans is a high-risk, high-reward task often fraught with peril. Our core advice—above all, do no harm. We are not trying to teach you how to exploit fandom. Quite the opposite, we want to teach you how to build a constructive relationship that respects and values the existing relationship between fans and any fan objects you may be working with.

There are also practitioners on the fandom side: the fans themselves and those who assist them. Fandoms are interrelated yet operate independently from the corporations and individuals that manage the objects of their fandom. Fans and fandoms sue companies, are sued by them, or sue each other. Fandoms are financially important. We also believe that they are culturally important.

We have both been working with organizations in these areas for decades, and our combined experiences lead us to believe that we can provide valuable information to better guide businesses and organizations alike—this is practical knowledge. Being useful requires us to blend the academic rigor of fan studies and consumer research with the pragmatic insights of brand management and marketing strategy.

The third purpose is to build on, promote, and try to further the new and important field of fandom relations. In both of our native academic fields—marketing and consumer research as well as communication and fan studies—researchers had been long sending back signals that consumers were far from the passive dupes, observers, and recipients that earlier theories and assumptions had made them out to be. Instead, fans, fandoms, consumers, and consumer collectives were enmeshed in complex and passionate relationships with the brands and franchises that shaped their lives.

We want the *Frames of Fandom* series to be a business guide, a source of inspiration for fan organizations, and more than just explanatory literature. In an attempt to match the reality of fandom today, we offer you a series that may shatter categories. We hope our efforts reflect our desire to build bridges between our respective fields. We aren't offering a rehash of established wisdom but rather a consolidation of original and, in some cases, we hope, truly controversial and novel thinking.

About this Book and its Authors

Most students could not name the authors of their textbooks. We assume that the textbook's author is an "expert." The faculty teaching the books surely knows who the authors are. But the textbook author's role is to write in a neutral voice, summarizing what the field knows rather than sharing the objects of their own passion and curiosity. They are not trying to make an original contribution. Their personalities are masked; most textbooks bore us to tears. They could have just as easily been written by artificial intelligence. Such prose, which seems lifeless to our eyes, seems inappropriate for the topic of fans and fandom, which is all about passion and personal investments. The field of fandom studies has long focused attention on the positionality of the researcher—that is, our relationship to the objects of our study.

This book grew from two lifetimes of conversations with media, family and friends, other fans, other scholars, and, perhaps most centrally, conversations with each other. As we are about to relate to you, we've recently had the privilege of developing those conversations much further while teaching a course called Fan Relations we designed together at the University of Southern California's Annenberg School for Communication and Journalism.

The resulting books constitute an ongoing conversation about the intersection of fan studies and marketing. We have been discussing how to make the book more conversational, and this is the result. Many multi-authored books hide the individuality of their authors, but it seemed like there was no way to do that with this book and no need to. The two of us have distinct voices, but the conversations we have always had were about bringing our viewpoints together into something new.

You may have noticed that this book series is self-published by the authors on Amazon. Although we have a wealth of experience working with academic publishers, we have been less than satisfied with our ability to get our message out in forms that were appropriate to us and our readers. We offer these books at a reasonable price and in a slim form that would have likely been impossible for us to arrange with a traditional academic publisher. As a further benefit, we could take control of book marketing and also, potentially, more fairly compensate ourselves for our efforts.

You may find one of our voices stronger than another in any given mini-book or passage, reflecting where these different conceptual frames come from. However, we both contributed to every text in this series. In order to continually signal our stakes in this research, we are, at times, holding onto the first person to describe our own experiences and insights. Where this happens, look for the phrase "Rob Here" or "Henry here" at the start of a subchapter. In other places, we simply refer to ourselves as "we" and offer our work in the third person. We hope this doesn't become too confusing.

Henry and Rob have both fan and professional interests in the topics discussed. One or another of us maintains social relations with most of the other scholars we reference here. They are our mentors, students, colleagues, and friends. We have learned from them, and they have drawn on our research within the network of knowledge production that constitutes any academic field. This is especially the case with fields like fandom studies and consumer culture research, both of which are relatively small by disciplinary standards. Although we will be discussing what we see as some key strands of research within our respective fields, we process them through the lenses of two lifetimes of active research and active participation within fan communities.

And now, we invite you to read and enjoy our exploration of the multifarious worlds of fandom with the third book of this series: **Fandom as Consumer Collective.**

CHAPTER 1
CONCEIVING OF CONSUMER COLLECTIVES

To ask "What is a consumer collective?" is to select a particular lens —a specific conceptual frame—through which to view the vast and complex world of fandom. Like an entomologist with a magnifying glass examining the intricate patterns on a butterfly's wing, each book in this series intentionally narrows its focus to illuminate a different facet of fandom. These frames are liberating, granting us the space to explore well-established aspects of fan activity in great depth. They are also, by design, constrictive, compelling us to see not only fandom but also the world through the unique theoretical language of that frame. The books in this series each focus their lens on different conceptual frames of reference from which we explore and discuss the many and strengthening forms of fandom across global societies.

The Bigger Picture

#	Title / Frame	Conceptual Focus	Key Contribution to the Series
1	Defining Fandom	**Foundational Definitions**: Passionate engagement, fanship vs. fandom, the fan object, aca-fan, auto-ethnography.	Establishes the core vocabulary and personal, auto-ethnographic voice of the series.
2	Fandom as Audience	**Reception & Interpretation**: Audience studies, media effects, active vs. passive models, interpretive communities, market segmentation.	Grounds the series in the history of media and communication studies.
3	Fandom as Consumer Collective	**Market-Based Identity**: Consumer Culture Theory (CCT) and other related concepts	Positions the marketplace itself as a primary resou identity and community.
4	Fandom as Subculture	**Resistance & Style**: Opposition to mainstream norms, bricolage, subcultural capital, fashion, language, and lifestyle as resistance.	Focuses on fandom as a site of oppositional identity construction through style and symbolic practices.
5	Fandom as Co-Creation	**Collaborative Innovation**: Value co-creation, fan labor, creative industries, business models, economics	Highlights the economic and creative value fans generate *with* and *for* commercial industries.
6	Fandom as Participatory Culture	**Grassroots Creativity**: Fan fiction, folk culture logic, "art worlds," connected learning, low barriers to entry.	Centers on creative output fans produce *for each other*, independent of commerce.
7	Fandom as Public	**Civic Engagement & Discourse**: Public sphere theory, forming public opinion, accountability, mobilizing around shared concerns.	Conceptualizes fandom as an active political force capable of influencing public discourse and holding industries accountable.
8	Fandom as Activism	**Social & Political Change**: Social movement theory, micropolitics, "save our show" campaigns, fan nationalism, fan feminism, civic culture.	Moves from discourse (Publics) to direct action, examining how fandoms function as vehicles for social and political change.
9	Fandom as Desire	**Affect & Embodiment**: Psychoanalytic and energetic theories, algorithms, utopian longings.	Drills into emotional and psychological drivers of fandom, focusing on passion, affect, bodies.
10	Fandom as Devotion	**Spirituality & Ritual**: Quasi-religious practices, veneration, pilgrimage, sacred texts, liminality.	Explores the relationship between fan practices and structures of religious devotion and belief.
11	Fandom as Agent of Globalization	**Transnational Cultural Flow**: Critiquing cultural imperialism, the "global shuffle", fans as translators.	Examines fandom's role in the global circulation of media, beyond a simple US-centric model.
12	Locations of Fandom	**Material & Geographic Spaces**: Cultural geography, tourism, local sites of performance	Provides "ground-level" perspective on *where* fandom happens, emphasizing place.
13	Fandom as Technoculture	**Historical Co-Evolution**: Long-term history of technology and fandom, technology mediation.	Historical view of technological affordances and fan practices shaping each other over time.
14	Fandom and Technocapitalism	**Economic & Algorithmic Power**: Platformization, monetization of passion, fan data, digital property.	Critical perspective on how digital capitalism quantifies and exploits fan engagement.
15	Fandom Relations	**Ethical & Utopian Futures**: Re-conceptualizing fandom as a core social structure, ethics of engagement, fandom as a resource for society.	A speculative and aspirational synthesis, proposing an ethical framework for a future where fandom is taken seriously.

Table 1.1: Comparing Conceptual Frames in the *Frames of Fandom* Series

Focusing on consumers and consumption as we do in this introductory chapter gives us an opportunity to discuss how each of the books in the *Frames of Fandom* series orbits a particular concept, drills down into its core meaning, and explores its significance. Table 1 presents a table comparing the epistemological and conceptual focus of each of the books in the series and highlighting its unique contribution to *Frames of*

Fandom. Although there is much in the series that overlaps, because these social categories intersect and interact in various (we think interesting) ways, this table should clearly illustrate how much is different about the topics treated in the fifteen books of this series and specify exactly where we believe their core contributions lie.

Each Frame Has Its Pet Concepts

For instance, when we view **Fandom as Audience**, we engage with the rich history of media and audience studies, exploring the tensions between media companies trying to manage "unruly" audiences and the rise of the active, interpretive fan. When we adopt the frame of **Fandom as Subculture**, our focus shifts to acts of resistance performed through the specific codes of style, fashion, and language. The lens of **Participatory Culture** brings grassroots creativity to the forefront, while **Cocreation** examines the collaborative, and often fraught, relationship between fan creativity and the commercial industries that feed upon it. **Fandom as Activism** takes the notion of resistance simmering beneath these other topics and places it on the front burner, analyzing fandom's power as a social and political movement.

This book, however, centers on what is arguably the most pervasive yet ideologically fraught context for modern fandom: consumer culture. More than any other volume in this series, this one focuses squarely on the interface of marketing, cultural studies, and fan studies. It pulls its core principles from the theoretics of Consumer Culture Theory (CCT), which can be understood as a family of theoretical perspectives addressing the ever-changing, fluid, yet often also highly structured cocreative relationships between consumer actions, the marketplace, and cultural meanings.

Building on theoretical foundations from Sidney Levy, Russell Belk, Emile Durkheim, Pierre Bourdieu, Lewis Hyde, Bruno Latour, Daniel Miller, and many others, **Fandom as Consumer Collective** integrates perspectives from fandom studies and consumer research to offer realistic and usable frameworks for understanding these collectives. Through numerous grounded case studies and an analysis of diverse fan groups—Apple devotees, Harley-Davidson riders, Quisp breakfast cereal enthusiasts, Titanic preservationists, geocaching aficionados, He-Man action figure collectors, and Star Wars loyalists, among others—the book illuminates how these collectives foster belonging, express meaning, and build connection across geographical and social boundaries. Along the way, we will encounter various roadside attractions, oddities, and ideas from consumer culture theory such as enchanted disenchantment, brand communities, linking values, consumption performances, subcultures of consumption, semiotic symbiosis, and others, applying their insights to inform our framing of fandom as a consumer collective.

Framing Fandom as a Consumer Collective

A consumer collective is any type of social grouping formed around a shared interest in a consumption activity, brand, product, or mass culture phenomenon. Thus, fandom could be considered an example or a sub-category of a consumer collective. By framing **Fandom as (a) Consumer Collective**, we are able to explore how market-provided resources—from brands and products to digital platforms—become the very building blocks for identity and community both in individual fanship and through the externalized connections of affiliative sociality that define fandom. This perspective promotes an understanding of the implications of fans' and fandoms' many intersections with the commercial world, some of which may be beneficial and others which may be harmful.

In cultural studies, conceiving of fans as consumers may be seen as controversial. However, there is no doubt whatsoever that fans are consumers. Their interaction with the commercial world of mass culture is the basis of the fanship that underpins their fandom. By looking at fans' interactions with their fanship and fandom's commercial aspects directly, the consumer collective frame examines how fans and fandoms interrelate with both the smaller (e.g., entrepreneurs like fan dealers or crafters on Etsy) and large-scale (e.g., team owners, Hollywood studios, record labels, toy manufacturers) market players. Whether applied to a Brazilian, Communist China, or American context, looking at consumers and their collective formations offers readers a vital and carefully detailed conceptual and pragmatic understanding of how we live and connect today. Human society is in an indisputably consumerist and capitalist phase. These are times in which fandom and passionate consumption phenomena like it play an increasingly central role.

The Paradox of the Consumer Collective

The very concept of a "consumer collective" presents a compelling paradox. At its core, consumption is often an intensely personal, even solitary, act. We experience fandom's foundational pleasures as individuals: the book read to oneself in the privacy of one's own mind, the television series streamed alone according to a personal schedule, or the music that feels like a private dialogue between artist and listener. The genesis of fanship lies in these intimate, individual affairs.

Yet this solitary experience is rarely the end of the story. Our social selves inevitably look outward, seeking connection with others. Specifically, the consumer self seeks out other consumer selves. Let's not be reductive and think of the "consumer self" as just a person who buys things. Consumers and consumption are so much more than that. To be able to consume freely, whatever one desires, say, that is a social signal of immense significance bound up with signals of personal worth. Knowing what and how to consume are also signals of legitimacy and class. But there are local legitimacies for consumption as well. For example, you might attend a concert or football game wearing the absolutely perfect, ideal shirt for the situation. Whether you consider yourself a socialist or a socialite, your consumption is a central expression of your social identity, and it comes complete with its own perceived status, rights, obligations, expected behaviors, and ideological assumptions. It is a framework through which we seek social legitimacy, attain fulfillment, and confer respect upon ourselves and others.

One key tension of this book, therefore, lies in what happens when the individualized, often self-oriented, consumer engages with the collective. This tension manifests across every level of our lives—as individuals, family members, participants in work networks, and citizens of nations. We do not engage with consumer culture superficially, merely as a "fan." Rather, our identity as a particular kind of consumer is entangled with our sense of conformity and status, our anxieties about legitimacy and attractiveness, and the push-and-pull between introversion and extroversion.

This personal struggle unfolds against the backdrop of a macrosocial world in which the marketplace is a rather cold, exploitative, and self-serving space, for the most part—the anonymous, industrial Gesellschaft. This coldness is especially salient when we are considering the marketplace as a potential buyer of our labor, a site of customer service needs, or, worst of all, a legal or other opponent. The corporations that create and control the products that embellish and enrich our lives can also mercilessly exploit and bankrupt us. Being a consumer, especially a passionate and loyal one, makes one particularly vulnerable to exploitation. Being a passionate consumer is a guilty pleasure, a dependency on profit-making corporations. Yet, when a piece of mass culture—a song, a game, a team, a book—speaks to you or seems to see you, it creates times you wish would go on forever. And by providing connection and collectives, it also provides a sense of belonging.

Consumption is Our Primary Source of Meaning(lessness)

This is the quintessential fate of the modern identity: in an era marked by the erosion of traditional faiths and communities, we can turn to the marketplace and find joy, pleasures, and camaraderie. Regardless of what language you speak, the color of your skin, or the cover of your passport, the cycle of productive labor and the joyful work of consumption become the primary source of meaning in the modern human experience.

When we consider the centrality of this cycle, we find the individual consumer seeking a collective consumption experience to be more than a sociological curiosity. It is arguably the latest evolution of well-established media consumption trends, now dramatically amplified by the connective affordances of platforms. The very act of searching for and then joining these passionate consumption-based collectives—be they style-based subcultures, brand communities, or fandoms—is both simplified and a profound response to a deep-seated (but largely unfulfilled in consumer society) human need for connection.

Writing as a critic of consumer culture at the precipice of the 21st century, the psychologist Philip Cushman identified this universal unfilled need for connection as the core pathology of our times. Blaming commercial society and the exploitativeness of the modern marketplace for the lack of meaning people feel, he wrote that the market has shaped a self that experiences a significant absence of community, tradition, and shared meaning. It experiences these social absences and their consequences 'interiorly' as a lack of personal conviction and worth, and it embodies the absences as a chronic, undifferentiated emotional hunger. The post-World War II self thus yearns to acquire and consume as an unconscious way of compensating for what has been lost: It is empty (Cushman, 1990, p. 600).

Feeling the emptiness of modern life after the decline of religious and other reassuring faiths (something Friedrich Nietzche and Jean-Paul Sartre also knew something about), and the breakdown of traditional sources of community [something Robert Putnam (2000) also investigated], those who primarily thought of themselves as believers and community members invested more of themselves into their identities as workers and consumers.

By locating the modern self in consumer identity, Cushman places consumer society at the center of modern life. Contestably, we think, he argues that this consumption ultimately is unsatisfying. Describing consumption more as an obligation and a consequence of habituation, Cushman asserts that once the pleasure of a purchase is spent, it leaves behind only a chronic, undifferentiated emotional hunger. One that cannot cover the basic emptiness in the modern human heart. And this hunger, the hunger of Cushman's empty modern self, initiates the fruitless and ultimately unfulfilling quest for the next temporary consumption satisfaction.

Cushman's theory is powerful, psychologically valid, and controversial. Although we use it as a touchstone throughout this book, we do not fully embrace or accept it. Cushman, who was writing about a pre-World Wide Web world that existed thirty-five years ago, misses entirely the fact that consumers today combine consumption and community. Contemporary consumers find within their collective consumption a communal experience that conceivably fills some, perhaps a significant amount, of the emptiness at the heart of (what he assumed was) individual and individualistic consumer behavior.

Wanting Contact

Whether we agree with Cushman's dire analysis or not, the evidence for our unfulfilled need for human contact manifesting itself through desperate acts of consumption is all around us. Peter Gabriel, a musician noted for his poetic and brilliant social observations, says it vividly in song.

> *Pull my chin, stroke my hair*
> *Scratch my nose, hug my knees*
> *Try drink, food, and cigarette*
> *Tension will not ease*
> *I tap my fingers, fold my arms*
> *Breathe in deep, cross my legs*
> *Shrug my shoulders, stretch my back*
> *But nothing seems to please*
> *I need contact*
> *I need contact, nothing seems to please*
> *I need contact*
> *Oh, I need contact*
> *Yes, I need contact*

PETER GABRIEL, I HAVE THE
TOUCH, 1982, WRITTEN AND ©
PETER GABRIEL

In our current consumer society, our need for contact is stoked vicariously and virtually by commercial entities such as brands, celebrities, and media franchises. It happens through the stories they tell, through our search for the next product to buy, and through our hard drives' collection of so much "information." Although we do not rely upon it as a literal or overarching truth, Cushman's empty self hypothesis helps structure the fundamental question motivating this book:

How and why has the marketplace become a primary arena for the modern search for community and self?

But if Cushman, like Nietzsche, stared into the abyss at the core of modern self and diagnosed its cause, the work of consumer culture theorists Russell Belk, Henri Weijo, and this book's own Rob Kozinets, maps the process through which the industrial marketplace promises to fill it. Belk, Weijo, and Kozinets identified this seductive and cyclical process as "disenchanted enchantment," a uniquely modern condition of simultaneous skepticism and willing participation in the market's magic shows, a state almost perfectly attuned to Cushman's empty self.

This jaded and sceptical consumer nevertheless suspends disbelief and continuously plays along with a procession of one technological magic show after another... In other words, consumers beguile themselves as much as they are beguiled by enchanting technologies and they are aware of their self-seduction. They do this both individually and jointly by, for example, speculating on the next version of a product on online forums. Disenchanted enchantment is the only possible form of enchantment in a late modernist world. (Belk, Weijo, and Kozinets, 2024, pp. 26, 29).

Devised to explain the constant allure of new technologies, the unending sideshow spectacle of the next latest and greatest innovation, this critical perspective also maps out the terrain of our investigation. Cushman postulates an "empty self," stripped of community and tradition, yearning to be filled. And we have a market that offers an endless parade of novel "magic shows" powered by "disenchanted enchantment." Included and bound up in these magic shows are movies, television shows, concerts, theme park rides, toys, concerts, teams, athletes, actors, musicians, and sporting events. The next television show, album, player, or sports season, coming soon, like the next technological offering, promises to be bigger, stronger, longer, with greater special effects, more action, more engaging plots, the most beautiful actors, the most attractive characters, more spectacle, and just all around better than anything we have ever consumed in the past. This attraction serves as the source of fanship.

When fanship extends to the seeking of contact that Peter Gabriel sings about, it reaches for fandom. Interpreted according to Belk at al.'s disenchanted enchantment perspective, the consumer collectives we see today, whether fan groups or brand communities or the genealogical networks we will explore in this book, are key arenas where this drama plays out. They are the new fellowships where the empty self seeks and (temporarily?) finds both meaning and connection, and where the rituals of disenchanted enchantment are received with the most seriousness, commitment, and fervor.

Consumption as Ideological Necessity

Our answer to the fundamental question of the market's psychic preeminence must also circle back to the definition of a consumer. Being a consumer involves our relationships with the material world, with things like food, smartphones, clothing, and so on. But being a consumer is, more accurately and extensively, the primary ritual through which the contemporary self is constructed, mediated, and, ultimately, controlled by social structures and institutional forces today.

Biological necessities serve as the foundation for these forces, yet their ideological reach extends far beyond them. Literally speaking, to stop consuming (food and drink) is, quite literally, to die. Our organismic reality is that we must keep consuming to live and so we are always on the lookout for the next thing we will ingest. This biological imperative is the consumption system's foundational hook, the panic-inducing vulnerability upon which the entire edifice of market society is seemingly built. However, this concept only serves as a foundation for the predatory forces that lurk within the competitive core of consumer society. In a blink, the need for bread and water is transmuted into the desire for a chocolate layer cake with chantilly and a decaf cappuccino. This transmutation is about combating insecurity and proving you are special (or better than) much more than it is simply about habituation, addiction, or "variety seeking." It is also a vivid illustration of what Pierre Bourdieu (1984) calls a game of distinction. It is where our consumption, still felt as a visceral need, becomes a declaration of our taste and status, our standing in the world.

We are no longer consuming to survive; we are performing our (social) position in the great, unwritten hierarchy that links people with things. Who sits upon the golden toilet? Through their consumption, you shall know them. Consumption is the terrain of judgment and the domain of materialized power, a royal fact that preceded, by centuries, Thorstein Veblen's (1899) naming of the notion of conspicuous consumption.

The things we own, therefore, are never silent. We imbue them with life and substance as if they were pets, our animist companions. Branded or not, they are artifacts dripping with surplus meaning, freighted with what the anthropologist Grant McCracken (1988, p. 131) calls "ballast against culture drift" that serves to anchor our identities. Our stuff, the things we hold onto, the things we collect, the memorabilia, the tokens or tickets, the pictures, manga, and magazines, all of them tell stories about who we are and want to be. Our toys are us; as Russell Belk (1988) tells us, they are our extended self.

Today, we might ask about how we—possessions and all—are made legible and visible in a world of social media? In previous eras, our possession-laden performances of self might have been confined to the physical homes, taking the form of the curated bookshelf, the display cabinet, or the carefully chosen decor. The digital world has exponentially expanded the stages at our fingertips. The digital realm demands not just that we *have* an identity anchored by our things, but that we actively and publicly *curate* it. This act of curation, which involves carefully selecting and displaying the material anchors of our identity for an online audience, is precisely where the macro theories of consumption collide with the micro-practices of everyday life. It is the modern arena for performing one's position in the great, unwritten hierarchy of culture that suffuses each one of us.

Introspection and Shelfies

To understand this performance, we must turn from the macro-level critique to the micro-level case study. We can accomplish this, as we have been striving to in this book series, visually and auto-ethnographically. We have been living for well over a decade now in the age of the selfie, where selfies are "digital images characterized by the desire to frame the self in a picture taken to be shared with an online audience" (Kozinets,

Gretzel, and Dinhopl, 2017, p. 1). There are many images in the book series of us, the authors, engaged in various activities relating to our fandoms and consumption.

In the next chapter, we turn first to a variation of the selfie called the shelfie. The term shelfie became popular in the early 2010s as a portmanteau combining the selfie with the word *shelf* (as in bookshelves). The goal of a *shelfie* is to photographically share the various objects people have on their shelves, whether books, souvenirs, toys, plants, or other things. Our next chapter opens with a shelfie of a fan object in one of the author's homes and continues with an exploration of a global genetics platform. Genealogy was once a solitary hobby but is now a globally platformed collective and family activity, a genetic treasure hunt that can expand one's very sense of family to include unknown relatives in distant countries. As we shift from the macro to the micro, the general to the specific, and the conceptual to the manifest, remember that these are more than just personal stories. They are case studies through which we can witness how individual and collective acts of consumption have become primary sites of pleasure, connection, expression, memorializing, discovery, and much else. By relating and then analytically dissecting these examples, we shall see how the market logic of a consumer identity and its intrinsic hunger for social contact are bundled into much of what we do and who we are.

CHAPTER 2
A FANDOM AND A FAMILY TREE

This is Rob. As we laid out in the former chapter, we are all immersed in consumer culture. Like fish trying to conceptualize this thing called "water," our immersion in consumer culture makes it very difficult for us to see it clearly or even discuss it as a topic. To understand this condition, to truly map and conceptualize it, we cannot remain at a theoretical distance. We must risk the charge of being self-indulgent, for it is only through a rigorously introspective chronicling that we can access the culturally grounded richness of the fan-as-consumer experience. We must examine our own attachments, our own "blips" of desire, to see how and where these forces show up.

Why do we, as social scientists, so often shy away from using our own personal consumption as a research topic? Why is introspection so rarely used? Perhaps many researchers are still uncomfortable stepping out from behind the authorial screen of implied impersonal objectivity. That and, as we have said, because there seems to be an implicit distaste, even a sense of guilt, that accompanies confessions of our own consumer behaviors. Perhaps because such a project necessarily reveals how deeply the authors are implicated in a capitalist society they claim to resist.

My own life is littered with these artifacts of desire, these totems of a constructed self. My book collection alone could serve as a testament to a lifetime of consuming identities, many as a fan and an aca-fan. I have mixed feelings as I write this, thinking remorsefully about the job of disposal someone will one day have. I feel sad at the thought of my things' dispersal and eventual resting place in the unmarked grave of a landfill. But for now, for this journey, we will be using a shelfie of an object that sits at the nexus of the personal and the collective, my analog past and digital present, a source of somatic joy and a commodified signifier.

My Little Jimmy

Let's start out by letting you have a look at my little Jimmy (see Figure 2.1).

Figure 2.1: 2006 NECA Jimmy Page Action Figure, sculpted by comic book author and artist Todd McFarlane's studio. Figure on display in author's bookcase. Photograph © 2025 Robert Kozinets. Image artificially extended with gen-AI.

My little Jimmy is a branded, limited-edition adjustable action figure, first released in 2006. It depicts Led Zeppelin guitarist Jimmy Page in his iconic black dragon suit—the one immortalized in *The Song Remains the Same* motion picture rockumentary—alongside his distinctive Gibson EDS-1275 double-neck guitar and a Marshall amplifier emblazoned with his personal sigil, "Zoso." I've placed the figure in a prominent spot in my home office, staged in front of Eric Davis's inspirational little 33⅓ book on Zeppelin's untitled fourth album and an assortment of other fandom-related books that happened to be stationed there.

But wait, there's more.

Figure 2.2: Various and sundry Jimmy Page fandom magazines, Led Zeppelin books, biographies, and academic and philosophical explorations from Rob's collection. Photograph © 2025 Robert Kozinets.

Relating specifically to Jimmy Page and Led Zeppelin fanship, I also have numerous magazines from the past, from Guitar Player magazines featuring interviews with Jimmy Page to Led Zeppelin special edition magazines devoted to the band. I have books about Led Zeppelin, Scott

Calef's edited volume *Led Zeppelin and Philosophy* (Calef, 2009), Chris Welch's (2017) Zeppelin book, and the Led Zeppelin illustrated volume by Real Art Press, along with biographies of Jimmy Page and Led Zeppelin lead singer Robert Plant. These are arranged in an image presented in Figure 2.2, which is not quite a shelfie (but might be termed a floorie?).

If you've read **Defining Fandom**, then you'll know my long history with Zeppelin fandom—especially with Page's virtuosic performances. If you've read **Fandom as Devotion**, you'll also recall the mystical significance I attach to my teenage midnight pilgrimages to Toronto's Danforth Music Hall to partake in the ritual partying and group watching of *The Song Remains the Same* projected on the big screen. So you can consider the figure on my shelf, taken out of its packaging and displayed, as part toy, part time capsule, part shrine–a devotional object that condenses years of transformative identity work into one compact scene.

Traveling down memory lane to teenage Rob's world, I remember myself as a devoted fan. I carried a pin of Pagey (as his bandmates called him) and a couple of Led Zeppelin pins on my jeans jacket, along with pins of other rock icons and bands (I still have most of them). I bought the bootlegs, wore the shirts, hunted down the interviews, and jammed the songs with friends in my basement. Then, my fan expenditures on Led Zeppelin were fairly modest, but collectively they were significant and consistent. I have owned all of the LPs, several of the cassettes, a few CDs, and several boxed sets.

But my fandom is not the same today. Now, Zeppelin remains a top-streamed band for me, though I ration them—like a sacred text whose familiarity demands reverence. I know that catalog far too well to listen to it all the time. Jimmy Page was an art student and his artistic eye influenced Led Zeppelin's alluring graphic design work. Today, they are licensed onto clothing everywhere. I wear my Zeppelin fandom on my sleeve, so to speak. Zeppelin t-shirts make me happy. I have a bunch. I kept my Robert Plant concert shirts, like the one for Pictures at Eleven and the one with The Honeydrippers. As I write this paragraph, I am wearing my Led Zeppelin hoodie with the band's licensed trademark symbols, including Zoso (a sigil both mystical and economic), on the sleeve and the back. My Led Zeppelin clock is on my wall and my Led Zeppelin comforter is on my couch. Perhaps the most consistent way I recharge my fandom now is by reading posts on r/ledzeppelin, the Reddit forum, and the Zeppelin posts that are all over my Quora feed. When I open my Reddit or Quora, Zeppelin and Jimmy Page are usually nearby, and there's usually something interesting to look at—a video, a question, a discussion, or some fun fact about the band members.

So what is the form of consumer collective expressed here? My relationship with Led Zeppelin is a part of my physical surroundings, whether in my closet, on my bookshelf, worn on my body, displayed as LPs, or posed like my Little Jimmy. It is part of my digital environment, in my playlists, on my newsfeeds. Throughout my lifetime, I have engaged in ongoing (if sporadic) product acquisition. But it is also a dance between my memories, my feelings, my material and digital reality, the stories I tell myself, and my various relationships. Fellowships of things like Little Jimmy, then, are not just about posing and photographing actual plastic action figures in bookcase shelfies. They are about communities, both imagined and real, that are organized around the felt significance of cultural texts, sounds, and figures. Jimmy Page in his dragon pants, holding his double-neck up high, is both a relic and a totem.

In this chapter, then, we begin with a single, seemingly trivial thing —a rock action figure. But we use Little Jimmy as a lens to reflect on how fandom operates through the realm of consumer objects and consumer identity. We leverage him to ask how these things link our materially embodied selves through marketplace actions and memories, personalities and desires, mass media, and personal meaning. We wonder how commercially created and beautiful things, creative works, and artistic things permit us, in moments large and small, to feel connected—to others, to ourselves, to a time when the music was new and omnipresent, and also to a present moment when a figure on a shelf can still summon a magical spell.

Little Jimmy sits on my shelf right now, playing Stairway to Heaven, a sculpture not entirely unlike Greek and Roman busts, a physical object forever capturing a time in the band's history and molding it into a colorful fan collectible. But let's stretch now what we mean by both fandom and consumer collectives. Let's push our definitions and turn our attention to a different type of consumption, a consumption of information and connection. Consider a collective built around platforms that share information about genetic material, a consumption experience of your body's informatics, your biological network, and your genotype's history and connections.

Consuming Family History

Consumer experiences are the vehicles that carry us through life. These experiences encompass everything from routine health clinic check-ups to transatlantic flights, from driving downtown to shop for a birthday gift to downloading a user-friendly new app for investing online. Consumer experiences encompass the thrill of a walk-off home run in a playoff game, the tension building in a concert that begins three hours late, and the crazed immersion of a 3 am shopping marathon on a vast new online site. To illustrate this point, we will elaborate on how a global genetics platform, Ancestry, became a vehicle for exploring the past and rewriting my family narrative.

The rising popularity of at-home DNA testing kits and online genealogy resources has fueled a surge of reality television shows centered on the theme of genetic testing and family heritage exploration. These shows tap into people's desire to understand their origins and connect with relatives, both close and distant. Popular programs like *Finding Your Roots* in the USA and *Who Do You Think You Are?* in the UK feature celebrities tracing their ancestry with the help of historians and geneticists, often uncovering surprising ancestral connections and hidden family histories (Saunders, 2024).

Other reality shows, like *Genealogy Roadshow*, bring the thrill of genealogical discovery to everyday people, showcasing the emotional impact of uncovering long-lost relatives or learning about ancestors' migration patterns and life stories. Some programs, like *Relative Race*, add a competitive element as contestants use DNA clues to locate relatives within a specific timeframe. This trend in reality television reflects a broader societal interest in identity and belonging, demonstrating how personal journeys of self-discovery can resonate with a wide audience.

The shows frequently highlight how DNA testing can unlock family secrets, break down genealogical barriers, and uncover unknown ethnicities or connections to historical events. Showcasing these features, reality television helps market the once niche pursuit of genealogy to mainstream audiences, potentially inspiring viewers to embark on their own ancestral explorations.

Why Do People Use Ancestry Platforms?

I'm going to use the pursuit of genealogy to illustrate and discuss the workings of a consumer collective in which consumption facilitates a social connection. A fandom, perhaps. My Ancestry experience transforms what might seem like a solitary act—researching my genealogical history—into a process of social and familial interconnection.

In her participatory genealogical ethnography about "virtual kinship in a postmodern world," Pamela Wilson (1999) identifies four key consumer motivations for using genealogy platforms like Ancestry. Wilson says that, first, consumers who use genealogy platforms are trying to understand themselves (or their spouses). Second, there are emotional payoffs, including a satisfying sense of continuity, learning, and meaning. Third, they can satisfy a need for social connections. Genealogy fosters community-building, both online and offline, as people come together to answer questions and fill in gaps in their family histories. Finally, there is an element of intellectual engagement that provides satisfying problem-solving opportunities. When Wilson notes that the participants in these genealogical activities are drawn to the detective-like challenge of piecing together fragmented histories, treating genealogy as an engaging puzzle, I clearly recognize the enthusiasm and commitment of my wife, Ulli, who is also researching and writing about numerous aspects of these genealogical journeys.

My curiosity has also been satisfied. Before Ancestry, I was aware of three of my grandfather's siblings but knew little about the rest. Supposedly, he was from a much bigger family. The Ancestry platform, however, allowed us to make contact with other people who were related to me in some way (finding out how we were related was the detective aspect). That process, when it worked, seemed almost miraculous. Family members who knew my grandfather, usually referred to as "Uncle John," would appear as if conjured from thin air.

The Genealogy of Genealogy

Some genealogy of the current genealogical industry may be in order. Wilson (1999) describes how genealogy for a long time was the domain of aristocrats, who would have access to their bloodlines to validate their lineage and the privilege it afforded. Genealogical research in Western Europe and the United States was thus historically tied to class and race privilege and used to gaslight and reinforce existing social hierarchies. However, the success of Alex Haley's *Roots*—a dramatization of the American author's tracking of his ancestry back to Africa—and advancements in technology sparked new interest among diverse groups, especially Black Americans, as they attempted to reclaim erased histories.

In her chapter, Wilson explores the role of the Mormon Church and its industrial-scale genealogical efforts, which have institutionalized these genealogical practices, resulting in the affordances of Ancestry. For several decades now, Ancestry has been on the leading edge of a type of revolution in popular genealogy rooted in the convergence of personal computers, databases, and internet access. Wilson was writing in the 1990s and she was talking about CD-ROM databases, not massive platforms and data centers. She was typing out these accounts well before smartphones and wifi. Nonetheless, she theorizes that contemporary genealogy takes place in what she calls "an elaborate interactive and noncommercial economy of knowledge exchange" (Wilson 1999, p. 190), a participatory culture in which users interact in digital spaces that are collaborative and communal.

Digital Genealogy and Fandom

Since the late 1990s, digital genealogy has continued to develop. Over 30 million people have taken a commercial at-home DNA test (de Groot, van Beers, and Meynen, 2021) and the rise of services like AncestryDNA and MyHeritage has reframed the practice of tracing ancestry, turning identity exploration into a type of consumption activity, a purchasable product with a platformized service extension. Commodifying family genetics, these companies have capitalized on the convergence of advanced DNA science, big data analytics, and digital consumer interfaces to create accessible and personalized experiences that seamlessly integrate with the broader identity projects of consumer culture.

Traditionally, genealogists relied on physical documents, archives, and field visits to uncover family histories. With the advent of smartphones and specialized apps, these practices have become more efficient, interactive, and collaborative. Apps such as Ancestry, FamilySearch, and FindAGrave facilitate data collection, connection with like-minded consumers, and the digital archiving of family histories. Heather Kennedy-Eden and Ulrike Gretzel (2021) offer an overview and taxonomy of related apps, illustrating how the discovery, collaboration, and navigation functions of mobile devices both enable and ultimately optimize genealogy research and travel. They also explain how technology enables a form of what they call "connectivism," a participatory culture-type pursuit in which genealogists act as both learners and teachers in online communities, sharing and seeking knowledge, capabilities that continue to extend through digital tools and artificial intelligence.

Wilson cites the sociologist Anthony Giddens (1991, p. 4), who characterized postmodern social life as one in which "disembedding mechanisms—mechanisms which prise social relations free from the hold of specific locales," recombine them, or allow us to recombine them, "across wide time-space distances." Wilson (1999) says she finds this recombination instantly apparent "in the creation of bonds of commonality across time (familial links over centuries) and across space (globally dispersed and electronically linked kinship groups) that I have found in the computer-based genealogy process" (p. 205). These processes seem much more like the deterritorializing and reterritorializing forces of assemblage theorists like Maryam Raminnia (2022).

However, the impulse to meticulously archive, interpret, and extend a core narrative is not unique to genealogy; it finds a powerful parallel in the complex world of fan cultures. Just as the digital genealogist pieces together scattered records to construct a coherent family history, so too do fans of media properties collaboratively assemble vast archives of knowledge. This participatory culture, a form of connectivism, thrives on digital platforms where fans act as both learners and teachers, lore-keepers and creators. They build intricate wikis that document every detail of their chosen fictional universe, write fan fiction that explores untold stories, and generate sophisticated analyses that rival academic critique. For both the genealogist and the fan, the study of genealogy is not a passive act of consumption but an active, often laborious, identity project. The process of tracing a bloodline or mapping a story world becomes a way of understanding one's own place, whether in a family lineage or a community of shared passion.

We can also understand these activities and interactions through the lens of disembedding mechanisms and assemblage. The genealogist confronts a deterritorialized archive, with records and relations pried free and disembedded from their original locales and scattered across time and space but missing vital connections and relationships. The work of digital genealogy is to reterritorialize these fragments, add missing connections, resolve inconsistencies in the historical record, and re-embed them into the meaningful structure of a family tree on a digital platform. Fan communities perform a similar function. They take a finished, canonical text—a movie, a book series, or a television show, for instance—and effectively deterritorialize it, finding missing or inconsistent plot points or explanations. On platforms dedicated to fandom, fans construct new connections, new explanations and facts that are not officially sanctioned but become widely accepted within fandom. These new, fan-originated interpretations are known as "fanon." In both cases, the result is the creation of powerful, electroni-cally linked groups whose bonds of commonality are forged not by geography, but by the shared, creative act of assembling a coherent story. In both cases, the identity and roles of the individual consumer are at the center of the action, yet the activities of a wider community, linked by overlapping interests and efforts, make possible the continuation and fruition of these searches for meaning.

Collectively Consuming and Creating Family Identity

Consumer collectives, such as fandoms, are often involved in creative or productive pursuits that they subsequently contribute to the group for the collective's benefit. Witness the Archive of Our Own (AO3) project, an example we keep returning to throughout this series. An analogous pursuit on the Ancestry site is the project of building family trees. When someone builds an extensive family tree and opens it up to public use, the result is a major research resource that is a gift of time and valuable ancestral information for some people using the platform. People spend a lot of time scanning family photographs and documents. Much like fans who create their own productions and share them at a convention event—a type of physical platform—amateur genealogists build new resources that add immense value to the type of information that Ancestry is able to offer. They are the detail filler inners, those who hold vital pieces of the genetic puzzles. The platform facilitates these interactions, allowing them to label their profile as a community resource: 'Ask Me Questions.'

Wilson emphasizes the collaborative and social dimensions of those early bastions of genealogy, particularly within online platforms like RootsWeb and GENWEB. For decades now, a range of online spaces have connected people with shared interests in surnames, geographical regions, or cultural heritage—and now with things like shared haploid groups from mitochondrial DNA. Like social media, or platforms themselves, genealogical sites are built for making connections.

Case Study: Auntie Dasha

In that collaborative and cross-platform digital space, I have connected with probably a dozen of these key family informant types across some wide time-space distances. One of them was Natasha K (not Kozinets), who lives in Texas. Natasha introduced us to her father, Alexander, who lives in Belarus, and who knows a lot of my family history. I have never met Natasha nor Alexander in person, but in an email that Alexander allowed me to quote, he told me that my great-grandfather, Nison, or Nathan, Kozinets is his great-great-grandfather.

He told me about Nathan's life in Melitopol. He was a tailor, a prominent and talented one who specialized in fashioning church vestments for the Russian Orthodox Church, before he and his family were forced to flee the country to escape religious persecution. And it was in this telling that I first learned the story of my great-aunt Dvoyra (a Russian version of Deborah), who was called "Dasha," my grandfather's sister, the oldest of his siblings.

Apparently, one day a customer, "an Orthodox priest with his son, came to him for a fitting, and the popovich [the son of the priest] met Dasha." Somehow, they fell in love. "Dasha was going to be baptized and marry him." But her parents were upset about this marriage and immediately married her off to another man named Isaac Y.

At the beginning of the 20th century, Nathan and his entire family emigrated to Canada—everyone except for eldest daughter Dvoyra. As the story goes, Nathan and Anna Kozinets went on to have more than thirty grandchildren, one of whom was my father. Dvoyra, who was left behind in Melitopol, went on to have nine children. She was also, like her father, Nathan, an expert seamstress and clothing designer. But by the spring of 1930, her husband had died and her children had all grown up. She went to Toronto to visit relatives, decided to stay a while, and made money sewing and seamstressing. In December 1930, apparently putting down roots in Toronto, she even registered a marriage with Joseph Shneiderman.

But it didn't last. In 1935, she decided she could stay away no longer. She returned to Melitopol. With money she had earned and saved, she bought a piece of land on Petrovsky Street, 12 and then put up two houses on it. She lived in one house with the family of her daughter Olga and rented out the other. This went on for six years, six difficult years to be a property-owning single woman living in Europe because, in 1941, Dasha sadly, and somewhat mysteriously, died. It happened during what Alexander describes as "a mandatory evacuation" with her daughter Olga's family on a train to Kazakhstan.

We will never know the exact circumstances of this forced evacuation from her home, which she had built six years earlier and lived in since then. The exact cause of her death, too, will likely remain a mystery. The story we are told is that after something horrible happened on the train, she was either rushed to a hospital, where she died, or, more likely, unceremoniously dumped and later buried in a hole that was hastily dug near the railway tracks. The unmarked grave in the Kazakh steppe remains forever lost.

However (and here is the silver lining to the story), many of Dasha's children survived, and that is how we learned this story. She had fourteen grandchildren, including Alexander's mother; eighteen great-grandchildren, including Alexander; and more than twenty great-great-grandchildren dispersed in Ukraine, Russia, Belarus, Latvia, Italy, the USA, and several other countries. And I know this story because of Natasha and Alexander's communication through my wife, Ulli. Ulli provided them with access to a very detailed family tree of that side of the family, including many images and links to many documents.

Connectivism is a learning theory that highlights the importance of networks and connections in contemporary processes of learning (Goldie, 2016). In a digital age, especially, learning occurs through the actions of networks of individuals, information, and technology. Learning becomes the capacity to traverse and string together the connections distributed throughout a network. We view the communications between my family members as a microcosm of the connectivist, participatory culture that defines these digital identity projects (and the projects of other types of fandoms). The story of Auntie Dasha, once a deterritorialized narrative fragmented across continents and generations, becomes the central "text" for a small, dedicated community of practice. Her life, pried from its original locales by persecution, migration, and war, is reassembled piece by piece through the collaborative labor of her descendants. Like fans meticulously piecing together the lore of a beloved character from scattered clues, building novel connections and filling in the blanks with fanon, we took the fragments provided by Alexander and Natasha and combined them with our documents and images. The result is a co-authored narrative, a reterritorialization of memory onto the new, stable ground of a digital family tree.

In this process, the digital archive became transformed into a type of living digital monument. Although Dasha's physical grave remains lost and unmarked in the vast Kazakh steppe, her story finds a permanent, accessible resting place online, in our hearts, and now, in this chapter.

The assemblage of emails, scanned documents, photographs, and shared memories reconstitutes her existence, giving it a presence and persistence that history sought to erase. I offer this story to you about someone who I never knew existed until my father and I sent our DNA specimens away to Ancestry's genetics laboratory. The shared and unexpected project that ensued created its own bonds of commonality, a kinship group formed not by proximity but by a collective emotional investment in a single, compelling story. Like a fandom dedicated to preserving its canon, this small family collective ensures that Auntie Dasha is not forgotten. Her difficult life and mysterious death are now reinscribed with meaning through the collaborative power of the network.

And Auntie Dasha's is just one of the family stories that we learned. Drawing on Giddens' (1991) theory of the "reflexive project of the self," Wilson discusses how genealogy exemplifies postmodern identity construction. The practice enables consumers to create "coherent, yet continuously revised, biographical narratives" (Giddens, 1991, p. 5) that blend personal and collective histories. This project both unifies and fragments the self. It connects, disconnects, and reconnects simultaneously. As Robert Saunders (2023) finds in his exploration of the platform, Ancestry's platform-based genealogical research is as much about shaping present identities as it is about uncovering the past.

Case Study: Hirschman and Panther-Yates' Consumption Ethnogenesis

My colleague Elizabeth, also known as Beth, Hirschman, had a considerably more dramatic genealogical experience than I did. Beth has always been on the cutting edge of research topics in consumer culture, and she was well ahead of the curve again when she pursued this topic. Her article "Suddenly Melungeon! Reconstructing Consumer Identity Across the Color Line," which she co-authored with Donald Panther-Yates (who was raised as an American Indian), offers the authors' personal and scholarly exploration of ethnic identity through the lens of Melungeon ancestry. Melungeons are a historically marginalized and racially ambiguous group in the Appalachian region of the United States, often perceived as having mixed Native American, African, and

European lineage. In the article, Beth and Donald recount their own genealogical discoveries, tracing their unexpected connection to Melungeon heritage through DNA testing and historical research. These revelations prompt an introspective journey that intertwines personal identity with broader cultural narratives of race, ethnicity, and belonging.

Their prior co-authored article, "Peering inward for ethnic identity: Consumer interpretation of DNA test results," discusses in more general terms how consumers use DNA results to construct narratives about their ancestry (Hirschman and Panther-Yates, 2008). Emphasizing the potentially life-changing disembedding that can happen, the authors discuss the identity disruptions that occur when results challenge pre-existing beliefs.

It may be tempting to categorize DNA testing as primarily a scientific endeavor due to its connection to cutting-edge genetics and biology. But we must also see it as a cultural phenomenon that constructs how individuals perceive race and ethnicity and how they learn about and enter communities associated with those identities. DNA testing services, in fact, have developed entire protocols to assist individuals who recently found out they are genetically unrelated to their close family members. These tests can both emplace and displace people from their familial, ethnic, and historical contexts. This deterritorialization and reterritorialization happens literally and can have a powerful influence on the evolving understanding of identity in contemporary times.

As I do in this chapter, Hirschman and Panther-Yates (2007) offer a personal narrative. It highlights the transformative power of genealogical discovery in shaping the authors' ancestral journey within a larger context of cultural redefinition, showcasing how marginalized histories can be reclaimed and even celebrated. In service of this celebration, the authors appropriate and develop Jonathan Hill's (1996, p. 1) concept of "ethnogenesis," described as "the historical emergence of a people who define themselves in relation to a socio-cultural heritage" and use ethnogenesis "as an analytical tool for developing critical historical approaches to culture as an ongoing process of conflict and struggle over a people's existence... within... a general history of domination."

They use the ethnogenesis concept in their ethnography to explore their personal, scholarly, and consumer-related relationship to their own newly discovered Melungeon heritage. Melungeons were most likely Sephardic Jews and Muslim Moors who superficially converted to Christianity to escape the Spanish Inquisition and then immigrated to the New World as colonists to escape further religious persecution. They settled around Appalachia and intermarried with the resident Indian population and, later, with free or escaped Black slaves.

Intriguingly, Hirschman and Panther-Yates assert that "learning to consume like a Melungeon" became a "key ingredient" in their ethnogenic process as the authors began re-evaluating their cultural and consumer choices in light of their new identity. They began consuming foods (kosher and halal style), musical styles, and herbal remedies deemed to relate to their newfound heritage, alongside books and artifacts linked to Appalachian and Melungeon history. These shifts reflected increasing engagements with their ancestral culture, which they began to prize and honor. "For example, the recollection that one's grandparents strictly avoided pork had not been previously recognized as indicating potential Jewish or Muslim ethnicity" (Hirschman and Panther-Yates, 2007, p. 245).

This process of "consumption ethnogenesis" illuminates a pathway of identity construction that runs parallel to the cultural logic of fandom. Hirschman and Panther-Yates, upon receiving their "revelation," act much like a new convert to a complex media franchise. They engage in an agentic and visible use of consumption to learn, perform, and embody their newfound identity. Just as a fan might purchase specific merchandise, learn inside jokes from tie-in materials, and adopt the styles of their favorite characters, the authors began to consume foods, music, and artifacts that signified "Melungeon." From the DNA test, the marketplace becomes the next station for identity exploration and the manifestation of material practices of belonging. Whether we use it for fandom, religious conversion, or to adopt a new ethnic identity, the market becomes a central place we use to demonstrate our fluency and commitment. Marketplace transactions help us transform a diffuse, abstract self into a real one.

This identity adoption stands in contrast to my own genealogical journey, yet it arrives at a similar destination. My experience reconstructing the story of my grandfather's eldest sister was a project of reterritorializing a narrative. Through the digital exchange of information with a dispersed family network, we assembled a coherent story from scattered fragments and even ended up finding and conversing with another new relative, Ivan, Dasha's great-great-grandson, who lives in Kyiv. Hirschman's journey, on the other hand, details the reterritorialization of a lived identity through her material practice of consumption. While my project resulted in a digital monument built from data, hers resulted in an embodied identity performed through marketplace choices. Both pathways, however, demonstrate the same fundamental process: using the tools and logics of our contemporary age—be it digital information exchange or the curated marketplace—to reclaim the past, construct new meaning, and forge powerful connections within our chosen kinship groups.

DNA AS FAMILY BRAND

In work that relates to her Melungeon identity tracking, Beth Hirschman builds on her experiences to link the idea of branding with family ancestry. "Evolutionary Branding" (Hirschman, 2010) argues that branding is interlinked with humanity's evolutionary drive to create symbolic markers that both construct and distinguish social groups. She examines branding narratives shaped by DNA testing and genetic ancestry, showing how consumers construct meaning and group affiliation based on DNA results, termed "brands of family."

She provides examples of "haplogroups as family brands" (p. 570), which include narratives connecting genetic subgroups to historical or mythological figures and communities. Intriguingly, Hirschman suggests that branding aligns with innate human drives for social cohesion and differentiation, making it a fundamental element of human culture rather than a byproduct of modern consumerism.

Genetic Roots and Global Routes

This is perhaps the most striking aspect of my engagement with Ancestry: the way it has enabled me to piece together genealogical records, census data, and DNA results and turn them into self-identity constructs, genetically based and verified. It brings us together with distant relatives we might never have otherwise known and their stories. And these people seem to tell me a bit more about who I am, what my heritage is, and where my capacities and blindspots may have recurred in family patterns. My personal act of consumption—ordering and interpreting a DNA test—catalyzed the formation of a dyadic family project: the discovery of my own identity and connectedness in the world.

As Beth Hirschman's work on consumer identities and ethnogenesis suggests, genetic testing businesses influence a wide array of industries, from health and wellness to tourism, with some consumers leveraging their ancestry results to guide their travel choices, food preferences, and even medical decisions. Heather Kennedy-Eden and Ulrike Gretzel (2022) explore personal heritage tourism as a niche domain of heritage tourism. Heritage tourism broadly encompasses visits to locations or communities that showcase folkloric traditions, cultural celebrations, and ethnic history. Kennedy-Eden and Gretzel define personal heritage tourism as individuals seeking connections with their personal ancestry and familial heritage, which includes visiting ancestral homelands, engaging with distant relatives, or conducting research into one's genealogical history.

A key feature of personal heritage tourism is its diversity. Kennedy-Eden and Gretzel classify personal heritage tourists into subgroups— roots, diaspora, genealogical, ancestral, and DNA tourists—with each one defined by distinct motivations and behaviors. Diaspora tourism often involves revisiting ancestral homelands and engaging with the culture, language, and traditions associated with one's ethnic background. For individuals whose families experienced displacement due to historical traumas like colonization, forced migration, or slavery, this aspect is particularly significant. For instance, the article highlights how some individuals of African descent try to reconnect with their heritage through visits to West African countries—Ghana is a popular destination. Diaspora tourists often must grapple with complex emotions tied to displacement or historical trauma. Examples of marginalized groups engaging in heritage tourism highlight the complexities of reconnecting with ancestral lands that may be fraught with colonial or post-colonial histories. It can also be a way to challenge historical erasure or racism and affirm ethnic pride.

On the other hand, European Americans often explore their roots in Ireland or Germany and trace the voluntary immigration of their ancestors. Genealogical tourists, in contrast, are on a type of treasure hunt focused on collecting historical records, such as birth or marriage certificates, and may visit libraries or genealogy centers. DNA tourists are motivated by a desire to understand their genetic identity and might explore cultural heritage sites that align with their genetic profiles or travel to connect with newfound relatives.

Kennedy-Eden and Gretzel explore how personal heritage tourism is shaped by access to resources, emphasizing the role of technology in democratizing these experiences. The financial and time investments required for extensive heritage travel may still exclude lower-income individuals, pointing to disparities in who can fully participate in this type of tourism. They also acknowledge the role of women in genealogical research, depicting women as central figures in family history projects, who act—just as my extremely capable wife, Ulli, does in my continuing genealogical journey—as memory keepers and organizers of family records. That gendered division of labor in heritage exploration is implied through examples of family-based research and the organization of heritage tours, which are often spearheaded by women.

Consuming the Collective Past

The journeys detailed in this chapter—my lifelong engagement with a rock icon, the digital reconstruction of Auntie Dasha's lost history, and Beth Hirschman's profound identity transformation—may seem disparate. Nevertheless, they are all variations on a central theme, best understood through the powerful, unifying lens of the consumer collective, with fandom as its archetypal form. Hirschman's "consumption ethnogenesis" is, at its core, a fannish practice. Her turn to consuming

Melungeon-related foods, music, and artifacts is a material practice of her newfound identity, a way to learn the culture and perform acts of membership. It is functionally very similar to my purchase and display of the Little Jimmy action figure. Both acts use the marketplace to acquire totems that make an internal, abstract identity tangible, visible, and real. This pathway of material consumption, of embodying identity by acquiring its objects, stands alongside the narrative pathway seen in the hunt for Auntie Dasha, where belonging was achieved not just by buying something but by co-creating a family story about my grandfather's long-lost sister.

Is there a hungry, empty self behind these activities? Subjectively, it feels more like a questing and curious self, a self putting out rhizomes into the world to explore and connect. My Jimmy Page action figure is a collectible toy and also an anchor to a youthful identity, a bulwark against the fragmentation of time. The Ancestry platform, a cold database, performs the almost miraculous act of conjuring lost relatives from the digital ether. Yet, unlike the enchantment/disenchantment paradox, these connections seem to bring me lasting joy. There is no furtive need for additional relatives or action figures. What I have is sufficient, but should another come my way, I expect I will be similarly delighted. There is no dark cycle of emptiness-fueled hunger and desire— Cushman (1990) and Belk et al.'s (2024) secret at the center of our modern condition—fueling my actions, at least as far as I can detect. This is me, living my life, assembling its meanings, enjoying its ever-unfolding quality.

CHAPTER 3
DIVERSE CONSUMPTION, DIVERSE CULTURES

L et's transition to the collective "we" voice of Rob and Henry. The last chapter contains three detailed examples involving the display of an action figure, the commercial use of DNA testing, and the adoption of the consumption habits accompanying a new ethnic identity. But, even if you don't have an action figure or use Ancestry to trace your family tree, you're probably part of a consumer collective.

This book concerns itself with consumer collectives as a particular type of social group, where a social group is composed of two or more people who interact, share similar interests, and possess some sense of having things in common. We should note that the nature of what constitutes a social group has changed rather dramatically since many classic sociological definitions were written. Earlier definitions tended to emphasize strong unity and shared beliefs, but we want to signal that these qualities are relative and contextual rather than absolute. Are two people who post to the same social media group part of the same social group? We think they are, but we also recognize that the bonds formed there are not the same, for example, as those formed by two people living together. Social groups, which we also call collectives, come in many forms, sizes, and types.

In a world of increasing individualism, one of the primary tools we have for building these social settings is consumer choice. The modern identity is a project constructed through a relentless series of consumption choices. The decision to wear a Led Zeppelin hoodie instead of a Joy Division t-shirt, to subscribe to one streaming service over another, or to buy organic instead of conventional are examples of these types of acts. They are public declarations of our values, our tastes, and our affiliations. The freedom to make these choices is central to the experience of being a contemporary consumer and is, in this respect, one of the key engines of our agency. Through the familiarity of our marketplace selections, we stitch together a personalized but recognizable self, signaling to others what kind of person we are and the collectives with which we wish to be affiliated.

Using the lens of consumer choice can also lead us to a heightened appreciation for the perspective of French sociologist Émile Durkheim (1893/1933). The brands, services, and media products we choose become what he would call "social facts"—things external to us that nevertheless profoundly influence our own and others' ways of thinking and feeling, shaping what he termed a "collective consciousness." Although consumer goods are often viewed and written about as tools for competition and status rivalry, they are equally signs of belonging and confederation. Their circulation leads to the creation of new social groups such as subcultures, brand communities, and lifestyles—concepts that we explore throughout this book and also in **Fandom as Subculture**.

However, while our choices are agentic, they are not made in a vacuum. To extend the metaphor, we are not choosing from an infinite wilderness of options, but rather from within the walls of beautifully curated gardens. Marketers and corporations are the landscape architects of these gardens. Marketers and brand managers, product innovators and makers and the companies behind them are the designers of many of the spaces we inhabit as consumers. They plan, select, create, and display the products that are available to us. They lay out the pathways that guide our experience within these walled gardens. We, as consumers, are not passive sheep being led through these gardens, either. We enter and leave them using our own free will. Once inside, we are active participants, free to wander, explore, combine elements in novel ways, and even cultivate our own small plots within this larger design. Nevertheless, our freedom is exercised within a pre-structured environment built to serve commercial ends. Moreover, paraphrasing what the French philosopher Louis Althusser (2006/1970) said of ideology, there is no activity that exists without consumer culture. Althusser believed one could only switch from ideology to ideology, never entirely escaping these embedded material practices. We find different types or lifestyles of consumption to be similar. We can choose between the offerings of the different walled gardens, but we find it practically impossible to escape from them. There is interdependence at work as well, for the architects need eager consumers to bring the garden to life with their energy and creativity. The consumers, for their part, appreciate having a beautiful, choice-filled, and well-organized space in which to enjoy their leisure time and connect with others.

That very human need for creativity and connection brings us to the core of Durkheim's enduring relevance. He was intensely interested in how modern societies maintain their coherence when traditional social and religious ties weaken. Even inside a commercially architected garden, the experience of "collective effervescence"—the shared energy and sense of unity felt at a concert, a fan convention, or in a thriving online forum—is entirely real and socially vital. This is the central paradox we must grapple with when we consider the topic of fandom as a consumer collective. For, although the creations of consumer culture may encourage individuality, the appreciation of their significance requires a collective recognition of their value. This recognition links them to some of the key dilemmas of contemporary capitalism, a subject we examine extensively in **Fandom and Technocapitalism**. Our consumption choices are therefore both acts of personal freedom and participation in a structured system; the goods we acquire are individualizing yet collective, separating yet connecting, and personal yet profoundly social.

Defining the Consumer Collective

We can now define a consumer collective as a social group of two or more people who connect around a shared interest in a brand, a form of consumption, or other mass culture products. As we explored in Chapter 1, conceptualizing fandom as a type of consumer collective requires us to closely examine the intersections of fan practice with consumer culture, economic structures, and methods of analysis. By framing these as specific types of social groups, we do not mean to suggest that they are monolithic. Rather, we envision a rich diversity of forms, members, and foci—the "multifarious qualities" we explore in **Defining Fandom**. The connections these various groups build are fluid and multi-layered, defined by ever-changing worlds of shared cultural references, diverse practices, and overlapping social networks.

Brands, services, and cultural goods animate these groups. Acting as social facts that are external to any single individual, yet still exerting a profound and social structuring influence, they move our focus beyond economic transactions. While some groups, like buyers clubs, form for purely pragmatic reasons—to aggregate buying power and negotiate better prices—the consumer collectives that are the focus of this book series are primarily concerned with meaning-making, information-exchanging, and the creation of social bonds. They are communities that draw people together by appropriating resources from the commercial economy and repurposing them for a vast variety of communal, social, and emotional ends.

To visualize this dynamic, we build on the conceptual work in **Defining Fandom**, which broadened the definition of fandom beyond traditional media to include diverse "fan objects" from tulips to Egyptology. The core relationship can be understood as a triadic structure, as illustrated in Figure 3.1.

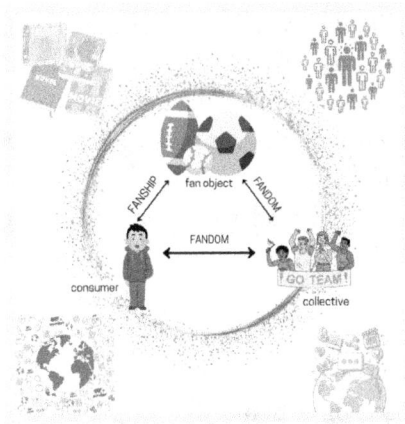

Figure 3.1: Triadic Structure of Consumer Collectives

This model focuses on the interplay between three key elements: the individual consumer, the fan object (which can be a sport, brand, musician, television show, and so on), and the collective itself. At the center of the relationship is fandom. On one hand, consumers develop a personal attachment to the fan object through "fanship"—the mostly individual experience of engagement, appreciation, and identification. On the other hand, fandom manifests as a social phenomenon, forging connections between individual consumers and the broader collective of fans who share a passion for the same object. This framework highlights how consumer collectives are sustained by global flows of media, commerce, and culture, situating them within broader societal forces and digital connectivity.

From Loyal Customer to Passionate Fan

Clarifying the often overlooked distinction between a "loyal customer" and a "fan" is a crucial aspect of our exploration. A loyal customer repeatedly purchases a particular brand or product, but their reasons for doing so can be varied and might even be dispassionate or habitual. This loyalty might be a function of simple pragmatism—a product that works well enough, a convenient subscription, or the high cost associated with changing. Economists and consumer scientists categorize such behavior under the umbrella of "lock-in," which includes mechanisms like "switching costs" that are explicitly designed by firms to enforce customer retention. We cannot, therefore, assume that someone who loyally buys the same laundry detergent or toothpaste is a "fan" of that product; their behavior may simply be a rational response to a given set of market structures.

However, within the broader category of loyal customers exists a vital and dynamic subset driven not by lock-in but by genuine enthusiasm, passion, and excitement. These individuals, whom we can call "passionate brand enthusiasts," feel a deep affective connection to the brand, product category, or consumption activity itself. Their energetic devotion might be focused on a brand like Apple or Coca-Cola, but their passion aligns them closely with fans of cultural phenomena like Blackpink, São Paulo FC, or Pokémon. This is our key point: these passionate enthusiasts exhibit distinctly fan-like qualities, channeling their energy into behaviors and attitudes that transcend simple repeat purchasing. When these enthusiastic consumers join together based on their shared passion, their consumer collectives become functionally analogous to fan communities. By the same token, fandoms themselves are a unique and powerful type of consumer collective, sharing traits with other collectives as well as with related concepts like audiences, subcultures, and publics—distinctions that are explored in depth in **Fandom as Audience**, **Fandom as Subculture**, and **Fandom as Participatory Culture** books.

Ultimately, it is crucial to recognize that every individual fandom and consumer collective has unique qualities. Just as no two people are alike, no two collectives are either; they are multifaceted social worlds shaped by a confluence of media, ideology, politics, morality, and much more. Within this patchwork, diverse cultural worlds emerge, each with its own distinct identity, social network, and creative expressions. Recognizing this diversity requires a deep understanding of lived human experience, which is why qualitative methods like ethnography and netnography are so essential. These methods allow us to capture the richness of fandom as both a social fact and a powerful aspect of contemporary life. In the following section, we showcase how these methods of cultural investigation reveal the resistance, richness, and diversity of consumer collectives.

Spaces of Connection and Rebellion: Rethinking Inclusion in Consumer Collectives

Consider a consumer collective with enough visibility and influence to be noticed even in today's fragmented world—a group that pushes against the "mainstream," however ambiguously that concept might be defined (see our discussion of post-subcultures in **Fandom as Subculture**). The vanlife "movement" is a prime example. At its core, it is a lifestyle centered around purchasing and converting vans, hitting the road, and embracing ideals of freedom, adventure, exploration, and reconnection with nature in settings that usually include varieties of group participation. The dominant narrative of vanlife has been critiqued for privileging white perspectives and lifestyles. Its guiding ethos, like that of many cultures, is perhaps unintentionally shaped in ways that include some while excluding others. Despite its presentation as a broad, inclusive community, vanlife's narratives often obscure the systemic inequities and barriers faced by marginalized groups, a critique that can be levied at many consumer collectives that also contain potentially exclusive social practices. The Academy Award-winning film, *Nomadland* (Zhao, 2021), takes us inside the culture of displaced people, moving from camp to camp, in search of work. They are also using vans as their homes, forming support communities wherever they land, with groups of people separating and coming together again. The nomads come from diverse backgrounds, but they share the common experience of a different form of "vanlife."

For these reasons, subgroups have arisen within the greater vanlife collective to better express the needs of these disenfranchised groups. The article *"Illusion of Inclusion: #BlackVanlife as Counter-Storytelling"* by Tatjana Walpersberger and Ulrike Gretzel (2024) explores the #BlackVanlife phenomenon as a form of counter-storytelling within the broader vanlife culture. Although #vanlife seemingly represents an average consumer experience, implying inclusivity, #BlackVanlife directly addresses the exclusionary practices hidden within its ideology. It highlights the barriers and inequities faced by Black vanlife participants.

Through videos, images, hashtags, and personal stories, participants in #BlackVanlife construct an alternative digital and physical community that fosters solidarity between its Black members. They use social media platforms not only to document their experiences but also to critique the structural inequalities that define their participation in vanlife. Narratives of "RVing while Black" in videos, images, tags, and stories reveal the systemic barriers faced by participants. Their narratives uncover how systemic barriers are intertwined with racialized experiences of travel and mobility, offering a counterbalance to the romanticized ideals and uncontested privilege of the vanlife lifestyle. The stories shared under #BlackVanlife highlight the systemic challenges its members face in accessing resources and navigating spaces, bringing to light the hypocrisies behind the idealized notions of mobility, freedom, and minimalism promoted by the mainstream vanlife narrative.

Dem Thrones

As a consumer collective, #BlackVanlife embodies a coded identity that intersects race, RV culture, and the ethos of traveling as a lifestyle. We might consider the example of a group of Black media fans inserting themselves into a mostly white narrative and redefining it towards their own ends: Sarah Florini's case study of Black *Game of Thrones* fans (Florini, 2019). At the time of the study, *Game of Thrones* was perhaps the biggest television series in the world, but it was one that had only a small number of Black characters. HBO was making minimal and somewhat patronizing efforts to court these minority fans through a campaign centered on hip-hop artists who were themselves fans of the series. So-called Black Twitter was being examined as an alternative set of networked practices that increased the visibility of Black voices but also sought to "enclave" itself, that is, to create a space where public opinion could develop within a minority community in the open but with limited interference from white platform users (Parham, 2021). We might also see Black travel as an example of "Black Twitter," related to Blackvanlife on Instagram, with all of these groups defining their identity and circulating counternarratives within social media platforms.

#DemThrones was a space where Black fans could reimagine *Game of Thrones* characters through a Black lens as well as play around with stereotypes of urban Black life and with "African American Vernacular English (AAVE)" in ways that turned the associations of the genre with European whiteness on its head. As Florini explains, "#DemThrones fans are able to shift their contributions to a parallel timeline, separating themselves from the fans using the official hashtags while still allowing them to utilize Twitter for synchronous co-viewing." She argues that such "sequestering" was both a means of self-protection and of inflecting fandom in a direction that allowed them to negotiate with the meaning of the series. As she notes, #Demthrones often reads "Black cultural specificity into a text with a notable absence of Black bodies" (Florini, 2019, n.p.).

Game of Thrones was, in turn, used to comment on contemporary Black life. She cites, for example, one post:

> All dese Black names, dog. C'mon. Tormund? I prolly play ball at the Y[MCA] with a nigga named Tormund...All these names sound Black. They be tryin' to pronounce it with that English accent like we don't know...All these names would not pass the résumé test. You put these names on a résumé, they be like, 'No, no, no, no. We are *not* gonna be hiring any Aryas. I think we know what that applicant gonna look like' (Florini, 2019, n.p.).

On #Demthrones, the *Thrones* houses were re-envisioned as rival gangs and the warrior figures were seen as "thugging." And they imagined how Black houses such as House Jackson of Detroitland would operate among the Lannisters and the Starks.

Carving Out Space: Gay Fandom in Mainstream Football

These examples of #BlackVanlife and #DemThrones illustrate how marginalized groups can form a "collective-within-a-collective," creating enclaves that offer both protection and a platform for creative reinvention. This dynamic is powerfully evident in the world of sport, particularly within the historically hypermasculine and heteronormative culture of English football. Here, we can observe distinct strategies for how marginalized fans navigate, challenge, and remake the spaces of their chosen consumer collective.

One strategy is to work from within the mainstream, carving out a space for belonging inside the established structures of fandom. The gay male football fandom studied by Rory Magrath (2021) provides a compelling case study. English football culture has historically been dominated by a "thuggish and violent form of masculinity, both on and off the pitch" (p. 981), creating a toxic environment where any alternative sexuality was explicitly rejected. In response, LGBT fans began to organize, forming official LGBT fan groups for nearly half of England's professional clubs. According to Magrath's research, these groups serve a crucial function, providing sexual minority fans with increased visibility, a sense of community, and a feeling of belonging in an environment from which they were traditionally excluded. They work directly with the clubs, assist in steward training, and organize social events, reforming the mainstream from the inside.

However, this hard-won inclusion remains what Magrath terms a "conditional acceptance" (p. 978). Despite feeling safer and noting a considerable decline in homophobic chanting, two-thirds of the gay male fans in his study still described football stadia as "unwelcoming" hypermasculine environments (p. 988). This feeling leads to tangible behavioral changes; almost a third of fans who attend matches with a partner will strategically avoid public displays of affection to prevent drawing unwanted attention. Their experience reveals a key dynamic of consumer collectives: a subgroup can achieve formal recognition and create a safer space, yet its members may still feel compelled to self-police their behaviors to conform to the dominant culture's unspoken rules. Like the Black Vanlifers, they have successfully carved out a space, but it exists within the larger, still-imposing architecture of the mainstream.

Building New Worlds: Queer Anarchism and DIY Football

A second, more radical strategy moves beyond seeking inclusion and instead focuses on building entirely new worlds within fandom. For some, especially those marginalized not only by mainstream society but also by more conventional gay and lesbian communities, reforming the existing structures is insufficient. Alice Hoole's (2024) research on queer DIY football offers a powerful glimpse into this alternative. Her study focuses on football spaces created from the ground up by and for women, transgender, and non-binary players who embrace a queer anarchist, Do It Yourself (DIY) ethos. Disillusioned with the rigid gender binaries and hierarchies of formal leagues like the FA Sunday League, they chose not to reform it but to abandon it altogether.

These groups engage in what is known as "prefigurative politics"—using radical, localized praxis to enact the kind of society they wish to see in the present (Raekstad and Gradin, 2020). A core tenet of these fans' practice is the deliberate decentering of competitiveness. They reject the mainstream sporting focus on winning, domination, and ability, and instead create spaces where "failure is not possible" and value is placed on friendship, community, and joy. They offer a fundamental reimagining of what football is for. Hoole (2024, p. 249) documents how these players, who often identify as "misfits" or "outsiders" even within queer culture, embrace "the absurd, the silly and the hopelessly goofy" (p. 252), finding a childlike freedom that stands in direct opposition to normative expectations of adulthood. Their goal is not to gain acceptance from the mainstream but to create "micro-utopias" (p. 254) that create networks of alternative practice and operate on entirely different principles.

Reforming from within versus building anew demonstrates a key strategic choice faced by marginalized consumer collectives. Magrath's LGBT fan groups illustrate a political struggle for recognition, safety, and inclusion within the existing consumer landscape. They are carving out a space in the established garden. Hoole's DIY teams represent a more revolutionary act of rejection and reinvention; they are leaving the curated garden entirely to cultivate their own, based on a different philosophy of what it means to play. Together, they reveal the profound potential of consumer culture not just to reflect societal norms, but to serve as a potent arena for their disruption and reimagination. The act of inserting racialized meanings into a white-dominated show, gay visibility into a hypermasculine stadium, or anarchist joy into a competitive sport reveals that when people are excluded, they will use the raw materials of culture to either demand a seat at the table or build a new table altogether.

Passion, Choice, and Consumption Collectives

In their influential overview, Eric Arnould, Adam Arvidsson, and Giana Eckhardt (2021, p. 415) define "consumption collectives as networks of social relations that arise around consumer goods, brands, and other kinds of commercial symbols, and digital platforms." Our concept of consumer collectives is indebted to this work. Their historical survey of literature on consumption collectives suggests a useful linear progression where early social theorists focused almost exclusively on the individualizing and alienating potential of consumer goods, with the collective dimension only being properly recognized by researchers in the latter half of the twentieth century. As Eric Arnould (2025) pointed out in a helpful explanatory email to us,

> scholars of consumption in marketing (because of the pernicious legacy of liberal economic thought) discovered [the culturally important collective dimensions of consumer behavior] in the latter half of the 20th century building from the near contemporaneous "discovery" of subcultures by the Birmingham school of sociology. Weirdly as Richard Wilk and I discovered in the 1970s, however, there was no anthropology of consumption at that time. Dannie Miller was the first to really plant that flag. The point is that consumption as collective practice rather than as a matter of individual demand or choice making was part of the enlightenment (small e) fostered by sociology and anthropology and taken up in marketing subsequently.

The idea that consumers could simultaneously be expressing a radical individuality and also participating in a vibrant, visible collective identity similar to a fandom thus has a long history and is a legacy that Arnould et al. (2021) track to advantageous effect. Our book series similarly treats this as a fundamental and timeless condition of consumption in the modern era.

This differing philosophy leads to a different understanding of the very nature of these groups. Arnould, Arvidsson, and Eckhardt offer the heuristic taxonomy of "packs, tribes, and bands" to classify collectives based on their structural characteristics, such as sociality, hierarchy, and territoriality. In their model, a rave is a pack, an online skater group is a tribe, and a Harley-Davidson subculture is a band. Their tripartite model's reliance on concepts like territorial stability and its specific associations with each collective type are perhaps not as aligned with the digital era as the ones we often encounter in this book series. As we see repeatedly through this book series, fandom manifests in stable, persistent spaces that are not necessarily, or exclusively, physical ones. A subreddit for a specific brand or a dedicated Discord server for a gaming subculture is stable territory where fandoms can formulate and flourish over time.

Packs, Tribes, and Bands

Another important fact is that these fanlike collectives are formed around market-mediated goods. These social aggregations are, in many ways, annexations of cultural spaces by consumer culture. It is important to integrate the role of corporate involvement, which can be a central force in the formation and maintenance of these collectives. Think of the way music companies and sports entertainment corporations have long managed their artists' and athletes' fan bases. These companies are active players, actively manage and foster a so-called "band" by creating and moderating official online forums, sponsoring events, or even directly overseeing community-building efforts to ensure brand loyalty. Similarly, the "ephemeral swarms" (p. 419) of a pack can be the result of algorithmic nudging and targeted marketing campaigns on social media platforms, transforming what appears to be a natural coalescence into a managed state designed to serve a brand's short, medium, or long-range goals.

The Arnould et al. (2021) framework usefully focuses on certain characteristics like ephemerality, stability, and organization, but it cannot focus on every element of this complex phenomenon (no model can). Throughout this chapter, we build on their work and also focus on other crucial elements, such as size and intimacy. The choice of criteria leads to particular types of representation of consumer collectives that may or may not be accurate or useful. The fleeting nature of a specific social event, such as a group of sports fans sitting together for a single game, may at times coexist with the deep, lifelong identity of being a fan of that team. Are the people sitting together at the game engaged in the short-term, transactional interaction of a "pack"? Or are these lifelong sports fans expressing the long-term, personal commitment of a "band"? We think they could be both. We also consider it helpful to differentiate between a massive, but still organized, collective and a small, intimate group with similar characteristics. That differentiation would likely prioritize the dimension of intimacy, which is central to understanding the nature of social bonds.

We would point out that, given the complexity of social life, any given fandom might fit into multiple categories. Packs, tribes, and bands are useful ways to think about consumer collectives, yet each may represent coexisting modes of interaction that thrive within a single, dynamic consumer collective (a reality that Arnould et al. certainly do not exclude in their article). Harley riders gather in small packs at local bars and in large ones at gatherings like Sturgis; they experience the intensely hedonic value of a tribe during a group ride on the open road; and they operate as a highly structured band within the formal hierarchies of their local chapters, complete with shared interpretive repertoires. Likewise, a rave can be also intensely tribal in its moments of cathartic, shared experience, while the dedicated groups of friends who travel together from event to event function as a tight-knit band. Pack, tribe, and band are not fixed categories but shifting modalities of experience that may coexist within any collective. Yet certain kinds of collective may lean towards certain kinds of experiences.

This fluid and human-centric model of consumer collectives may help us formulate a vision of the future of community in an increasingly algorithmic age. Arnould, Arvidsson, and Eckhardt rightly point to the rise of algorithmically defined "taste communities" (p. 421), such as the thousands of micro-clusters Netflix uses to categorize its viewers.

Drawing on Dalli (2021), they pose the critical question of whether the concept of "community" is still relevant when physical human relations matter less than the devices, platforms, and software that connect us. It is an important question, and one we address directly in **Fandom as Technoculture**. Nobody can predict with certainty whether we will be further atomized into a passive audience, controlled by machine logic, or if we will experience unprecedented empowerment. We struggle with, examine, and analyze these concerns throughout the book series. For the most part, we see the human drive for connection as a powerful counterforce constantly working within and against these algorithmic structures.

The story of Auntie Dasha is a testament to this indomitable and human algorithm. The massive, anonymous DNA database of Ancestry is the ultimate algorithmic collective, connecting millions of people who will never interact. Yet for my family, this supposedly soulless platform became the tool we used to forge a deeply personal kinship group across continents, allowing us to reconstruct a lost history and construct a digital monument to memorialize a forgotten relative. The algorithm provided the initial link, but it was pure human passion, curiosity, and our desire for a coherent and meaningful narrative that ultimately drove the creation of a genuine community. The future of consumer collectives will likely involve other complex stories of human community struggling against the challenges and sheer power of machinic and mediated connectedness. We are especially attuned throughout this series to the efforts of people to creatively repurpose the ever-more-powerful tools of the pack to satisfy their timeless, unshakeable need for the effervescence of the tribe and the solidarity of the band.

CHAPTER 4
OF ORANGES AND ODYSSEYS

I n the preceding chapters, we explored the nature and conception of consumer collectives and provided numerous examples of ways that consumer and collective behaviors intersect with fandom, including action figure display, online genealogical search, RVing, and sports fan communities, among others. These discussions laid the groundwork for understanding the diverse nature of consumer collectives and their cultural underpinnings. In this chapter, we turn our attention to the historical evolution of consumer behavior, focusing on how the study of consumers has shifted from individualistic, utility-driven models to more culturally and socially embedded understandings.

Before we embark on that historical journey, it is important to situate this exploration within the broader aims of our book series. Our analysis, which is deeply rooted in social and cultural theory, seeks to also be extremely useful to practitioners. Marketers, public relations professionals, brand managers, and any leader who works with or seeks to engage passionate groups of consumers will discover significant value in understanding the intellectual lineage of these ideas. To effectively connect with any given consumer collective—be it a fandom, a brand community, or a lifestyle movement—a manager must move beyond simplistic demographic targeting and grasp the deeper forces of meaning, identity, and community that underlie and motivate it. This chapter provides that essential context, revealing how decades of research have built a sophisticated understanding that offers a powerful toolkit for contemporary practice.

Furthermore, although Chapter 1 provided a justification for studying fans within the traditions of fan studies and communication, it is crucial to acknowledge that a parallel and highly influential field of inquiry has long been doing this type of research within businesses, in industry, and, most importantly, within business schools and their rigorous academic publications. As this chapter will show, the field of consumer research has undergone its own remarkable evolution. In some ways paralleling developments in communication and cultural studies, it gradually branched off from its pragmatic roots in economics and sales management, moving further and further away from a view of the consumer as a rational, utility-maximizing actor. Over time, it developed a profound appreciation for the agency, creativity, and diversity of consumers, becoming more sociological and anthropological in its outlook and methods.

As the world has changed, so too have the ways of and the reasons for consumer connection. A scholarly recognition of the collective capacities of consumer groups situates them within the broader contexts of economic, cultural, and technological transformation. From the rational utility-maximizing individual posited by classical economics to the nuanced, culturally rich, and symbolically laden perspectives advanced by the current generation of groundbreaking scholars, the field of consumer culture research has developed powerful methods and theories of its own. This chapter traces key moments in that metamorphosis from economics offshoot to productive subfield, exploring key milestones such as the rise of cultural approaches in consumer research, the influence of advertising as a cultural force, and the emergence of qualitative methodologies like ethnography and netnography.

A key focus here will be the increasing recognition of the collective aspects of consumption as it is shaped by shared identities, symbolic systems, and social connections. This chapter highlights how foundational thinkers like Sidney Levy and Russ Belk reshaped the field by emphasizing these dimensions of consumer behavior, laying the groundwork for contemporary studies of consumer collectives, including fandoms. Additionally, the chapter examines how shifts in media and technology, such as from traditional advertising to digital platforms, have created new opportunities for collective consumption practices to grow and develop.

By taking this historical lens, we not only uncover the intellectual lineage of research into collective consumer behavior but also foreshadow its broader significance in understanding fandoms as a type of consumer collective. Bridging past and present, these insights from the history of consumer culture research cast new light upon the complex consumer landscapes we engage with today. As the book progresses, we will build on these foundations to explore how fandoms exemplify the cultural and symbolic power of consumer collectives to offer new ideas about their role in shaping society, markets, and culture.

Utility Maximus

Economists initially framed consumer behavior as an individual, rational process governed by utility maximization. Rooted in classical and neoclassical economic theories, this perspective posited that consumers make choices by weighing costs and benefits to achieve the greatest satisfaction, or "utility," from their purchases. Utility curves were developed to represent these decisions, reflecting how individuals allocate limited resources based on their unique preferences and constraints. For instance, a consumer might decide between spending on luxury goods versus necessities based on the idea of diminishing marginal utility. Although it was elegant in its mathematical simplicity, this influential model of consumer behavior largely ignored the many social, cultural, and emotional factors that shape actual consumer decisions in the real world. For example, it wasn't until the formal founding of the consumer research field in 1969 that it started to become obvious how much consumption was driven by family membership and the need for a sense of status, meaning, and belonging, rather than the functionalist individual decision-making that was previously presupposed. Later investigations by a range of psychologists, including those calling themselves "behavioral economists," revealed just how supposedly (and predictably) "irrational" consumer decision-making could be (Ariely, 2008).

The study of consumer collectives by consumer researchers has evolved in parallel with shifts in socioeconomic, cultural, and technological landscapes. When media consisted largely of a few channels and a few big newspapers, society was far more unified, and consumers could be classified and targeted in ways that seemed far more straightforward and direct than the multiple (or "omni") channel advertising and distribution models of today. As digital platforms proliferated and expanded into online social spaces, researchers began to notice that they were creating new opportunities for consumers to connect, participate, and build collectives. All the while, studies of these proliferating consumer collectives were starting to look more and more like the studies of fandoms coming from the cultural and media studies scholars embedded in communication schools.

Figure 4.1 presents a parallel timeline showing the developments of fandom studies and consumer research from the 1950s to the present day and noting the numerous similarities between the two fields. The timeline compares the two fields and highlights their shared roots. Beginning in the 1950s, cultural studies and marketing scholarship laid the groundwork for both fields. Raymond Williams' (1989) foundational work, "Culture is Ordinary," challenged elitist views of culture, while Sidney Levy's (1959) "Symbols for Sale" explored the symbolic nature of consumer goods, foreshadowing the core themes of consumer culture research.

1960 and 70s – EARLY STIRRINGS

In the communication field, media studies and culture studies (popular culture) sub-branches develop; increasing interest in popular culture and challenges to elitist views of television

In marketing scholarship, consumer research sub-field develops; increasing interest in context effects that question rational economic decision making models

1979-Dick Hebdige's Subculture: The Meaning of Style is published; book is very influential in both fields

1990s – FIELDS EMERGE

Fandom studies splits from audience studies. In communication and media studies, Camille Bacon-Smith, Constance Penley, and Henry Jenkins publish fandom ethnography books.

In consumer research, increasing interest in postmodernism, popular culture, and consumer resistance. Fandom and consumer research begin focus on role of gender and sexuality

In consumer research, Eileen Fischer, Julia Bristor, Susan Dobscha, Linda Tuncay Zaher, and others open up feminist consumer studies. Susan Fournier founds consumer relationship brand studies and John Schouten and Jim McAlexander publish their Harley Davidson subcultures ethnography

2015s and beyond–CONVERGENCE

Fandom studies and consumer culture theory research increasingly institutionalized and legitimate. Scholars in fandom studies and consumer culture research fields both turn their attention to issues of race and globalization.

Scholars in fandom studies and consumer culture research start to become more aware of each other's works and slowly build ties between their respective fields and shared scholarly interests

1950s – FOUNDATIONS LAID

1959-Raymond Williams publishes "Culture is Ordinary," a foundation of cultural studies that challenges elitist views of culture; the same year, Sidney Levy publishes "Symbols for Sale," which explores the symbolic meanings of consumer goods and foreshadows many of the key concerns of consumer culture research

1980s – SEEDS SOWN

In communication and media studies, Stuart Hall publishes "Encoding/Decoding" in 1980, triggering increasing interest in subcultural and popular culture topics and qualitative methods. Increasing interest in qualitative and ethnographic methods as Consumer Behavior Odyssey demonstrate their power in consumer research. .

2000s – GROWING IMPACT

Consumer culture theory splits from consumer research field. In 2001, brand community concept introduced by Al Muniz and Tom O'Guinn; in 2002, Robert Kozinets develops netnography and Steven Kates theorizes gay and queer consumers; in 2003, Eric Arnould and Craig Thompson introduce Consumer Culture Theory as a sub-branch of consumer research

Fan and fandom studies gain wider acceptance within media studies and cultural studies; fields begin to increase their focus on the political and social implications of fandom. In 2006, Helleksen and Busse publish volume on fandom and the internet. In 2008, Henry Jenkins publishes Convergence Culture signaling increasing attention to the impact of technology and also increasing engagement with the creative industries.

Internet becomes decisive force in both fandom studies and consumer research.

Converging Timelines between Fandom & Consumer Studies

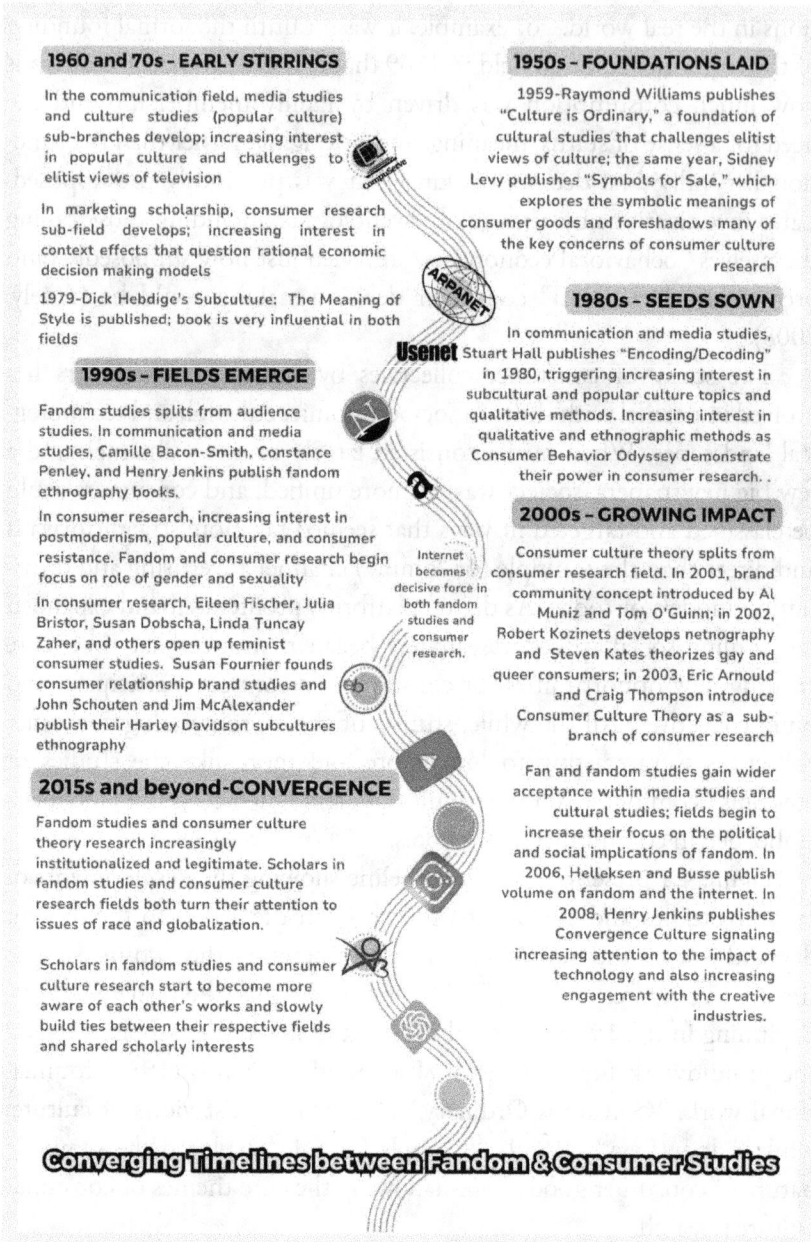

Figure 4.1: Fandom Studies and Consumer Culture Research's Parallel Timelines

Throughout the 1960s and 1970s, media studies and marketing science cultural studies gained traction. Both communication and marketing fields were profoundly impacted by the publication of Everett Rogers' (1962) *Diffusion of Innovations* book. That book clarified that the then-expanding field of mass media did not always directly influence audience members or consumers but, instead, these people were influenced by their observation of their local peers. Roger's study found that farmers in Iowa watched the crops of their neighbors who had adopted new hybrid seed corn and saw that it grew faster and better than their own crops. That, rather than news reports or advertising, is what most power-fully convinced them to order the new seed next year. The publication of Dick Hebdige's (1979) work on subcultures also sparked interest in popular culture and subcultures in marketing and cultural studies, as we explore further in **Fandom as Subculture**.

The 1980s and 1990s witnessed the growth and formalization of both fields. Fandom studies gained legitimacy through works like those by Camille Bacon-Smith, Constance Penley, and Henry Jenkins, which examined fandom as creative and resistant. Meanwhile, consumer culture research expanded to explore consumer resistance and brand-focused ethnographies. The mid-1990s marked the emergence of subfields, including Robert Kozinets' (1997) introduction of netnogra-phy, which bridged consumer research and fan ethnography. As digital technologies transformed both domains in the late 1990s and 2000s, fandom and consumer culture studies began addressing the social and political implications of this computer-mediated revolution and also featuring increasingly diverse voices and global perspectives. By the 2020s, greater collaboration was starting to emerge, with both fields increasingly recognizing their overlapping interests in studying online communities and collective consumption practices.

Active and Passive Consumers

To understand the contemporary consumer collective, we must first grapple with the historical stereotype it pushes against: the image of the passive consumer. This narrative begins to take shape with the great "consumer revolution" (Trentmann, 2016) that swept through much of the Western world, including France (Williams, 1982) and the Ottoman Empire (Karababa and Ger, 2011), during the eighteenth century—a transformation influenced, in part, by earlier developments in Ming China (Brook, 1998). This period saw a dramatic rise in the availability of consumer goods, spurred by expanding market economies, international trade, and the economic growth of colonial activities. As goods became more accessible, consumption began to emerge as a central force in social life, creating new possibilities for identity and association.

However, as industrial production ramped up over the next century, a powerful dichotomy took hold in social thought. Production was framed as active, valuable, and socially productive—and, not incidentally, associated with masculinity. Consumption, in contrast, was often cast as production's negative opposite: a passive, mindless, and feminized act of simple acquisition and use. This view framed consumers as solitary shoppers or end-users, devoid of meaningful social contribution beyond their role in absorbing the output of industrial economies. This stereotype, while lacking strong evidence, represented a powerful daydream for producers and advertisers: an ideal state in which they could sell products to a compliant public simply by placing ads on the radio or television and ensuring the goods appeared on retail shelves.

This general stereotype of the passive consumer found its most potent and enduring icon in the figure of the American housewife in the early-to-mid twentieth century. This viewpoint is popularly known as "Selling Mrs. Consumer," the title of a 1929 book by home economist Christine Frederick (Lavin, 1995). In this heavily marketed vision, the ideal woman's life was dictated by household chores and raising children, her agency expressed primarily through brand-loyal shopping for her family. This image of the homebound and brand-dependent female consumer was so powerful that it was eventually generalized, creating a broader view that all consumers—male, female, young, and old—were fundamentally passive and domesticated, beholden to their favorite brands and willing to do whatever paternalistic corporations and their persuasive advertisers told them to do.

The cultural historian Jackson Lears (1995), in his work *Fables of Abundance*, masterfully explains the cultural engine that powered this worldview. He demonstrates how the advertising industry, particularly in America, realized quite early on in their history that they were actually in the business of building and selling mythologies, aspirations, and dreams—not just products. By harnessing powerful symbols of abundance, progress, and magical transformation, advertising created a cultural framework where consumption became the primary pathway to achieving a better self and a sense of belonging. This linkage of goods to personal and social ideals helped cement the notion of a consumer whose desires could be shaped and guided by marketers. Today, it is commonly accepted that these commercial and media ecosystems interact with our lives in myriad ways, with branding and advertising serving as powerful tools for both identity construction and social connection. However, just as Stuart Hall's (1980) work on encoding and decoding deconstructed the assumption of a passive media audience, the history of consumer research reveals a parallel journey: a move away from the myth of the passive shopper and toward a recognition of the active, creative, and profoundly social consumer.

This movement is also related to the established literature on "active leisure" within leisure studies, public health, and sport sociology, which is often contrasted with "passive leisure." In that literature, passive leisure refers to seemingly sedentary activities like watching television or browsing social media, while active leisure includes physically or mentally engaging pursuits that require effort, skill, or focused participation. These range from sports, exercise, outdoor recreation, and dance to hobbies, volunteering, and creative arts. The literature approaches active leisure from multiple angles: its role in promoting health and well-being (Caldwell, 2005; Godbey, 1999), its sociocultural meanings and accessibility (Iso-Ahola, 1980; Chick, 1998), and its place in broader debates about the commodification of leisure and the blurring of boundaries between work and play (Rojek, 1995; Blackshaw, 2010).

Active leisure links directly to the themes of fandom and consumer collectives because many fan engagements have been deemed participatory and active. Sports fandom can involve physically playing the sport; music fandom often extends to dancing, performing, or traveling to live events; media fandom may lead to cosplay, fan art, or organizing conventions. Even when the object of fandom originates in the cultural industries, the leisure it inspires frequently takes on the qualities of "serious leisure" (Stebbins, 2007). Just as consumer researchers have been complicating the view that sees consumers as passive and isolated, so too have active and serious leisure researchers emphasized that leisure is productive, creative, and socially embedded, operating as a site where consumption and production merge.

The Levy Legacy

Contemporary thought about consumption and brands owes a lot to the work of Sidney J. Levy, who spent most of his career at the Kellogg School of Management at Northwestern University in Chicago. A product of interdisciplinary doctoral education at the University of Chicago, Levy promoted a view of brands that pictured them as cultural symbols. In a time when economists viewed brands as signals of quality, utility, and consistency, Levy argued that they are part of the fabric of society, reflecting and being reflected by cultural narratives, myths, and values. In one of his lesser-known articles, Sidney tied his interest in marketing to his life experiences growing up as the son of a Chicago grocery store owner (a "green grocer" as they were called). When he was nine years old, Sidney relates how he began to work in his father's grocery store and noticed that most of the produce was unbranded—the foods were commodities. However, his young mind began to rank the foods. He found the apple to be "considered a touch biblical" and, relating it to advertising campaigns like "an apple a day," healthy for daily consumption. However, he found one fruit special: oranges.

> Oranges were more special. As one consumer said in a later marketing research study, 'Oranges are a Godpackaged juice.' Oranges were rare, seasonal, and expensive. Then I became aware that oranges had names. Among them were the Florida kind, those that were pale, juicy, and somewhat tart. The greatest oranges had a more specific and evocative name: Sunkist. They were big, bright orange, and sweet, and sort of amazing, as they had navels and no seeds. Their belly buttons made them look kind of sexy, while the absence of seeds

suggested a scientific miracle, although one that had been kissed by the sun (Levy, 1996, p. 164).

Levy's soliloquizing on the virtues of oranges gives us a taste of his theorizing, which pulled back the curtain on the symbolic and cultural realms of consumption as a lived experience rich with difference and meaning. His short tribute to Sunkist oranges reveals the role of brands and branding, and his descriptions of the "belly buttons" of oranges as "sexy" prefigure the sexualized oranges of Seth Rogen's (2016) *Sausage Party* and (2024) *Sausage Party: Foodtopia*, demonstrating how cultural impressions of consumer goods can lead to narratives about them in popular culture.

Writing in the 1950s in a way that was well ahead of his time, Levy's work marked a profound shift in how we understand consumer behavior, emphasizing the symbolic, cultural, and emotional dimensions of consumers' behaviors. It was, in fact, revolutionary in 1959 when, in his *Harvard Business Review* article "Symbols for Sale," Levy linked sociological and historical analysis with marketplace trends, forming the foundations upon which consumer culture studies were built. He wrote that, as people had become less concerned with matters of their own survival, the more abstract their considerations become, and these more abstract considerations were reflected in their consumer behavior. "As behavior in the marketplace is increasingly elaborated, it also becomes increasingly symbolic" (Levy, 1959, p. 117). What this means is that "sellers of goods are engaged, whether willfully or not, in selling symbols, as well as practical merchandise" (ibid).

Proposing ideas that would become core principles of branding, Levy's insights made it clear that people were not consuming products simply for their functional benefits or utility. Instead, consumers were engaging with brands and products, and they were often doing it in emotional and socially connected ways that were central to their identities and their participation in society.

Early Developments in Consumer Science

Sidney Levy's work opened the door for later researchers with a cultural bent to theorize more directly about the role of advertising and celebrity endorsers. The cultural anthropologist Grant McCracken for example, studied the movement of meanings from marketers to consumption objects to consumers. The job of advertising, McCracken theorized, was to associate broader cultural meanings—such as having high status or being healthy—onto products. When consumers consumed the product, they would also integrate those meanings into their individual and collective identities. Advertising using celebrity endorsers was doing the same thing, McCracken (1988) asserted; it transferred meanings associated with the celebrity onto brands, like George Clooney transferring his brand of sophisticated suave onto the Nespresso brand of coffee maker.

In an important statement around the time of the founding of the field of consumer research, the marketing professor William "Tom" Tucker (1967) compared the way marketing researchers, like the ones who worked for a company, would look at consumers versus the way a consumer researcher would gaze at them. For Tucker, professional marketing researchers looked at consumers the way a fisherman looked at fish. They were interested in learning about consumers mainly because they wanted to learn how to catch them: what bait they like, what lures to use, and where they hang out. Instead, consumer researchers were the equivalent of marine biologists, interested in consumers and consumption as a source of intriguing psychological, cultural, and social insights and valuable in their own right.

It was not long before creative scholars like Morris Holbrook and Beth Hirschman were building on these ideas to explore how consumption involved consumers' experiences, which included ideas of fantasies, feelings, and a sense of fun and even the then-novel idea of researching "more diverse exploration—such as that involved in exposure to entertainment media," explained as a playful or "ludic" behavior (Holbrook and Hirschman, 1982, p. 136). It is worth noting the terminology here. Holbrook and Hirschman were writing for a research audience that was still deeply immersed in the quantitative economic models and the information processing theories of psychologists. The idea that people were "exposed" to entertainment or media—as if in a laboratory study by a white-coated technician—reflects this prevalent perspective.

Holbrook would go on to write several articles about music consumption, nostalgia, and movies, and many would contain the quantitative researcher's quest for clear causal patterns. He did, however, go on to publish an intriguing symbolic analysis of the movie *Out of Africa* that examined some of its tendencies to materialism (Holbrook and Grayson, 1986). Some of Hirschman's work also explored the media, including her structural-syntactical analysis of the ideologies contained within the *Dallas* and *Dynasty* television shows (Hirschman, 1988). Their book, *The Semiotics of Consumption* (Holbrook and Hirschman, 1993), includes numerous other examples, such as the interpretation of the *Beverly Hills Cop* and *Gremlins* motion pictures. Despite breaking new ground in consumer research by studying entertainment, Holbrook and Hirschman primarily focused on interpreting its inherent symbolism. The study of actual media fans and fandoms remained unexplored.

The Odyssey

At this point, we need to introduce Russell (or Russ) Belk, a former psychology researcher who abandoned a promising career as a consumer psychologist—the field he had been trained for—to adopt and develop qualitative research methods in the fields of marketing and consumer research. Belk's (1975) psychology work on the importance of "situational variables" in consumer psychology gradually led him to forsake the psychologist's stimulus-response model that treated consumers as organisms and to recognize not only the importance of their agency but also the complexity of the social and cultural environment in which they acted.

Context matters, Belk the psychologist argued and the results of this recognition ramified through the field of marketing and consumer behavior. After struggling to fit a nuanced view of situational contexts into psychological methods like experiments, diaries, and multidimensional scaling, Belk began adopting the qualitative methods that could follow the nuances of the social human environment, beginning with analyses of magazine ads and comic books. Along with him, the sociologist Melanie Wallendorf, the anthropologists John Sherry and Eric

Arnould, and others, the field began introducing what they called "naturalistic" and "interpretive" methods into consumer research. John Sherry also helpfully called the move a "cultural turn." This humanist vision of consumer research was methodological and conceptual; it built on early work by Levy, Holbrook, Hirschman (the latter called these "humanistic methods") and several others who were working in marketing at that time, and it lay in sharp contrast to the prevailing tendencies of the 1970s and 1980s that leaned heavily towards positivism and quantitative methodologies.

Promotional Buyways

Belk had a showman's talent for promotion, and he used it in the research field to good effect. In the mid-1980s, he spearheaded an ambitious research project that he termed, with a sideshow barker's bombast, the Consumer Behavior Odyssey. The Odyssey, as it came to be called, was not simply a research endeavor but an actual physical journey of ethnographic consumer researchers through the highways, "buyways," and back alleys of American consumer culture. Belk's vision for the Consumer Behavior Odyssey was expansive, and he didn't embark on this journey alone. Accompanying him was a group of intrepid scholars who shared his passion for exploration and naturalistic research—and who had formal backgrounds and experience in unstructured interviewing and ethnographic work.

For the entire summer of 1986, Belk, along with Melanie Wallendorf, John F. Sherry Jr., advertising historian Rick Pollay, and a wider group of fellow researchers who joined and then left, including Tom O'Guinn, Morris Holbrook, Debbie Macinnis, and ten others, collected data in their travels across the United State. The focal point of the journey was an RV, donated to the group by a member of the Marketing Science Institute, Vince Barabba of General Motors. In personal correspondence, Melanie Wallendorf recalls that Mr. Barabba reportedly told the board "something like 'I think sending a team of researchers out there to actually talk to people is a great idea.'" And actually talking to people was exactly what they did. The researchers centered on conducting ethnographic studies, interviewing consumers, taking copious fieldnotes and photographs, and pioneering consumer videography techniques. Their goal was to gain a more profound understanding of American consumer culture while also providing proof of concept for the types of qualitative research techniques the Odyssey was designed to demonstrate.

Throughout what follows, we find ourselves thinking about particular kinds of vehicles—such as those shaping the collectives being studied and those employed by the people doing the research. In this case, there is the rented RV. The anthropologist James Clifford has noted that in accounts of the ethnographic process, "The means of transport is largely erased—the boat, the land rover, the mission airplane, etc. These technologies suggest systematic prior and ongoing contacts and commerce with exterior places and forces which are not part of the field/object. The discourse of ethnography ("being there") is too sharply separated from that of travel ("getting there")." (Clifford, 1992, p. 101). In this case, we are discussing heroic journeys through the American heartland, not some exotic elsewhere and how we get there is part of the fun. So many of these references to transportation were invisible to Rob when we were first writing this section but popped for Henry as someone still new to the field of consumer culture research as he read it for the first time. As we continued with the writing, we have foregrounded them more, but it is interesting to us that transportation is the central lens through which to understand **Fandom as Consumer Collective** and is also prominent in **Fandom as Location,** while sartorial fandom becomes the core for understanding **Fandom as Subculture**.

Tales from RV Land

An RV set the backdrop for the Odysseans' collective journey, as Figure 4.2 amply illustrates. The RV assumes a larger-than-life identity in the Odyssey narrative. In the tales recorded in the archives and in rumor and gossip, the Odyssey RV becomes central intelligence, the professor's research office on wheels, a kitchen, dining room, bedroom, something like a light academia Mystery Mobile, a mobile research lab, a discussion hub, and a site of the researchers' metamorphosis from embedded city dwellers to aca-nomads. ". The desk that was used for typing fieldnotes during the day dropped down to become someone else's bed at night," Melanie Wallendorf recalled. The RV becomes like a boat charting new waters, a train taking on new passengers in every city, or a hop-on/hop-off research bus.

Plate 1.
The Odyssey rental van exterior in Wyoming, with (left to right) Russ Belk, Melanie Wallendorf, Rick Pollay and Joe Cote

Source: Consumer Behavior Odyssey archive, Marketing Science Institute, Cambridge, MA

Figure 4.2: The Odysseans, Circa 1986. Photograph © Russell W. Belk, Source: Belk 2014, p. 383 and Marketing Science Institute.

The RV, a symbol of travel and exploration in American culture, perfectly symbolized the group's nomadic intent, or aca-nomadicity. As a 'home on wheels,' the RV saw them navigating the vast stretches of America, making spontaneous pit stops, and living amidst the consumers they were studying. The Odyssey was always much more about the journey itself than it ever was about any of the destinations. Big shopping malls, retailers, or retail chains were not included among its many stops because the researchers would have required permission to interview people in the privately owned space of retail outlets. However, they stopped at numerous festivals such as country fairs and at some recognizable shopping districts like the Hollywood Walk of

Fame. The RV was a dedicated site for sociological and cultural observation and related academic discussion.

As Belk, Wallendorf, and the rotating crew of fellow Odysseans traveled, the RV became a melting pot of ideas, with researchers engaging in intense discussions, debates, and reflexive introspections. At times, the writing about the Odyssey was as much travelogue as it was social science. The sense of movement—geographic, conceptual, and even methodological—was palpable in the ethnographic notes provided in the Odyssey texts, as the following example from John Sherry's journal attests.

> Red Mesa Swap Meet is an excellent venue for observing family behavior in a consumer culture. I find myself having very angry reactions to some of the ways that children are socialized in particular subcultures. So much potential can be obliterated so easily that it literally makes your head swim. After today, I find myself missing my own wife and kids. Despite the regional cast of our fieldsite, it is interesting to note how often religion-as-product/ministry-as-service transcends geography. That ideology can be marketed as effectively as durable goods is an issue that the summer project might explore in depth. I find my concern with blitzkrieg ethnography being tempered somewhat by the phenomenon of high-tech equipment as license. Both researchers and informants can become disinhibited, not just inhibited, in the presence of video equipment. (Belk, Sherry, and Wallendorf 1988, p. 452)

We can see from these journal notes how richly insightful the trained ethnographic eye is when it enters into marketing and observes its cultural contexts. John Sherry is a talented anthropologist and he offers here a rich account that reflects on numerous matters: the frustrating state of childhood education and socialization in America, self-reflection about how he misses his wife and children, and observations about how ministry religion is commoditized and marketed. We also see one of the core methodological tensions of the group, which originated in the fact that the team was moving through places at a rapid pace and consequently was unable to fully appreciate what was going on in any of the locations. Comparing it to the rapid-as-lightning battle tactics of the German army at the beginning of World War II, Sherry uses the term "blitzkrieg ethnography," which anthropologists at that time were using to critique George Markus' idea of the multi-site ethnography.

We consider it noteworthy that Sherry links the acceleration of ethnographic time to ethnographers' adoption of "high-tech equipment," speculating (in the mid-1980s) that technology might speed the process of disinhibition and make qualitative research work more time efficient. As Sherry publicized its perils, blitzkrieg ethnography became a concern for consumer culture qualitative researchers. Post-Odyssey, researchers were asked in conference presentations and in submission reviews about the depth of their immersion and the need for prolonged field engagement when doing ethnographic work.

In notes to the authors, Melanie Wallendorf explained her stance on this methodological limitation and how she sees it represented in consumer culture research to the current day.

> I also share John's concern about the lack of sustained engagement. For the swap meet paper, we were deliberately dipping in for a few days to show MSI [the Marking Science Institute, a key sponsor of the Odyssey] how we would approach a site. However, I found it frustrating on the summer project to constantly be moving on. In response to this, I stayed in touch with two sets of informants and did follow-up visits with them: a couple who sold at swap meets that I originally met at what we called Red Mesa, and a set of women we interviewed about their home interiors. On the revisit with the women, I went with Morris [Holbrook] and Jeff Durgee, as I recall. I think this lack of extended engagement has spilled over into CCT's frequent use of stand-alone interviews without any extended period of observation, something that concerns me. I'm more interested in watching what people do than in just listening to them talk about what they think they do and are willing to tell you about.

These concerns were situated in and around the work of applied anthropologists advocating multi-sited ethnography (Marcus, 1995), which the Odyssey certainly was. It long preceded the tourism studies focus on the RV-centered Vanlife movement and the Black Vanlifers studied by Walpersberger and Gretzel (2024). From garage sales in the Midwest to shopping malls in metropolitan areas, from Native American reservations to vacation spots like Las Vegas, the Odysseans' twentieth-century journey covered a diverse array of consumer environments and locations. The sampling strategy was wide rather than deep, but this was precisely the point. The research team devoted themselves to their sites, immersed themselves in the local milieus, participated in activities, struck up conversation after conversation, and used video cameras and tape recorders to document both mundane and profound moments in people's lives in public marketplaces. They had enough material to make the first widely known consumer research videography, planting the seeds for what would become an important representational form in the field. Blitzkrieg ethnography or not, they were innovating pragmatic and time-sensitive, yet rigorous, ethnographic methods that, years later, would become commonplace in marketing research firms worldwide—due in no small part to the role of anthropologists like Rita Denny and Patti Sunderland, who have worked tirelessly for decades to help bridge the academic-practitioner divide in ethnographic marketing research. Interested individuals are directed to their helpful book, Doing Anthropology in Consumer Research (Sunderland and Denny, 2016).

For next-generation consumer researchers like Rob (who was still ten years away from completing his doctorate), the Odyssey provided a combination of inspiration and methodological guidance. It legitimized a path of inquiry that emphasizes empathy, context, and cultural theorizing. It laid a visible foundation for qualitative research methods in a field that had been dominated by quantitative, economic, and psychological models—and, in fact, is still dominated by them to this day.

Life among the Winnebago

Playing with the double entendre of ethnographic studies of Indigenous tribes and of the Odyssey's RV-centricism, Russell Belk's doctoral student John Schouten wrote a poem entitled "Life Among the

Winnebago." In the poem, which was published in the *Highways and Buyways* book (Belk 1991), Schouten summarizes an Odyssey experience in a way that allows us to comprehend its physicality and links with brand mythologies, as well as its ties to entertainment culture and the pastime of shopping. Following is an excerpt from the poem.

> *Wooden Indians,*
> *mechanical miners,*
> *barkers with beards and bad teeth*
> *bid us enter and buy;*
> *women with legs like bread dough*
> *and men with John Deere*
> *caps or Epcot Center belt buckles*
> *amble through curio shop doors*

The images of men wearing baseball caps sporting the logo of John Deere—an Illinois-based brand of tractors and other agricultural and forestry equipment—and Epcot Center belt buckles draw together the role of industrial and entertainment brands and also provide a glimpse of affiliations both ordinary and aspirational. In the next chapter, we will again encounter John Schouten and his keen ethnographic sense—along with his lifelong research partner and friend Jim McAlexander—responding to the call for post-blitzkrieg consumer ethnography and subsequently developing one of the hallmark studies of a consumer collective.

The work of Russell Belk, alongside such major consumer research figures as John Sherry, Eric Arnould, Beth Hirschman, Linda Scott, Linda Price, Melanie Wallendorf, Annamma Joy, Morris Holbrook, Tom O'Guinn, John Schouten, and Jim McAlexander, brought to life Levy's key foundations about the rich cultural experiences of everyday consumers. Leaving behind the mathematical econometric models, the psychology labs, and student research pools, these researchers took their investigations into the field and spoke to real consumers as they shopped around, outfitted their trailers, or buckled their pants with an image of Buckminster Fuller's geodesic dome, which Disney named, in deference to his influence, Spaceship Earth.

Whether investigating Black vanlifers, queer football activists, hip hop event planners or the places these groups of people gathered, these communities of scholars (who, Eric Arnould reminds us, also came from sociology and anthropology, as well as communication, cultural, and subcultural studies, human geography, tourism and leisure studies) collectively blew open the door to the cultural approaches that would dramatically deepen our understanding of consumer collectives, including fandoms.

CHAPTER 5
THE SUBALTERN AND THE SYMBIOTIC

W here the Odysseans had decided to favor multiple-site ethnography that took them roaring across America in an RV, their work inspired others to follow more closely the anthropological model of prolonged engagement and participant observation. It was with this mentality that John Schouten and Jim McAlexander conducted research with the Harley-Davidson company among the consumers of its motorcycles. Although we describe the theoretical contributions of that important work in **Fandom as Subculture**, we use this book as an opportunity to delve into some of that foundational work's other methodological and conceptual advances.

Riding the Boundaries of Belonging

Schouten and McAlexander's work is a timeless example of consumer ethnography. The research was sustained and multi-phase, transitioning from non-participant observation to full-time ethnographic immersion among the same group of related biker sites over a period of three and a half years. Seemingly configured as an antidote to the blitzkrieg approach of the Odyssey, their work aimed to understand the cultural and social dynamics of a consumption subculture by progressively deepening their engagement with its community and members.

In the initial phase of their research, Schouten and McAlexander (1995) engaged in non-participant observation, attending events such as the annual Sturgis rally and Daytona Bike Week as what they called "tourists." They introduced themselves as researchers and explained their relationship to the Harley organization while they busily cataloged symbols, observed interactions, and conducted initial interviews to identify safe entry points into the subculture. As Schouten and McAlexander describe, the emotions they felt during this period included fascination, fear, and heightened self-consciousness. Their internal discomfort reflected their outsider status. Over time, however, they transitioned to a more seasoned part-time involvement with the groups, during which time they began socially interacting with key informants, participating in numerous kinds of events, and becoming more integrated into the group's social structure. This phase moved them beyond the experiences typically available to those whose participation was more temporary or superficial (i.e., what they might see in a blitzkrieg-style set of ethnographic interviews). They began to recognize various categories within the subculture, such as the lesbian "Dykes on Bikes" offshoot, noting core elements of the different subgroups and observing various acculturation practices.

Passing as Harley Bikers

The final stage of their research involved full-time ethnographic immersion, during which Schouten and McAlexander became accepted by, and began considering themselves to be, Harley bikers. Schouten and McAlexander describe "'passing' as bikers" (p. 44) as a core element of their ethnography's legitimacy. In Schouten and McAlexander's case, their internal and external adoption of the Harley-Davidson subculture's rituals and practices enabled them to internalize the culture, and their critical self-reflection and rich data collection ("making a conscious effort to maintain scholarly distance from the phenomena we are constantly experiencing and observing") turned this emic (empirically and culturally experience-close) practice into an etic one (a cultural experience interpreted through the conceptual lens of scholarly categories). That type of patient, gradual, and internalized progression enabled them access to the emotional and relational underpinnings of the subculture, culminating in a nuanced understanding not only of how the Harley-Davidson brand promotes a sense of self-worth, belonging, and shared meaning among its enthusiasts, but also of how subcultures in general could do so. For example, Schouten and McAlexander's work linked the various symbols, including brand symbols, and the affordances of the motorcycles to an emancipatory ideology of personal freedom from the mainstream and its confinements. We can see from the following passages how this liberatory and oppositional ethos, that we also explore in **Fandom as Subculture**, becomes linked to commercial brands and the social groups that emerge around some of them.

> The Harley-Davidson motorcycle/eagle/steed stands for liberation from confinement. For bikers the Harley is the antithesis of all the sources of confinement (including cars, offices, schedules, authority, and relationships) that may characterize their various working and family situations. Similarly, symbols such as the tattoos, long hair, and bushy beards of many bikers, especially working-class members of the baby boom cohort, signify liberation from mainstream values and social structures. The myth of the Harley and its supporting symbolism is one of total freedom. The reality of daily life is usually one of multiple sources of confinement. For the biker, it is the reality of confinement that makes the myth of liberation so seductive and the temporary experience of flight so valuable. It is ironic that members of

the HDSC commonly choose, in joining formal organizations, to accept rigid new structures, new codes of conduct, new pressures to conform, and new sources of authority. (Schouten and McAlexander, 1995, p. 52)

The authors astutely note that Harley bikers' desire for freedom propels them into new social structures with their own sets of rules and strictures. This is a core paradox of social life. We crave association and a sense of belonging, as well as personal freedom and individuality. That fact means that we are constantly balancing the need for individual expression with the desire for group belonging. Subcultures of consumption, like other core social constructions, are places where individuals collectively work through some of these tensions as they conquer their loneliness through various forms of sociality but also must deal with their consequences.

Werther Fever and the Development of Capitalism

In many ways, this work builds on the intellectual heritage established by Johann Wolfgang von Goethe, the German poet and novelist. Goethe proposed the theory of elective affinities in his 1809 novel of the same name. According to Goethe's now firmly established idea, people are drawn to each other because they share common interests, values, and experiences. Unlike ascribed social categories and attributions such as kinship (your family), race, social class, religion, geographic location, or ethnicity—and the connections, friendships, and relationships that accompany them—these connections were elective because people freely chose them. In a utopian slant, Goethe expressed that the ability to choose affinities in society might one day overcome some of society's most formidable cultural impediments.

Goethe's 1774 novel, *The Sorrows of Young Werther*, written when he was only twenty-three, gave him an in-depth experience of such affinities. The book generated what we might today call a fan following, stimulating what writers of the period called "Werther fever" as young men imitated the lead character's distinctive style of dress. Marketers attached themselves to the phenomenon to sell perfumes, porcelain, and prints. More grimly, waves of youthful suicides spread across Europe, with people using similar guns and leaving copies of the novel nearby. The idea that the book made these youths kill themselves is one of the many charges that has clung to the notion of the fan through the years, contributing to the perception that fans' lack the ability to distinguish fantasy from reality and may be compelled to act upon the psychic force of their fantasies in dark and destructive ways.

Interestingly, and like Georg Simmel (who was writing at around the same time), Max Weber used the elective affinity concept to explain the rise of capitalism, the development of bureaucracy, and the formation of social classes. These historical synchronicities might suggest that, as modern capitalism and consumer culture were emerging and mass media communication was both isolating people (from ascribed and traditional categories) and bringing them together (through novel and chosen forms of connection), elective affinities arose as a type of grassroots social glue. For Weber, in particular, elective affinities between Protestant entrepreneurs and lawmakers drove the unstoppable rise of capitalism. It may be reasonable to consider fandoms and other grassroots supporters of media and corporate interests as a type of economic floor that supports and sustains local, regional, national, and global forms of capitalism. Fandoms, capitalism, and bureaucracies and institutions of various sorts were all built on the bulwarks of elective affinities, that magnetic attraction between people that held the social glue together when so many other connections were melting away.

Elective Affinities in Subcultures

The theory of elective affinities has been used to explain marriage, friendship, and social group formation, and it is in this latter sense, particularly, that we can also use it to explain how subcultures, fandom groups, and other consumer groups are drawn to specific consumption activities (e.g., playing pickleball), product categories (e.g., wristwatches), or brands (e.g., Labubu). Schouten and McAlexander's concept of subcultures of consumption offers us a framework for examining how elective affinities ground consumer collectives and lead to their relational, cultural, and symbolic dimensions. They define a subculture of consumption as "a distinctive subgroup of society that self-selects on the basis of a shared commitment to a particular product class, brand, or consumption activity" (p. 43). The key link to elective affinities is the idea that the members of subcultures of consumption "self-select" based on "a shared commitment."

The link to consumer culture comes in the form of that shared commitment. For Weber, the rise of capitalism happened because of the affinities between Protestant entrepreneurs and lawmakers. For Schouten and McAlexander, the Harley Davidson subcultures of consumption happened because groups of men who felt confined in their work (and perhaps home) lives joined together around the imagery and experience of the modern biker as someone free, rebellious, and macho. As a result of these brand-negotiated and advertising-promoted affinities and self-selections, the Harley subculture developed unique social structures, shared values, and symbolic expressions. They organize around shared practices, rituals, and ethos, which serve to bond members while also delineating hierarchies of authenticity and commitment.

The Harley Owners Group (or H.O.G.), which is operated by the Harley Davidson company itself, offers us a powerful example of how an ancillary commercial service can market a sense of community. H.O.G. acted as a rich site of identity construction and meaning-making for middle-class men who wanted to affiliate themselves with biker culture but were not interested in embracing the full-time or outlaw-related biker life. The sanitized corporate vision of the community still allowed its members to navigate the subculture's ethos of freedom and masculinity through symbolic acts, such as gathering together, drinking beer, customizing their motorcycles, or participating in communal events like rallies. These practices, according to Schouten and McAlexander (1995, p. 50), create "a sacred domain within the everyday life" of participants, highlighting the spiritual and transformative dimensions of consumption and their interrelation with a sense of the communal.

"Symbiosis" of Marketers and Consumer Collectives

Marketing institutions interconnect with subcultures. According to Schouten and McAlexander, the general biker subculture and especially the H.O.G. corporate community illustrate how brands like Harley-Davidson cultivate "long-lasting, symbiotic relationships" (p. 57) with these groups by aligning their strategies with the subculture's ethos and values. The passage is important because it explicitly draws on well-known subcultures (like punk) and fan groups (the Deadheads) for its comparisons.

"Subcultures of consumption, in their devotion to and ritualistic consumption of certain products, tend to patronize marketers who cater to their specialized needs. It is possible for a marketer who understands the structure and ethos of a subculture of consumption to cultivate a long-lasting, symbiotic relationship with it. Harley-Davidson has maintained such a relationship with the HDSC [Harley-Davidson subculture of consumption]. Other examples of such symbioses include those between Deadheads and the Grateful Dead organization (Pearson 1987), between bodybuilders and the Weider brothers' empire (Klein 1985, 1986), and, to a lesser degree, between small proprietorships such as punk bars and their regular subcultural clientele (Fox 1987)."

However, the concept of "symbiosis" between subcultures and marketing institutions, as described by Schouten and McAlexander in the context of Harley-Davidson, merits additional scrutiny. The term suggests mutual benefit and alignment. However, it could also be used to obscure the inherent tensions and power dynamics that characterize these relationships. Harley-Davidson's cultivation of its biker subculture and the Harley Owners Group (which it owns) demonstrate how companies with passionate followings seek to integrate themselves into consumer collectives by adopting—some might say appropriating—their values, symbols, and ethos and turning them into for-profit social networks. This strategy is positioned as a type of harmonious partnership between customers and the company that reinforces brand loyalty and creates a sense of shared identity. However, portraying it as "symbiosis" may mask exploitative practices that, in the long run, tend to serve corporate interests more than those of the consumer collectives.

Consider a social post titled "HOG membership is losing value fast," posted in May 2024 in the r/Harley subreddit. The post, which garnered 164 comments, details user experiences with the owners' group and offers us a brief critical lens through which to examine the concept of "symbiosis" between Harley-Davidson and its consumer subcultures about thirty years after the original ethnography. The subreddit poster, let's call him "Nicolass," describes how the value of his "lifetime membership" to H.O.G. has degraded over time. Although the "pins and patches" are still nice, they "no longer send a printed magazine," and the quality of the roadside assistance has significantly deteriorated. Harley-Davidson's actions, such as moving to online-only offerings and directing members exclusively to authorized dealerships, suggest a shift toward prioritizing corporate convenience and profit over maintaining the cultural and relational bonds that underpin the H.O.G. subculture. This shift reflects a clear divergence in interests: although the brand seeks to streamline operations and maximize revenue, members of the collective value authenticity, support, and the shared cultural practices they use to both bond with each other and reaffirm their identity and loyalty.

The post also reveals the emotional labor and expectations embedded within these consumer relationships. Various commenters on Nicolass's post have their own critical comments about the quality of the H.O.G. experience. "HOG culture is the reason people are not buying Harleys like they did in the past," said one poster, and several others chimed in with stories about how they "refuse to go to any of the meet ups" now and how some of the newer members are sloppy riders who might endanger the people they ride with. Nicolass expresses not only frustration with the service failures but also a sense of betrayal, particularly when his concerns were dismissed by H.O.G. representatives. The communication breakdown amplifies the disconnect and a lifetime member of H.O.G. turns to Reddit to warn others not to join the group, as he finds that membership fees and loyalty have been disregarded by the company.

Commerce Commandeering Community

In fact, Harley-Davidson's reliance on the H.O.G. to foster loyalty and market differentiation depends on maintaining the illusion of an authentic community while simultaneously ensuring corporate control over its boundaries and operations. For Harley-Davidson, aligning with the biker subculture was a calculated business strategy. The company's marketing efforts—ranging from branded merchandise to organized events—commandeered the subculture's aesthetics and values, assimilating them into a corporate framework. While consumers gained communal experiences and a sense of identity, these were often mediated and monetized by the brand. The tension arises because the company's primary objective is profit, whereas the subculture's goals may center on authenticity, freedom, and resistance to mainstream norms.

The broader implications for fandoms and consumer collectives are significant. While the notion of "symbiosis" is invoked to describe the broader relationship between marketers and their devoted consumers, this case illustrates how the term can be used to mask deeper conflicts and inequalities. In fandoms, media producers and fans engage in an often uneasy dance of co-creation (see **Fandom as Co-creation**) but, time after time, their motivations conflict. Producers seek to monetize fan enthusiasm, controlling intellectual property and dictating the terms of engagement. Fans, by contrast, value the freedom to create, control over their community's organization, and a wide range of participatory liberties. These differing priorities can lead to friction, as seen in disputes over fan fiction, unauthorized merchandise, and creative reinterpretations of source material. The producers' dominance in these relationships often enables them to exploit fan labor and loyalty while presenting their actions as part of a mutually beneficial partnership. In nature, parasitism is a type of "symbiosis." When both sides benefit, it is called "mutualism."

Returning to Harley-Davidson, we can read their narrative of symbiosis as a reflection of Schouten and McAlexander's own position within the research context. They were aligned with the company during the ethnography, and their corporate bosses would likely have been interested in seeing how Harley-Davidson was represented in the published work. Additionally, marketing departments instruct business students how to become marketers, a process that is accompanied by an ideological agenda suggesting that 'marketing is good for society.' Both elements may have influenced the symbiosis interpretation, leading to the framing of corporate-community relations in a favorable light. Moreover, these were the relatively early stages of H.O.G.'s establishment in 1983. In 1990, when their ethnography started, the company might have placed a greater emphasis on member happiness than it does now. In an email to us, John Schouten (2025) affirmed that this was the case. He said that, especially during the 2000s, the company "turned its priorities and its loyalties from Main Street to Wall Street." When he and Jim McAlexander originally wrote about the company, it was more symbiotic than it later became. Judging from current subreddit discussions, that unfortunate decline continues.

There is always a need for critical but fair-minded distance in analyzing such relationships, as what appears symbiotic may, in fact, involve significant asymmetries of power and benefit. Recognizing these tensions allows us to devise a more nuanced understanding of consumer collectives and to better appreciate the effects of their interactions with marketing institutions.

John Fiske and Blue Jeans

Henry's mentor, John Fiske, began his 1989 book, *Understanding Popular Culture*, with an essay on blue jeans, reflecting on the various meanings this widely shared garment acquires and the ways they have been tapped by branding strategies. The cover of the book's second edition has a striking photograph of jean-covered legs, showing the ways that the jeans are altered in countercultures through slashing them with razors and marking them up with ink pens and magic markers. Fiske's blue jeans essay provides a sense of how some of the most advanced thinkers in cultural studies were reflecting on brand cultures even as consumer cultural research was beginning its climb. Fiske remained in the realm of meaning, always important for cultural studies, while consumer culture researchers had pulled their focus towards communities and their material practices.

Fiske's research began with an informal survey of his students where he found that 118 out of 125 young college students at 'a major Midwestern university' (Madison, I suspect) were wearing jeans to class on a given day and continued through close readings of what students wrote about why jeans were meaningful to them and of advertisements for jeans that mobilized around particular meaning clusters. Fiske begins by dismissing the idea that the choice of jeans was purely "functional" or "rational": "of course, jeans are supremely functional, comfortable, tough, sometimes cheap, and requiring 'low maintenance'–but so, too, are army fatigues" (Fiske, 1989, p. 1).

Rather, he argues, jeans are so widely valued because of their openness to a range of associations and values. He discusses how clothing is designed to convey both personal (individualistic) meanings and shared social meanings, though as always, cultural studies is most interested in collective meaning-making. Fiske maps a range of meaning clusters that shape how we engage with jeans: For example, he explores the ways that jeans carry meanings of "physical labor, ruggedness, activity, physicality." These values might well be associated with the people who join motorcycle clubs, yet he never gets there, since his analysis assumes all of the meanings could be accessed by anyone who chose to wear jeans that particular morning.

Fiske also maps these meanings in relation to each other, showing the different meanings that cluster around regular "generic" jeans and designer jeans. Advertisers tap the range of meanings that have encrusted around jeans as a symbolic object and mobilize them in ways that reinforce some, may route around others, but build on the consumer's prior associations. Under Fiske's model, consumers may prefer some meanings over others, may resist certain meanings through various expressive activities, or may embrace some meanings [think about Stuart Hall's (1980) reading positions from **Fandom as Audience**], but there is no sense here of a brand community that might collectively shape these meanings and make demands on those who produce the brand. See Table 5.1.

GENERIC JEANS	DESIGNER JEANS
Classless	Upscale
Country	City
Communal	Socially distinctive
Unisex	Feminine (or more rarely, masculine)
Work	Leisure
Traditional	Contemporary
Unchanging	Transient
The West	The East
Nature	Culture

Table 5.1: Comparing the Meanings of Regular Jeans and Designer Jeans

From Subcultural to Digital Realms

Rob here. I used Schouten and McAlexander's (1995) concept of subcultures of consumption to introduce fan studies into consumer research. As Ph.D. students sometimes (dare I say *should*) do, I also went through that paper as if it were gospel. The authors' incorporation of technology into their consumer ethnography intrigued me. In their article, the Harley ethnographers presented a post "from a Harley-oriented computer bulletin board on Internet" (Schouten and McAlexander, 1995, p. 49) that presented several key descriptions of the less authentic subgroups of the subculture. During my dissertation work, I had also read about the use of bulletin board and newsgroup data in online fandom studies by Nancy Baym (1993), Henry (Jenkins, 1995), and Susan Clerc (1996).

I used the subcultures of consumption framework to position my fan studies work within the consumer research literature. I saw in fan discourses so many of the familiar hallmarks that Schouten and McAlexander had identified as essential to a subculture of consumption: distinct values, specialized knowledge, and collective rituals. By engaging with episodes and merchandise in online discussion forums, fans were using digital means to visibly and efficiently perform acts that other fans were doing in person: collectively constructing and displaying evaluative standards, sharing symbolic vocabularies and communal identities, and much more. As they did, they negotiated their aesthetic preferences, belief systems, and even sacred experiences—practices that aligned closely with Schouten and McAlexander's findings on how subculture members were constructing their identity and community through shared practices around the Harley brand. Establishing a link between consumer research and fan studies allows us to see the significant overlap between consumer collectives and fandoms.

Virtual Collectives and the Evolution of Consumption

My early work on online fandom led directly to other works in which subculture concepts became woven into the fabric of digital consumer research methods and theories. It led directly to the concept of "virtual communities of consumption" (Kozinets, 1999). As we will explain in **Fandom as Technoculture** with a look into Howard Rheingold's (1993) influence, the term "virtual community" was then the accepted way to refer to online communities. Today, we might just call them social media users or posters. Regardless of the terminology used, I utilized that article to create a stronger foundation for extending Schouten and McAlexander's ideas about consumption subcultures into the digital realm by emphasizing how Internet technology was reshaping social interactions and consumption practices.

The deeper parallels between subcultures of consumption and virtual communities lie in the ways that they enable consumer collectives, platforms, and marketers, too, to build social structures around enthusiasm and knowledge for something particular and consumption-related, be it a brand, product category, or consumption activity. Yet the digital context introduces new layers of complexity. For instance, the anonymity and asynchronous nature of online interaction allow for broader participation while challenging traditional notions of authenticity and proximity central to physical subcultures. These gatherings, much like subcultures of consumption, serve as vital spaces for identity construction and collective meaning-making in an age of fandom and online community. However, they also introduce new dynamics of fragmentation and fluidity as members navigate diverse platforms and rapidly shifting allegiances. This flexibility fits perfectly within a broadened conceptualization of consumer collectives, where individuals move through overlapping and intersecting networks defined by shared yet volatile cultural touchpoints.

Thus far, this book has explored the concept of consumer collectives, first by developing key conceptual elements, then by discussing a variety of cases such as action figure displays, genealogical pursuits, and Black Vanlife. In the prior chapter and this one, we extended these discussions by examining the historical trajectory of consumer behavior studies, from the rational, utility-maximizing individuals of classical economics to the dynamic, culturally embedded perspectives that have reshaped the field into a thriving global arena of consumer culture theory. In this chapter, we continued to track the profound transformations brought about by social change and digital platforms. Next, we shift our focus to the diversity and complexity of consumer collectives, building on themes introduced earlier. The next chapter deepens our understanding of the different forms of consumer collectives, expanding our core frameworks to encompass their varied and evolving manifestations and setting the stage for a more multifaceted exploration of their cultural and social significance.

CHAPTER 6
VARIETIES OF CONSUMER COLLECTIVES

B oth here. In the opening chapters of this book, we began exploring some of the diverse qualities of consumer collectives. LGBT football fan groups, #Demthrones, and #BlackVanlife illustrated not only the resistance and reinvention present in these social spaces but also served as examples of the diverse subgroups within them. In this chapter, we move deeper into an appreciation of the varieties of forms that consumer collectives take. We will explore how dimensions such as size, intimacy, internal structure, and official affiliation shape these groups, but our ultimate goal is to demonstrate how these different dimensions intersect and influence one another. This chapter will build a more comprehensive framework for understanding the fluid, complex, and often paradoxical nature of collective life in contemporary consumer culture.

We begin by mapping collectives along the foundational dimensions of size and intimacy, revealing how these factors influence the nature of interaction and social bonding. We then turn our attention to the transformative impact of digital technologies, exploring how online spaces create new possibilities for connection that challenge traditional relationships between scale and closeness. Finally, by examining the tensions between structured and unstructured collectives, as well as the impact of official versus unofficial affiliations, we will uncover some core organizing principles. By the end of this chapter, these distinct analytical lenses will be brought together to provide a more holistic and dynamic model for making sense of the rich variety of consumer collectives.

Dimensionalizing Consumer Collectives

Size and intimacy provide two useful initial dimensions for thinking about the variety and nature of these diverse consumer collective forms. The size of a collective, measured in the number of participants, fundamentally shapes the types of interactions that are possible within it. A small group of three or four people fosters immediacy, directness, and personal connection, while a group of thousands requires different mechanisms to manage the anonymity and distance that can result. Fanships are usually expressed in small groups and fandoms in larger ones. Intimacy, by contrast, captures the depth of emotional or relational connection among members of the collective. It is less about how many people are involved and more about how closely they are bound together. Intimacy has numerous qualities, reflecting the many types and depths of relationships available. Thus, relational depth can manifest in various ways, from the affective intensity of a shared peak experience to the enduring social cohesion of a group with a long history to the solidarity that emerges from a common purpose. Intimacy lives in shared stories and secrets, common history and experience, mutual trust, and a sense of vulnerability.

The two dimensions of size and intimacy are not stable factors; they are constantly shifting and overlapping, and at times, their relationship can be contradictory. Intimacy, for example, does not always fade as size grows. In some cases, particularly where technologically mediated interactions are involved, we can see new forms of intimacy emerging at previously unimaginable scales. For this reason, it is tempting to rely on familiar categories like "community" or "subculture" to explain collectives, but these terms often come preloaded with assumptions that we must carefully examine. Communities, for instance, evoke images of tightly knit groups with deep connections and a shared sense of place, yet many consumer collectives do not fit this characterization. Subcultures bring connotations of distinctiveness, often rebellion, within a larger societal frame, but many collectives defy such tidy demarcations. The reality of collective life—its flexibility and fluidity, its overlapping boundaries, and its ever-evolving passions—calls for more flexible tools of analysis.

Mapping the Unmappable

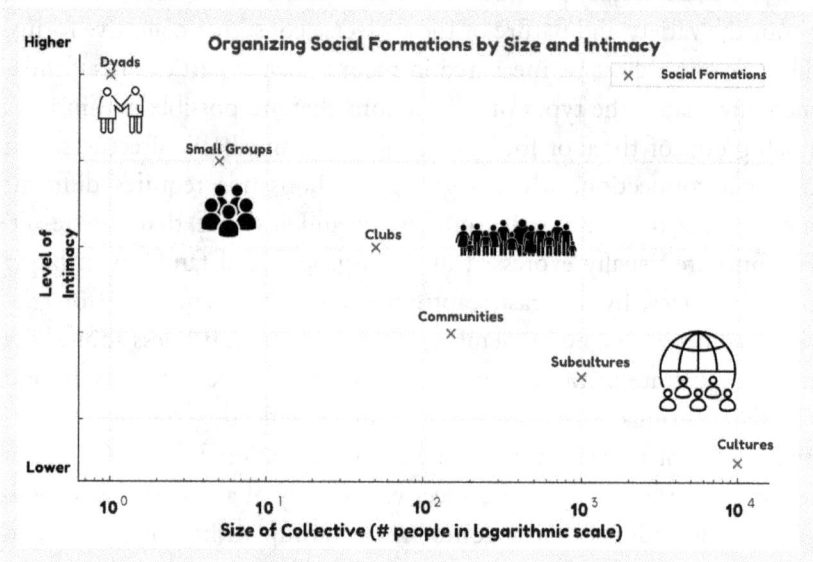

Figure 6.1: Varieties of Consumer Collectives

With Figure 6.1, we introduce the idea of mapping collectives along the two dimensions of size and intimacy as a way to resist the rigidity of fixed categories. A diagram that places dyads, small groups, clubs, gatherings, subcultures, and cultures on this dual-axis framework helps clarify their relational positions but avoids reifying any of them as "the" definitive form of a consumer collective or fandom. The horizontal axis represents size, ranging from the smallest formations to vast cultural systems, and it is plotted on a logarithmic scale to capture the exponential growth in numbers. A dyad, such as we might observe in a dedicated in-home sports fanship, consists of only two people, while a small group might include three to fifteen. Clubs and gatherings expand this dimension further, potentially reaching hundreds, while communities and subcultures can span thousands or millions. Cultures—those amorphous, more encompassing entities— represent the largest size category and often defy precise quantification.

The vertical axis represents intimacy, a qualitative concept that measures closeness, trust, and emotional connection. This axis is intended to capture the depth of a relational bond, which could be related to physical proximity or frequent interaction, but is much more than that. Dyads are usually at the apex of intimacy: two individuals engaged in a shared passion, where vulnerability and trust are heightened by the exclusivity of the relationship. As size increases, a certain type of direct, personal intimacy often decreases, but not always. Some friend groups, clubs, and even certain digital subcultures maintain high levels of relational closeness despite their size, sustained by powerful shared rituals, values, and practices and by affordances that enable the sharing of secrets and vulnerabilities.

This dual-axis framework allows us to map the relative positions of various collectives. Dyads occupy the upper-left corner—minimal in size but maximal in intimacy. Cultures appear in the bottom-right, representing the inverse: large, diffuse collectives where intimacy is shared across symbols and archetypes rather than direct relationships. In between, we place formations like small groups, clubs, and gatherings, each finding a pragmatic equilibrium between closeness and scale. Clubs, for instance, may have higher intimacy than more transient gatherings, as their membership is often more exclusive and their interactions more structured. This hints at how a collective's internal governance—a dimension we will explore in detail later—profoundly shapes its position within this relational map. Together, these two axes help us to conceptualize the ways collectives organize themselves in relation to these two critical dimensions.

Considering Digital Collectives

It is crucial, then, to consider the question of online groups within our conception of consumer collectives. These are social formations that often straddle boundaries and complicate traditional ideas of collective life. Are they (online, virtual) communities? Networks? Assemblages? To answer these questions, we must consider what it means to participate in a collective when the spaces of interaction are virtual. Online groups, like those on MacRumors or Reddit, can bring together hundreds, thousands, or even millions of participants. These are undeniably collectives in size. However, the experience within these online groups is often quite different from a distanced collective, as participants typically interact through discursive message threads that resemble dyadic or small-group conversations. On a site with millions of members, many may see a single post, a smaller percentage might like or upvote it, but only a few might engage in the conversational activities that build social links resembling communal exchange.

Furthermore, the anonymity and pseudonymity offered on many social media platforms can foster a unique kind of connection, leading people to disclose innermost thoughts and otherwise secret experiences, thereby building closeness and trust with a group of strangers. These novel and accessible affordances allow the intimacies of technological interactions to challenge the conventions of physical proximity. On a forum, a person can engage in a deep, sustained conversation with someone they will never meet in person, building a sense of connection that might rival the closeness of a neighborhood community or workplace team. In the same online space, thousands of others may hover on the margins, reading the dialogue but remaining no less present as part of the collective atmosphere. The very architecture of these digital spaces —their formal rules, informal norms, and technological features— becomes a primary factor in mediating the relationship between a collective's size and its capacity for connection, a theme of structure and governance we will return to.

Let's now move to a second version of the chart that includes online groups (see Figure 6.2). By including online groups, we complicate the traditional assumption of a simple inverse relationship between size and intimacy. The signifiers "online," "digital," and "social media" are slippery; they can refer to anything from personal text messages to comments on a YouTube video seen by millions. The group sizes one interacts with can range from one other person to tens of millions. Green points, spanning both axes, represent the diversity of online groups. Smaller and more tightly knit online forums, such as a private Discord server for designers fascinated by generative AI, cluster closer to the high intimacy of small groups. Larger communities, like MacRumors or fandom-specific Reddit subforums, span the mid-range of intimacy while reaching thousands or even millions of participants.

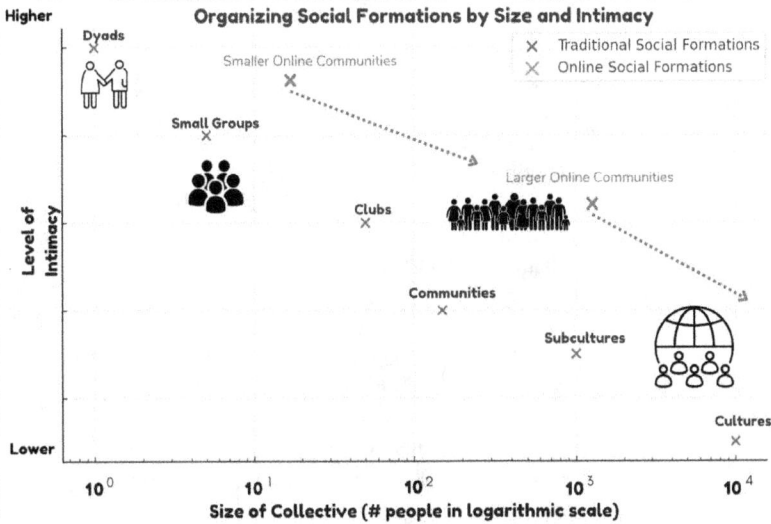

Organizing Social Formations by Size and Intimacy

Higher

Dyads

Smaller Online Communities

× Traditional Social Formations
× Online Social Formations

Small Groups

Larger Online Communities

Clubs

Communities

Subcultures

Cultures

Lower

Level of Intimacy

10^0 10^1 10^2 10^3 10^4

Size of Collective (# people in logarithmic scale)

Figure 6.2: The Variety of Consumer Collectives, with Online Groups

The chart demonstrates how digital groups resist neat categorization, often creating spaces where intimacy is not sacrificed for size. Technology enables relationships that are deeply personal yet scalable, a dynamic that redefines what collectives can be and what they can achieve. For instance, an online Harry Potter forum may serve thousands but still foster deep, supportive interactions among some of its members. A virtual game world might house hundreds of thousands of players, but those players could also form packs or, in game parlance, guilds with tight social bonds that predate, or are formed and maintained by, their digital connections. By incorporating these digital collectives, the framework becomes a more inclusive tool, capable of mapping the broad range of both traditional and contemporary social formations.

VARIETIES OF CONSUMER COLLECTIVE: THE APPLE EXAMPLE

The Apple ecosystem provides a vivid context for applying these measures of size and intimacy, while also hinting at the dimensions of structure and affiliation we will soon explore. Consider a range of Apple-related collectives:

In a family Apple account, size is small—two to six people on average—and intimacy is exceptionally high, as members share daily routines and personal data. In their study of household device sharing, Tara Matthews and her colleagues offer a taxonomy of six distinct sharing types—borrowing, mutual use, setup, helping, broadcasting, and accidental sharing—each with unique practices (Matthews et al., 2016). Apple's ecosystem, with features like iCloud and Family Sharing, facilitates these interactions, creating a highly intimate, unofficially structured collective that operates within an officially managed commercial framework. Friends and small groups who all use iPhones to access iMessage or FaceTime form a similar type of close-knit and Apple-enabled collective, their social bonds reinforced by the brand's technological infrastructure.

In a local Apple Store, the size of the collective grows to thousands of visitors per week, and the overall intimacy drops, as most interactions are transactional. However, pockets of connection and even intimacy emerge.

There can be what Linda Price and Eric Arnould (1999) call "commercial friendships" between customers and the service providers hyperbolically known as "Geniuses."

Price and Arnould found that service encounters were defined by spatiality, temporality, and intimacy.

Thus, a shopper discussing an upgrade with a Genius or a fan live-tweeting during a keynote is not simply engaging with the brand but is also sharing that engagement with another person, creating fleeting moments of shared experience that may involve a sense of genuine human contact.

A MacRumors forum, with its tens of thousands of active users, combines a large scale with surprising pockets of intimacy. Here, individual passion for the brand broadens into collective enthusiasm as participants gather to speculate on product launches or troubleshoot issues. Despite the size, interactions often feel personal. Regular contributors build reputations as experts or empathetic advisors, creating islands of communal connectivity within this large, unofficial space. Frequent posters and readers recognize one another and may even remark on each other's familiar patterns. Passion for the brand transforms into a form of social currency, driving dialogue and a sense of shared identity.

Finally, an Apple product launch can reach millions worldwide, its intimacy largely diluted by its immense scale. This is a highly official and structured event, orchestrated by the brand to generate collective excitement directed more toward the new product than between individual viewers.

The study of an iPhone launch by Gabriela Căpățînă and Florin Drăghescu (2015) explains how these events harness collective identity to create an aspirational narrative, with Apple products serving as a cultural touchstone that unites people under the banner of the brand.

Each of these collectives occupies a unique position on our map, configured by the intersection of size and intimacy. However, our examples demonstrate that their internal structure and their relationship to the official brand also define them. Thinking about how these dimensions work together provides us with a richer understanding of not only the individual collective forms but also how they relate to one another within broader networks of social organization.

Learning From Foundational Fandoms

Although the dimensions of size and intimacy provide a valuable map of the relational landscape of consumer collectives, they do not fully explain how these groups function internally or what governs the interactions within them. The Apple example hinted at how a collective's internal organization and its relationship to an official brand profoundly shape the experience of its members. To understand these crucial dimensions of structure and affiliation, we can discover no better foundation than in the formative debates of early fandom studies. It was here that scholars first grappled with describing the complex, often unwritten rules of emergent, passionate communities, providing us with the intellectual tools we need to build our next framework.

One of the foundational works in fandom studies is Camille Bacon-Smith's *Enterprising Women: Television Fandom and the Creation of Popular Myth* (1992). While she was arguably more embedded in fandom at that stage than Henry was, she constructed herself as a perpetual outsider—'The Ethnographer'—and framed her project as taking fandom to the 'outside world.' Her background as a folklorist and ethnomusicologist shaped her writing, evident in the anthropological rhetoric that permeated her prose. (For a glimpse into this early moment in the development of fandom studies, see the transcript of Henry and Camille speaking at Gaylaxicon in 1992, published as Jenkins, 2010).

Early in the book, Bacon-Smith attempted to dissect what she saw as the structures of the fan community. The section begins by describing the choices fans make as they enter the fan world: "Does the incipient fan prefer science fiction, fantasy and horror books, television and films?" (Bacon-Smith, 1992, p. 7). This passage may seem innocent, but it implies a rational choice model where the decision to become a fan precedes the fan object rather than emerges as a reaction to the affective force of that object. It also suggests such a choice is necessary—that you can only be a fan of one object and not find yourself engaging in various ways with multiple objects.

Bacon-Smith continues, "When outsiders think of fans, they usually think of clubs, which they imagine as a cross between a mailing list producers use to encourage viewer enthusiasm for their stars and products and the 4-H club from their youths" (p. 8). She acknowledges that many, but certainly not all, fans participate in formal fan clubs, but she sought to push beyond such official organizations to identify the hidden and informal structures of fandom—what she calls "fan circles." Bacon-Smith's fan circles fell somewhere between the openly networked and the more tightly structured. We might situate the early fandom studies researchers along a continuum from Rob, whose research included and was positive about fan clubs, to Henry, who was deeply suspicious of fan clubs as imposing top-down dictates on a more participatory form of culture. Henry's *Textual Poachers* saw fandom as a series of informal, intersecting networks, as did Rob's work, which also emphasized online participation in fandom.

Bacon-Smith continues, "Unlike more traditional and geographically fixed communities, including clubs, the fan world structures itself
around a series of conventions, held in a 'mobile geography' of hotels all
over the world. Conventions temporally and spatially organize the interaction between the community and potential new members and serve as
formal meeting places for the various smaller groups of fans who follow
the convention circuit" (p. 9). Here, Bacon-Smith is discussing the
"weekend-only world" that Henry described in *Poachers* (1992).
Drawing on a song popular among science fiction fans, *Textual Poachers*
ends with a passage that talks about social relationships among people
who came together around a few conventions a year and who maintained intense and intimate relationships with each other that differed
from those they had with people they might encounter much more
frequently in their everyday lives at work or school. Bacon-Smith writes,
"Local clubs organize most of the larger conventions... but that does not
mean that all of the participants at the convention are club members"
(p. 11).

Bacon-Smith writes, "Interest groups are not so much a collection
of like-minded individuals as they are a cluster of circles, groups of close
friends who come together to participate in a particular interest group....
At house parties, fans talk, watch videos, laugh, read fanzines, talk dirty,
talk story, dissect character development in the source product or the
fan fiction, and generally form the interpretations that will guide the
continuity in establishing standards of appropriate behavior and
response" (p. 26). In *Textual Poachers* (Jenkins, 1992), Henry traces the
operation of one such circle and its Saturday morning creative activities:
"Four *Quantum Leap* fans gather every few weeks in a Madison,
Wisconsin apartment to write. The women spread out across the living
room, each with their own typewriter or laptop, each working diligently
on their own stories about Al and Sam... The clatter of the keyboards
and the sounds of a filktape are interrupted periodically by conversation" (Jenkins, 1992, p. 152). As the passage continues, Henry cites the
ways they might consult each other, pooling expertise or soliciting feedback on what they are writing: "As the day wears on, writing gives way
to conversation, dinner, and the consumption of fan videos" (p. 154).

Bacon-Smith saw these circles as organized around a core of two to five members with various creative skills and somewhat interlocking interests. She discusses the trade of goods and skills within and between circles, the stability of these circles, the ways they function as support systems at conventions, and the ways these informal structures intersect with the more formal convention structures. All told, it is one of the more impressive sections of the book, except that, at the time the book was released, many fans did not recognize their community as depicted here. They argued that the structures and norms were too formal and rigid to account for the fluidity of their movements through fandom. We were on the cusp of a much more open culture, which crystallized when fans encountered the internet. Many of the fans recognized themselves more in the porous and fluid language of networks rather than in traditional structures.

Circles, Lines, and Consumer Collectives

These early debates within fandom studies focus our attention on several new concepts for understanding consumer collectives beyond their size and intimacy. The foundational tension in that scholarship—between Bacon-Smith's more structured "circles" and Henry's more fluid networks—provides the perfect entry point for developing a framework based on a collective's internal governance and its relationship to commercial or institutional power. From this debate, we can derive two new, intersecting dimensions for our analysis: the spectrum from *Structured to Unstructured* and the spectrum from *Official to Unofficial*.

The *Structured-Unstructured* spectrum highlights the varying degrees of formality within these collectives. Attempts to nail down the singular "structure" of fandom in those early days often imposed a structuralist model at the cost of understanding the idiosyncratic and fluid nature of fan participation. What had struck Henry at the time was how relatively unimportant formal fan clubs—with membership cards, rules, and hierarchies—were for the fans he communicated with, and how much freedom they enjoyed to move through the fan world, interacting with whomever they chose. Nevertheless, structure of some kind is unavoidable. Even the most informal gathering develops norms, and the most rigid organization contains pockets of unstructured sociality. These dimensions, then, are not a binary but a spectrum of emphasis.

Let's turn to the other dimension. The *Official-Unofficial* dimension is vividly illustrated by the fan convention circuit. On the official end of the spectrum, we might think of the commercially run conventions, such as the Creation-Cons, which benefit from their direct access to official channels. Such an affiliation involves complex trade-offs. Established in 1985, Creation Entertainment was a commercial company which produced fan conventions, hosting at its peak roughly 20 events a year across as many cities, frequently centered around particular television series and organized to bring the stars and producers to their fans. A Creation-Con event might allow fans unparalleled access to celebrities, but only under very controlled circumstances; what happens on an autograph line, for example, is carefully regulated. The presence of celebrities often comes at the cost of access to fan-made goods, which is a hallmark of more fan-centric events. For example, MediaWest was, at the time *Poachers* (Jenkins, 1992) was written, the key event for the release of new fanzines and the centerpiece of a fan-driven economy. The Creation-Con might provide access to insider information or exclusive merchandise, but it does so at the expense of the more informally structured and fan-led discussions that are the defining trait of fan-run conventions such as Escapade, a California-based convention that attracts only a few hundred participants each year for more intimate exchanges among fans only.

By broadening these concepts beyond fandom, we can see how they apply to many different kinds of consumer collectives, from tech enthusiasts in online forums to local communities centered around ethical consumption. These collectives resist static definitions, thriving instead on their adaptability. This flexibility underscores the complexity of consumer relationships in contemporary culture, which bridge the formal and informal as well as the structured and unstructured in ways that continually reshape social engagement.

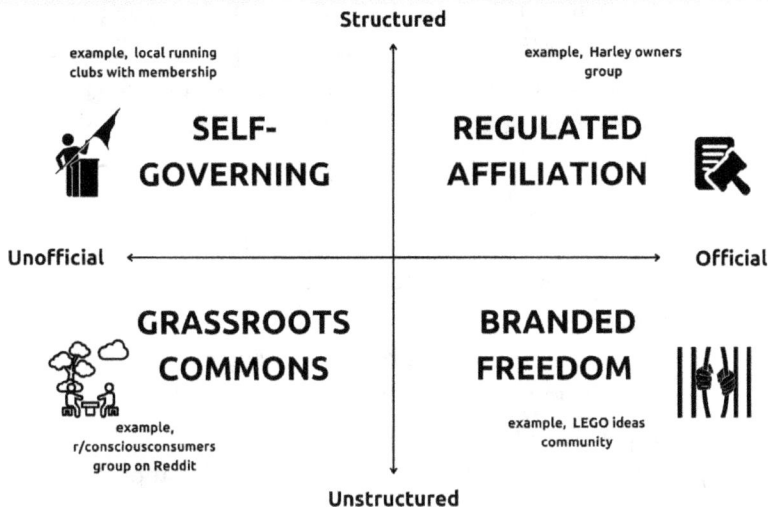

Figure 6.3: Structural and Official Dimensions of Consumer Collectives

Figure 6.3 presents a 2x2 diagram that maps these two new dimensions, creating four ideal types of consumer collectives. The horizontal axis represents the **Official-Unofficial** dimension, while the vertical axis captures the **Structured-Unstructured** dimension. We must view this framework not as a replacement for the Size and Intimacy map, but as a second, intersecting layer of analysis. Any collective in these quadrants also has a size and a capacity for intimacy, which are, in turn, profoundly shaped by its structure and affiliation.

In the top-left quadrant, we find **Self-Governing** consumer collectives, which are highly structured but remain unofficial. Local running clubs are a perfect example. They often operate with formalized schedules, training plans, and leadership hierarchies, yet they maintain their independence. This quadrant can contain collectives of vastly different scales and relational depths. A local running club might be a small group of twenty people with high intimacy, while a national, unofficial athletic association for the same sport, like the Road Runners Club of America (RRCA) is a much larger community of 200,000 runners with more diffuse bonds, yet both organizational forms remain self-governing.

In the bottom-left quadrant are **Grassroots Commons** consumer collectives, which are both unstructured and unofficial. Here, the range of size and intimacy is perhaps at its most extreme. A grassroots commons can be as small and intensely intimate as a private group chat among a few friends—a dyad or small group—sharing links about sustainable products. It can also be as large and anonymous as the r/consciousconsumers subreddit, which serves as a vast community or "pack" where intimacy is found in brief, dyadic, or group conversations among thousands of otherwise disconnected members.

The bottom-right quadrant is home to officially sanctioned but largely unstructured **Branded Freedom** consumer collectives. The LEGO Ideas community is an exemplary case. As an official platform, it constitutes a large community of almost 3 million users. However, its unstructured nature allows for the spontaneous formation of smaller, more intimate collaborations—small groups or project-based dyads— that coalesce around specific design submissions to offer feedback and support. The official platform, therefore, enables the organic emergence of high-intimacy pockets within a low-intimacy, very large-scale collective.

Finally, in the top-right quadrant are **Regulated Affiliation** consumer collectives, which are both official and highly structured. The Harley Owners Group (H.O.G.) is a prime example. At a macro level, H.O.G. is a massive global culture of over one million members with relatively low intimacy between them. However, the genius of H.O.G. lies in its regulated, hierarchical structure, which intentionally fosters intimacy at the micro level. The entire global organization is built upon a network of 1,400 officially sanctioned local chapters whose groups function as highly intimate and socially cohesive clubs and small groups that hold regular rides and events. This scenario demonstrates perfectly how the dimensions intersect: the official and structured nature of the larger organization is what enables the creation of a vast network of inti-mate small groups.

VARIETIES OF CONSUMER COLLECTIVE: THE
NAPOLETANO EXAMPLE.

Fandom, much like brand loyalty, thrives on
the interplay of intimacy, scale, structure,
and passion. The devotion of families in
Naples, Italy, to their home team, SSC
Napoli, offers a perfect illustration of how our
integrated framework can illuminate a single,
complex collective. Here, an object of
devotion—a team, a player, and a sport—
serves as the focal point for connections
that ripple through every quadrant of our
models. The sacred presence of Diego
Maradona, enshrined not only in memory but
also in the spiritual life of the city, highlights
the transcendent aspects of this fandom.

In Naples, the intimacy of fandom often
begins at home, in the smallest and most
unofficial of collectives.

Parents teach their children not only how to
play but also how to love the game,
recounting tales of Maradona's triumphs as
if passing down sacred lore.

In these familial settings—a dyad or small
group—the shared experience of Branded
Freedom is intensely intimate and largely
unstructured, connecting generations and
binding the family to the city's storied
history.

This foundational passion then scales up.
Small groups of friends amplify the intimacy
as they ritualistically gather to watch
matches in cafes, their cheers and
commiserations producing deep social
bonds.

These regular meetups can evolve from a
loose, unstructured get-togethers into a
more self-governing formation, like an
informal neighborhood supporters' group
with its own traditions and meeting places.

If that neighborhood fan group had regulations about, say, gathering times and places, appropriate food, and leadership structure, it would be an example of a Self-Governing fan collective.

On match days, the city's collective heartbeat seems to synchronize with the rhythm of the game, and at the Diego Armando Maradona Stadium, tens of thousands of fans are transformed into a singular fan assemblage. This is the consumer collective at its largest scale, providing a powerful experience of tribal effervescence.

Yet, this experience is facilitated by a Regulated Affiliation—the official club, SSC Napoli, which structures the event, sells the tickets, and manages the space. Globally, Napoli fans who cannot be in the stadium connect through online forums and social media, forming a vast and unofficial Grassroots Commons.

On those forums, a fan might post a tribute to Maradona, participating in a massive, low-intimacy pack of global supporters. But within those commons, they may also engage in an intimate, dyadic conversation with a fellow fan from the diaspora, forging a deep connection of napoletanos across continents. The reverence for Maradona, a vital cultural resource, sparks a never-ending dialogue that unifies these varied collective forms, from the most intimate family ritual to the most regulated public spectacle.

A Multidimensional View of Collective Life

This chapter began by seeking a more flexible and accurate way to understand the rich variety of consumer collectives. We started by mapping these social formations along core dimensions of size and intimacy, a useful lens that nonetheless proved insufficient on its own, especially when confronted with the complexities of digital life. By turning to the foundational debates within fandom studies, we uncovered two more crucial dimensions—the spectrum from structured to unstructured and from official to unofficial. The goal was not to replace the first model with the second but to integrate them into a more powerful and multidimensional framework.

The key insight of this chapter is that no single dimension can explain the dynamic nature of these groups. A consumer collective is not just large or small, intimate or distant, structured or unstructured, or official or unofficial. It is a fluid assemblage that often embodies all these characteristics at once. The power of our integrated framework lies in its ability to hold these seeming contradictions together. It allows us to see how a massive, official, and highly regulated collective like the Harley Owners Group is built upon a global network of small, intimate, and self-governing local chapters. It helps us understand how a sprawling, unstructured, and unofficial grassroots commons like a subreddit can simultaneously be a space for anonymous, pack-like behavior and the birthplace of intensely intimate, dyadic friendships.

The Apple and Napoli examples demonstrate the analytical power of this approach, revealing how a single brand or team can foster a complex ecosystem of interconnected collectives. Ultimately, this multidimensional perspective provides us with a more sophisticated and realistic toolkit. It allows us to move beyond static categories and appreciate the true adaptability, fluidity, and profound capacity for connection that characterize the consumer collectives that give shape and meaning to our contemporary world. Armed with this more robust understanding of the varieties of these groups, we can now turn to the deeper question of how they function as sites of cultural production and change.

CHAPTER 7
A BRAND CALLED WE

E very other day or so, Rob goes into his garage, sits on his stationary bicycle and does what over six million other people across the US, UK, Canada, Germany, and Australia do: he joins the Peloton "community." The brand name Peloton already contains collective meaning, drawn from a cycling term that refers to a group of riders who coordinate to protect each other from the wind. Peloton, a New York-based fitness company with over 50 instructors who run various live cycling, yoga, strength training, and other health and fitness classes every day of the week, leverages those meanings to encourage its user base to think of themselves as a community, a group whose members encourage each other to work out regularly and to get the most out of their fitness experience. The company's website states their intention clearly: "At Peloton, we believe that the power of our community is unmatched in its ability to inspire each member to reach all of their goals."

While riding, Rob can see the pseudonyms (and possible photos) of other riders, such as "RockingRicardo" or "VancouverMom," on the "Here Now Leaderboard," which displays everyone currently taking a class and allows users to filter participants by age, gender, or other tags. Participating in a live class, a member can compete against other members on the leaderboard. Groups form based on mutual interests, following certain instructors, or enjoying certain kinds of music, like house or 90s rock. Members can also give each other "high fives" through the Peloton app, and instructors will call out to members to wish them a happy birthday or to congratulate them on milestones such as reaching 500 rides. Users can add friends, follow one another, share tips, encourage each other, and even link to their Facebook pages to reveal their identities—and to partake in a Facebook group with over 470,000 members. Subgroups can be substantial as well. The Peloton Mom Group, for example, has over 42,000 members. There are also live group workouts at fitness clubs in New York and London and an annual homecoming event that is open to all members.

In their study, Brandon Boatright and Karen Freberg (2023) investigate Peloton instructors as types of "corporate influencers" who leverage their personal narratives and different motivational styles to bridge the gap between the corporate identity of Peloton and the individual experiences of its users. This dynamic fosters a participatory culture, where members feel seen, valued, and inspired to actively engage with the brand and one another. In their classes, instructors blend physical training with personal storytelling, humor, and affirmations, creating a space where fitness goals are intertwined with emotional support and community-building. Outside the virtual studio, instructors maintain this connection through their social media platforms, amplifying the reach of the brand community and reinforcing its values of inclusivity, self-improvement, and resilience.

The multiple levels of engagement blur the lines between brand ambassadors and community leaders, empowering Peloton instructors to act as central nodes within a collective that thrives on shared values and mutual support. As a result, Peloton's community exemplifies the characteristics of a powerful consumer collective. Instructors serve not only as motivators but also as facilitators of social connections among members, encouraging them to share their progress, challenges, and successes within the Peloton ecosystem. These actions help create a self-sustaining community that also strengthens Peloton's market position.

Peloton is an example of a company that has deliberately engaged its customer base with one another in what has become known as a "brand community." The term brand community is one of the best-known of the consumer collective concepts to emerge from marketing and consumer research scholarship. The concept was developed in the dissertation research doctoral student Al Muñiz did at the University of Illinois Urbana-Champaign with his supervisor, Tom O'Guinn and they defined it as "a non-geographically bound community, based on a structured set of social relations among admirers of a brand" (Muñiz and O'Guinn, 2001, p. 412). Their positioning of the idea of a "non-geographically bound" community seems to be a result of the timing of their study after the technology boom that led to the Internet's early growth. Muñiz and O'Guinn were trying to incorporate the fact that many consumers were beginning to use digital means to share information, ideas, opinions, and connections, similar to Rob's work among fandoms and Schouten and McAlexander's use of a bulletin board in their subcultures research.

However, by simply stating that these communities were not geographically bound, the paper seemed to suspend itself in a strange netherland where it could not differentiate between the physical gathering of living, breathing face-to-face humans and the digital gathering of discourses and textual artifacts—almost as if that difference no longer mattered—even though their dataset and much of their theorizing from it are dominated by in-person gatherings. In the next section of this chapter, we elaborate on the complex intersections of commerciality and community encompassed by the brand community term, exploring some of the important and under-explored ramifications of this popular concept.

Gemeinschaft und Gesellschaft

The article that Muñiz and O'Guinn jointly authored from Al's dissertation spends a significant amount of time considering the concept of community. Community, they tell us, "has been a staple of political, religious, scholarly, and popular discourse" for "a century and a half" (p. 412). Citing German sociologist Ferdinand Tönnies' 1887 classic, *Gemeinschaft und Gesellschaft* (which translates roughly to "Community and Society")—a popular citation in consumer research about community—they noted how his work distinguished between the traditional, familial, emotionally close, and often rural community and the more mechanistic, individualistic, and contractually driven urban society. "The essential notion underlying this discourse was that something more natural and thus real (community) was being replaced by a more depersonalized, mass-produced, and less grounded type of human experience (modern society)" (Muñiz and O'Guinn, 2001, p. 413). Building on Tönnies' work and other community-focused sociological literature, the article argues for a shift from understanding brands as simple entities for exchange or quality signaling to seeing them as focal points for individual and collective identities and thus as an important site of contemporary relationship-building and meaning-making.

While acknowledging the variety of definitions of community, they then try to pin down the three "core components or markets of community." The first and most important marker they called "consciousness of kind." Members of any kind of community possess an awareness of themselves as part of an extended group, just as members of a neighborhood or religious community identify themselves as belonging to it. Because they share an identity, they also feel or have an inner connection that distinguishes them from non-members. This shared recognition leads to a sense of a distinct "communal identity"—such as being a member of the "Peloton community" in our opening example. Other prominent examples of contemporary brand communities are Apple diehards, who also call themselves "Appleheads" or "iFans" or the Harley Riders and H.O.G. members studied by Schouten and McAlexander. Because this inner identification, or consciousness, is presumably a voluntary choice and not some sort of corporate assignment, the brand community concept draws heavily from the notion of elective affinities and the self-selection criterion of Schouten and McAlexander, although that link is never explicitly made by Muniz and O'Guinn.

The second marker they identify is "shared rituals and traditions." This market sits at the borderline between definitions of cultures and communities, both of which emerge through common narratives, traditions, and practices. Like the work on subcultures that preceded it, the brand community concept acknowledges that rituals and traditions can include those organized around brands. For instance, before the release of new products, Appleheads congregate outside Apple stores for hours or even days. Rituals and customs strengthen the social link between users of the brands while also recalling the brand's history, sharing stories about the brand and brand use, and celebrating and trying to live up to the brand's ascribed ideals.

"A sense of moral responsibility" serves as the third marker. Because of their shared identities and social ties, the members of most communities feel and express a moral duty to one another. Muñiz and O'Guinn extend this idea to the world of brands, asserting that the members of brand communities take care of one another. Their example is that a Saab driver will stop to help another Saab driver if they see them in a car broken down on the side of the road. Harley riders and Tesla drivers might similarly look out for one another. Appleheads may help each other troubleshoot problems on their devices or learn to use new features. The sharing of information and assistance in user groups, and especially online, is perhaps a more common form of collaborative activity. The core assertion is that brand community members feel a heightened sense of responsibility for the well-being of other members and may go to great lengths to guide new customers or assist those experiencing problems with the brand.

Ambivalence and Discomfort

To illustrate brand communities in the real world, Muñiz and O'Guinn (2001) conducted a "study" with two phases: a face-to-face "ethnographic" (p. 412) component and a phase "conducted entirely in environments of computer-mediated communication" (p. 415). It focused on two types of automobile enthusiasts, those of Saab (RIP 2011) and Ford Broncos, as well as the devoted users of Apple Macintosh computers and other Apple-branded products (note that this was several years before the iPhone was introduced). As Schouten and McAlexander did, they studied how brands could serve as a nexus for user enthusiasm, inspiring the formation of groups that went beyond simply using or consuming the brand to a variety of activities, including celebrating, discussing, critiquing, and creating. Casting their contribution more as a sociological understanding of the changing ways that community was manifesting in postmodern society than as a marketing strategy to be advocated or embraced, their article demonstrated the three traditional sociological markets of community in action within the three brand-based communities they studied.

Beyond that, they offered tantalizing insights about the ambivalences of brand community members' passion and the inclusiveness of the communities themselves. They found a "self-awareness and sensitivity concerning the commercial nature of the community" that bordered on discomfort, driving brand community members to "joke about their level of commitment" (p. 421). "These consumers know that their membership may be taken as signs of shallowness, fanaticism, materialism, and hedonism. Yet most feel that such judgments reveal an ignorance of the real value of the brand and its community" (ibid). They also related that they found brand communities generally to be more democratic and inclusive than many traditional face-to-face communities. Brand communities, they wrote, were places where membership was open and (somewhat surprisingly, given what has been written elsewhere) where one's race, gender, and class do not matter. However, contradicting their latter point, they backtracked and later said that these groups were still under the influence of social stratification effects.

Why Brand Managers Were Delighted With Brand Communities

In the growth phase of the internet of the 2000s, brand managers across Corporate America and in other countries were struggling to figure out how to incorporate the Internet into their marketing, public relations, advertising, and other corporate communications practices. The Internet had boomed, then it had busted. Like a phoenix emerging from the ashes, "Web 2.0," which evolved into social media behemoths like Alphabet, ByteDance, and Meta, rose. Hinting at the importance and impacts of the rapidly emerging online world but passing on engaging with its more manipulative implications, Muñiz and O'Guinn conclude their article with a weighty statement—almost a pronounce-ment—that casts the online world and the role of brand communities within it in a positive light.

> At this moment we seek to understand community's existence, persistence, endurance, and constant reinvention in the post-modern consumption space where enormous changes in human communication reside. At this nexus we introduce the idea of brand community. We believe brand communities to be real, significant, and generally a good thing, a democratic thing, and evidence of the persistence of community in consumer culture. (Muñiz and O'Guinn, 2001, p. 428)

In those heady days, brand managers were struggling to apply busi-ness principles to the mysterious and off-putting world of emotional outbursts, rampant free speech, and technocultural weirdness that char-acterized the emerging online world. These managers were drawn to the terminology and perhaps even the concept of brand communities. They were attracted because it aligned neatly with their desire to extend intel-lectual property into the social realm, opening new worlds of advertising and promotion and casting the new online realms as collaborative spheres of drummed-up consumer enthusiasm.

Beyond the fact that it provided general support for managers to use the Internet, the excellent thing about the brand communities is that they focus explicitly on the company's products or services, giving marketers a framework for cultivating and maintaining consumer rela-tionships—branding for the long term that transcends mere short-term transactions or order taking. A tale of brand communities centered on shared admiration and passion for a company's own, fully owned intel-lectual property. That was music to the ears of these managers. Soon, advertising would become much more than sales pitching. It would become the online facilitation of social interaction. No longer commercial, the brand manager's job was transforming into the careful crafting of potent narratives and strategies that would further align corporate goals with people's needs and introduce something even more powerful: a sense of communal belonging that they would also control.

These "default social" ideas later became grafted onto the structure of social media itself in the use of terminology like "sharing," "liking," and "friending" in Facebook and other platforms—as communication and platformization scholar José van Dijck (2013) notes. For marketing managers, the brand community framework is especially appealing because it implicitly grants them a degree of legitimacy not only in fostering but also in managing these social groups. In the hands of brand managers, whose job, after all, is to manage, a brand community becomes another asset. Brand-centered groups and discussions shift from the self-governing and unofficial communities of the pre- and early Internet days to become official and structured regulated affiliations. The community morphs from the more subcultural concept of an independent, perhaps at times even resistant, gathering of enthusiasts who have their own interests and their own views of authenticity and becomes more like an extension of corporate influence into the lives of the brand's most loyal consumers.

Symbiotic or Symbiotes?

That vision contrasts sharply with the subversive undertones present in the subcultures of consumption and the virtual communities of consumption concepts that predated the idea of brand communities. For example, although they profess the possibility of symbiosis, Schouten and McAlexander's framework clearly shows how subcultures appropriate brand symbols and practices for their own purposes rather than strictly following the intentions of the brand and its management team. Kozinets (1999, p. 258) is even more explicit about this resistance, arguing that the ability of online consumers to communicate and organize among themselves implies that "power is shifting away from marketers and flowing to consumers." Rob's research found consumers increasingly using the online medium to expose and resist forms of marketing they find invasive or unethical. Social media, from its very beginning, was becoming an important arena for organizing consumer resistance and acts of activism around advertisements, advertising in general, marketing, capitalism, and many other topics (Kozinets and Handelman, 1998; Kozinets and Seraj-Aksit 2024).

In an example of the way online consumer collectives try to undermine the commercial activities of brands they find unethical, Caitlin Lawson (2021) explored the mobilization of the online beauty community in response to racial insensitivity among beauty influencers and brands. Her study detailed how consumer collectives utilize social media platforms to call out and critique brands and influencers for racist actions or lack of inclusivity, such as insufficient diversity in product ranges. For instance, when beauty brands like Tarte release products that do not cater to a wide range of skin tones, the community responds with significant backlash, utilizing social media platforms to amplify their disapproval. Influencers play a crucial role in these scenarios by refusing to review or promote such products, pressuring brands to make substantive changes. The article emphasizes the international implications of such controversies, noting that the effects of callouts resonate well beyond the U.S., affecting global markets and international consumer perceptions.

The brand community concept presents a picture of seamless cooperation, where consumers and corporations collaborate to create a new community that aligns with the brand's image. The framework thus risks simplifying or erasing the sometimes uneasy dynamics between corporate power and consumer agency. The brand community concept's pragmatic core is the calibration of shared consumer enthusiasm to corporate goals. But by centering on corporate needs, it marginalizes the more contentious, independent, and unpredictable behaviors that the subcultures of consumption and virtual communities of consumption frameworks hold to be central to the very nature of contemporary consumer collectives.

Fandom's Moral Economy

In 2013, the *Journal of Fandom Studies* asked Henry (Jenkins, 2014) to identify some topics that the field needed to explore in the years ahead. He outlined an ambitious agenda in "Fandom Studies as I See It," including many themes we have developed more fully across the *Frames of Fandom* series. One key area—fan morality—continues to trouble him. He cited a passage from research on hobbyists by Paul Hoggett and Jeff Bishop (1986): "[T]he values [...] are radically different from those embedded within the formal economy; they are values of reciprocity and interdependence as opposed to self-interest, collectivism as opposed to individualism, the importance of loyalty and a sense of 'identity.'" (p. 280)

If fandom studies had engaged more closely with consumer culture research from the start, we might have made more progress in understanding fandom ethics, given how much early consumer culture research was focused on how consumer collectives were holding companies—the beauty companies in the example above—accountable for their violations of the fan community's shared ethical norms and values (such as the commitment in this example to supporting diversity). Henry's own efforts to address these questions drew on the work of British historian E.P. Thompson (1971), another key figure in the development of cultural studies. Thompson used the term "moral economy" to refer to social norms and mutual understanding that make economic exchanges possible. Thompson introduced the concept in his discussion of eighteenth-century food riots, arguing that when the indentured classes challenged the landowning interests, their protests were most likely shaped by some "legitimizing notion": "the men and women in the crowd were informed by the belief that they were defending traditional rights and customs; and in general, they were supported by the wider consensus of the community" (p. 78). Relations between landowners and peasants—or, for that matter, between media producers and fans—reflect the perceived moral and social value of those interactions. All parties involved need to feel that they each are behaving in a morally appropriate fashion.

Henry (and his collaborators, Sam Ford and Joshua Green) offers his fullest discussion of the concept in their book, *Spreadable Media* (2013). There, they use it to consider the Napster debate, where music sharing and piracy were used as opposing moral discourses ("sharing is caring" vs. "sharing is piracy") to legitimize and stabilize the moral economy in the midst of profound technological and economic disruption. Readers interested in the topic might also want to see Markus Giesler's (2006) detailed netnography of the Napster community, which we explore later in this book.

Earlier, in his first essay on fandom, "Star Trek ReRun, Reread, Rewritten" (Jenkins, 1988), Henry used the concept of "moral economy" to explain some of the tensions then shaping the norms of fan fiction writing. Slash, homoerotic fan fiction, was then relatively new and the larger culture had not yet made peace with the push for gay rights. He found sharp divides among fans as they reacted to stories where Kirk and Spock were depicted as lovers, debates that centered on the "right way," the most appropriate ways that fans might build on canonical media stories and what kinds of stories constituted "character" or abuse of the source materials. Many rejected K/S (a Kirk/Spock romance) because they did not find it "plausible." By the time, just a few years later, he published *Textual Poachers* (Jenkins, 1992), these debates had largely died down, slash had become more normalized, as had been more resistant relations with the source material. The concept of a "moral economy" seemed less pressing, and these ideas about the moral economy of fandom lay dormant until the publication of *Spreadable Media*. Even now, few have built on this framework. There is ample space for other ways to theorize the moral and ethical relations between fans (such as what can one borrow from another fan's fictions in constructing your own story or whether it is ethical to profit from the sale of fan fiction) or between fans and producers (such as when fan engagements with celebrities intrude upon their privacy or when producers go too far in commodifying their interactions with fans).

Things Get Nasty

Another important and lasting contribution of the brand community framework is the development of the out-group effects of what they term "oppositional brand loyalty." Oppositional brand loyalty is a social process integral to the dynamics of brand communities, consumer collectives, and fandoms alike. It operates as a mechanism through which members reinforce their collective identity by positioning themselves against competing brands, communities, fan objects, or fandoms. In essence, when they identify and discuss a shared "enemy" of the community, members derive an essential aspect of their community experience and a significant component of the brand's meaning. This opposition clearly delineates what the brand stands for. It also distinguishes who the brand community's members are—and, perhaps even more crucially, who they are not. The discussion of anti-fans in **Fandom as Audience** directly relates to the concept of the "oppositional brand," serving as its doppelgänger within fan studies.

The power of oppositional brand loyalty lies in its ability to unite community members around a perceived threat or competitor. Communities often experience their strongest bonds during periods of perceived threat or distress. Drawing on studies of neighborhoods and social groups, researchers like Bensman and Vidich (1995) observe how opposition can forge unity as a group rallies to resist a dominant institution or another powerful community. In such cases, a countercommunity's very existence is defined by its opposition to the perceived dominance of a rival group. That same dynamic applies equally to consumer collectives and fandoms, where the presence of a competing fandom, product, or company intensifies intra-group cohesion.

We can see from these instances that oppositional brand loyalty serves a dual purpose. It solidifies the internal bonds of the community by creating a shared adversary. Simultaneously, it enhances the visibility and significance of the brand or fan object's symbolic meaning. Members' collective defense against external threats reinforces their identification with the brand or cultural product, fostering a more profound emotional engagement and sense of loyalty. Although it may be empowering for the community, the results—a thing built of fear, threat, anger, unity, and rivalry—can be quite unpleasant. Throughout this series, we will be confronting and explaining this seemingly unavoidable side of contemporary fandom.

One of the issues may be the focus on a singular "brand" within the concept of brand communities. When individuals focus their devotion on a single brand or fannish object, such as a specific football team or media franchise, we can expect these oppositional dynamics to intensify. The exclusivity fosters a clear "us versus them" mentality, where allegiance to one brand inherently positions other brands—or their communities—in a competitive light. If you win, we lose; what was a business narrative about consumer needs satisfied becomes one of power, politics, and even military conflict. The more the identity of the collective becomes deeply intertwined with the brand or object itself, the more that rival brands or groups become perceived as existential threats. We can see this logic at work in sports fandoms, where devotion to a home team often escalates into outright hostility toward rival teams and their fans. At its extreme, the oppositional mindset can shade into destructive phenomena such as hooliganism, where the lines between support, rivalry, and aggression blur dangerously.

In broader consumer collectives or fandoms organized around more general interests—such as a shared enthusiasm for a consumption activity or a genre like science fiction—the dynamics are often more inclusive, omnivorous, and nomadic. Fans and consumers in these spaces engage with a wider range of products, texts, or brands, and their identities are less likely to be tied to an exclusive brand that needs to be defended against offense or disrespect. That multiplicity of interests, which we might see in a subculture of consumption or virtual community of consumption's shared commitment to a product class or consumption activity (rather than a specific brand), is much more likely to foster a cross-pollination of ideas and affiliations, encouraging dialogue and exploration instead of antagonism. Rob and Henry, as lifelong fans of both Star Wars and Star Trek (and yes, we know it is shocking to some), try to role model this more inclusive style of fandom.

Online, the oppositional focus manifests in the form of cyberbullying, toxic gatekeeping, and factionalism, as individuals and groups seek to protect their chosen object of devotion from perceived threats or outsiders. Although these oppositional logics can serve important binding and defining roles for communities, they can also fracture broader social and cultural contexts.

Linking Values

This overview of consumer collective concepts is not exhaustive, but it would be remiss for it to proceed without acknowledging the important contributions of Bernard Cova in developing the notion of linking value. Cova's 1997 article "Community and Consumption: Towards a Definition of the 'Linking Value' of Products or Services" is widely regarded as a foundational contribution to the consumer tribes and the overall consumer collective framework. In this article, Cova draws our attention to products and services themselves, asserting that they may hold what he termed "linking value"—an ability to create and sustain social bonds among consumers. He quotes an estimate that the average consumer is in contact with thousands of commercial objects every day, perhaps as many as 20,000, and that people who had not given up on their desire for community were, in some compensatory manner, often satisfying it through consuming mass-produced products and services.

The goods and services which are valued are mainly those which, through their linking value, permit and support social interaction of the communal type. . . . Ephemeral tribes which need to consolidate and affirm their union are, in fact, on the look-out for anything that could facilitate and support the communion: a site, an emblem, the support of a ritual of integration, or of recognition, etc. Thus, to satisfy their desire for communities, postmodern individuals seek products and services less for their use value than for their linking value. . . . it is not the producer who decrees that their product has a linking value, it is the people who are going to use it who will give it this meaning. Moreover, as the meanings of objects are no longer fixed and connected with their functions, but free floating, each individual may ascribe different meanings to the objects (Cova, 1997, p. 307).

The conceptualization of linking value marked a departure from traditional marketing models that focused primarily on the functional or symbolic value of goods for individual consumers. Instead, Cova emphasized their relational aspects, showing how goods act as mediators of social ties within transient and loosely structured groups. That emphasis on goods focuses consumer culture on the materiality of the physical world of things, which, as we will discuss later, displays its own co-constitutive processes with individuals and collectives.

Consumption Tribes

These early studies also cast what Cova called "consumption tribes" as distinct from both traditional communities and brand-based communities. Emphasizing both linking value and advocacy at the concept's center, Bernard and Véronique Cova define a consumption tribe as "a network of heterogeneous persons—in terms of age, sex, income, etc.—who are linked by a shared passion or emotion; a tribe is capable of collective action, its members are not simple consumers, they are also advocates" (Cova and Cova, 2002, p. 602). In ways that seem related to the differences between audiences, market segments, and publics we talk about in **Fandom as Audience** and **Fandom as Public**, they also contrast a consumption tribe with a 'segment,' defining the latter concept as "a group of homogeneous persons—they share the same characteristics—who are not connected to each other; a segment is not capable of collective action, its members are simple consumers" (p. 603). Unlike traditional communities, consumption tribes are not defined by stable structures or long-term commitments; they are ephemeral, situational, and often built around shared rituals and passions. Unlike brand communities, consumption tribes are not confined to a single brand or product. Instead, they engage in collective practices that may span multiple brands, genres, or categories, blending and reinterpreting these elements to fit their unique cultural expressions.

Cova's collaboration with the sociologist Michel Maffesoli was particularly influential in framing the aesthetic and emotional dimensions of these consumer collectives. Maffesoli's emphasis on shared emotions, rituals, and the communal experience of "being together" was crucial to Cova's theoretical grounding. By incorporating consumption into the neo-tribal concept's strong emotions and social bonding, they developed the consumption tribes concept. Tribal consumption also emphasized the interconnectedness and tensions between commercial and communal realms. Although tribes often appropriate and reinterpret the meanings of brands and products, they are not entirely oppositional. Rather, they operate fluidly, creating hybrid spaces where market logic and a communal ethos coexist.

Not coincidentally, the meaning-making processes ascribed to consumption tribes overlap significantly with those of participatory culture, where consumers are active agents in the co-creation of value and meaning but expand into even wider sociopolitical and industrial spheres. The use of the term "tribe," however, carries significant historical and cultural baggage that is unwelcome in the current day. We discuss some of these concerns in **Defining Subcultures.** Rooted in colonial anthropological discourse, its application to contemporary phenomena such as brand-related and online gatherings risks erasing the rich complexities of Indigenous social systems. Critics such as Jodi Byrd (2014) argue that this framing perpetuates colonial hierarchies, subsuming Indigenous identities into Western consumer narratives. More recently, Cova repudiated the tribal concept for a different reason: because the term is now associated with "extremely polarized clan forms in which moderate positions have disappeared," thereby losing its "liberating dimension" and becoming instead "an unconscious driver" of "consumer conformity" (Cova and Barès, 2024, p. 2). Because of this new set of meanings, Cova and Barès propose a reinvigorated emphasis on the concept of linking value.

This chapter provided the framework for a deepened understanding of fandoms and brand communities, illustrating how companies like Peloton leverage digital platforms to foster a sense of belonging and identity among users. These groups, which are grounded in shared interests and built through regular interactions, embody the modern incarnation of Tönnies' concepts of Gemeinschaft, transforming consumers into social and active participants in ongoing brand narratives. Through examples like online beauty communities, Apple, and Tesla, we have explored the defining traits of brand communities, such as shared consciousness, communal rituals, and moral responsibility toward fellow members. Ultimately, the chapter presents brand communities as phenomena that offer important new insights into the evolution of social forms and socialities, with key implications for consumer behavior, corporate strategy, and communal engagement.

CHAPTER 8
CULTURES OF CONSUMPTION

T his chapter examines the intricate relationship between global
consumer culture and its local manifestations, exploring how the
passions of fans and consumers are shaped by and, in turn, shape the
world around them. We will investigate how vast, international flows of
media, brands, and ideologies are received, interpreted, and given new
meaning within the specific contexts of personal lives and local communities. To navigate this crucial relationship between the global and the
local, this chapter will introduce and develop the concept of "cultures of
consumption" as our primary analytical tool. By using this lens, we will
synthesize insights from consumer research and fan studies to explore
how fandoms contribute to, and are constituted by, the broader
consumer culture landscape.

Using the "cultures of consumption" framework (Kozinets, 2001), we will explore the rich internal diversity and heterogeneity within what might otherwise appear to be a monolithic group, using the Harley-Davidson community as a prime example. This next step leads us to examine the intersectionality of identities within these subcultures, particularly focusing on how feminist perspectives can challenge traditionally male-dominated narratives. The chapter will then consider the crucial role of digital platforms and social media in accelerating and shaping these consumer cultures, emphasizing the global reach and local specificity of contemporary fandoms. Finally, we will consider the power dynamics at work, exploring how consumers use market resources not only to forge collective identities but also to challenge or reinforce prevailing social norms.

Cultures of Consumption

It was against the early backdrop of the the ethnographic Consumer Research Odyssey work (Belk et al., 1988, 1989), the subcultures of consumption (Schouten and McAlexander, 1995), and virtual community (Rheingold, 1993) studies that Rob undertook his ethnographic dissertation work on Star Trek fandom (Kozinets, 2001). Attempting to mind-meld the perspective of consumer research and marketing with thinking from the emerging field of fan studies—especially the work of Stuart Hall (1980), John Fiske (1989), and, of course, Henry (Jenkins, 1992)—Rob relied heavily on the work of Belk and his colleagues on active consumers (for example, Belk et al., 1988), on Schouten and McAlexander's (1995) subcultures of consumption concept, and on the emergent literature on virtual communities by thinkers like Howard Rheingold (1993). Using the pieces of this conceptual puzzle, Rob found himself challenged to build a broader understanding of consumer culture and to explicitly develop the role of fandom within it. His solution was to view the cultural and subcultural construction of consumer meanings as a "culture of consumption," which he defined as:

> a particular interconnected system of commercially produced images, texts, and objects that particular groups use—through the construction of overlapping and even conflicting practices,

identities, and meanings—to make collective sense of their environments and to orient their members' experiences and lives (Kozinets 2001, p. 68)

The "culture of consumption" concept moves beyond frameworks like subculture or community by shifting the primary focus away from the group of people itself and onto the interconnected system of commercial products—encompassing images, texts, and objects—that those groups use. This conceptual lens also permits a large degree of flexibility and acknowledges internal conflict. Members of these groups do not simply affiliate without reason; they do so because participation leads to a wider cultural outcome that matters in their lives. They use the resources of the culture of consumption as part of their own sense-making and meaning-making practices.

Embracing Heterogeneity and Diversity

This emphasis on the connection between mass-mediated images, texts, and objects and the social practices of specific user groups is what gives the "cultures of consumption" concept its distinct analytical power. Unlike the "subculture of consumption" framework (Schouten and McAlexander, 1995), which often emphasizes a single group's unified commitment to a brand, the culture of consumption is a more flexible frame. It allows us to see a brand or cultural property not as the anchor for one group but as a vast, interconnected system of commercially produced images, texts, and objects. Within this system, numerous different groups can construct overlapping and even conflicting practices, identities, and meanings. The Harley-Davidson culture of consumption, for instance, is not just the subculture of bikers; it is the entire commercial ecosystem of motorcycles, branded apparel, marketing mythologies, and historical narratives. It is within this sprawling system that diverse subgroups—from hardcore bikers and weekend warriors to Christian motorcycle clubs, veterans' groups, and the LGBTQ+ group "Dykes on Bikes"—find the resources to build their distinct worlds.

Partnering with the feminist consumer researcher Diane Martin, who takes on the lead author role, Schouten and McAlexander (2006) co-authored another article after Schouten and McAlexander (2005). That article was "Claiming the Throttle: Multiple Femininities in a Hyper-Masculine Subculture," which offers an illuminating illustration. The "traditionally hyper-masculine domain" they re-examine is actively produced and sustained by the Harley-Davidson culture of consumption through its dominant commercial images of rugged masculinity. The authors explore how women riders navigate, engage, and resist this dominant narrative. Their ethnographic findings show that these women are not simply adopting masculine traits; they are engaging in a creative struggle over the meaning of the core commercially produced object: the motorcycle itself. The idea of "claiming the throttle"— moving from the passenger seat to the driver's seat—is a powerful metaphor for this process. It represents the appropriation of a key cultural object and its re-inscription with new meanings of female autonomy, strength, and personal freedom.

The lived experience of these women is foregrounded in their ethnographic data. As one rider, Caroline, recalled of an incident at a club bar where she was being harassed: "'I had a beer and one of the guys started bugging me, and another one said 'You don't want to mess with her, she rides her own bike'" (Martin, Schouten, and McAlexander 2006, p. 178). This moment reveals a negotiation over the meaning of the object within the collective. As the authors explain, "Women who ride have significantly more status in hard-core motorcycle clubs than women passengers. When women take the front seat, their status in relationship to outlaw clubs takes a dramatic turn." By riding their own bikes, as opposed to clinging to the backs of male riders, these women use a central icon of the Harley culture of consumption to assert control over their identities and social spaces, demonstrating how gendered performances can simultaneously challenge and reinforce the norms of this commercially produced world.

This process of negotiating meaning within a commercially managed system is also evident in the context of bilingual brand communities. In their article, Dino Villegas and Alejandra Marin (2022) investigate how brands adapt their social media strategies to engage Hispanic consumers. Their findings reveal that brands create different "interconnected systems" of images and texts for different segments of this heterogeneous demographic. A strategy of "deep cultural integration," for instance, is an explicit attempt by a brand to build a specific culture of consumption for a subgroup by aligning its commercial symbols with their unique cultural values and traditions. This demonstrates that cultures of consumption are not only created from the bottom-up by consumers; they are actively co-produced and managed from the top-down by marketers seeking to harness their power.

The inner diversity of consumer collectives is revealed within the world of fandom as well. The Doctor Who fandom—or "Whovians"— provides a clear example of how different groups form around their engagement with distinct elements of a sprawling culture of consumption. The "Classic Whovians" build their identity around a specific set of commercially produced texts: the episodes that aired between 1963 and 1989. "NuWhovians," in contrast, attach themselves to the post-2005 revival (Peer, 2014). Other subgroups, like TARDIS builders or fans of the Big Finish audio dramas, form their collectives around their interaction with very specific objects (the time machine as a design) or ancillary texts within the larger commercial ecosystem. These are not just differences in taste; they represent distinct communities that draw upon different parts of the same vast cultural system to orient their lives.

Although traditional sociological frameworks might slot people into neat categories, the "cultures of consumption" concept allows us to appreciate this diversity. It acknowledges that different groups, subgroups, and even individual members may interpret, use, and derive meaning from the same set of commercially produced artifacts in divergent ways. The concept spotlights the dynamic and negotiated nature of meaning-making within consumer contexts. It considers how the meanings attached to consumer objects are continually shaped by broader cultural and industrial influences, as well as by the particular social situations in which consumption occurs. Most importantly, it highlights the productive tension between the personal and collective investments people make in consumer goods and the powerful commercial forces that produce and market those goods in the first place.

The Cultural Turn: Theorizing Consumer Culture

The work of Russ Belk and the Odysseans revealed consumers as active cultural actors within the material world of products, services, brands, and experiences (Belk et al., 1988, 1989). As sociologists and anthropologists were drawn to the marketing field by Levy's (1959) broadened perspectives and his professional recruitment efforts at Kellogg/Northwestern, a body of new work began to emerge demonstrating how consumers were actually misnamed. To these thinkers, consumers were not simply people who use things up or buy; instead, they are participants in rich cultures that include patterns of consumption reflecting broader societal values as well as individual tastes. Viewed from this new perspective, consumers were builders, growers, cultivators, and multipliers of meaning. As the work of early consumer ethnographers like John Sherry, Eric Arnould, Melanie Wallendorf, and others permeated the field, it began to concentrate around the notion of culture, recognizing the key situational context in which its studies had been embedded: consumer culture.

Building on this foundation, Eric Arnould, Craig Thompson, David Crockett, and Michelle Weinberger (2023, p. 2) define the concept of consumer culture as "a dynamic network of material, economic, symbolic, and social relationships or connections that function both as a sense-making device (or worldview) and a cultural blueprint." This macro-level framework explains how consumer culture shapes our perceptions of trends and desirability, influences our expectations of the "good life," and links them to a set of images and values. It also provides a set of behavioral scripts and norms for activities like dining in fast-food restaurants or the ritual formats for gift exchange. This overarching consumer culture is not monolithic; it consists of various meaning systems, often conceptualized as subcultures, that are differentiated by social factors like age, gender identity, and social class. The Arnould et al. consumer culture framework sets the boundaries for what actions, feelings, and thoughts are possible when people operate together from within consumer culture as their lived reality, a state of existence in which certain types of consumption behaviors are far more likely and others are practically unthinkable, much like how players navigate the rules of a game.

From a Shared Culture to Diverse Cultures of Consumption

Although Arnould et al's macro-level "consumer culture" framework is key for understanding the broad rules of the game, our book series is particularly interested in how the game is actually played by different groups on the ground. To analyze the diversity, fluidity, and sometimes disruptive qualities of these groups, we require a more focused lens. This is where the complementary concept of "cultures of consumption" becomes valuable. A culture of consumption is more specific; it is a *particular* system of commercial elements that groups and their members use. To visualize this crucial distinction, Figure 8.1 illustrates the relationship between the overarching consumer culture and the various specific cultures of consumption that operate within it.

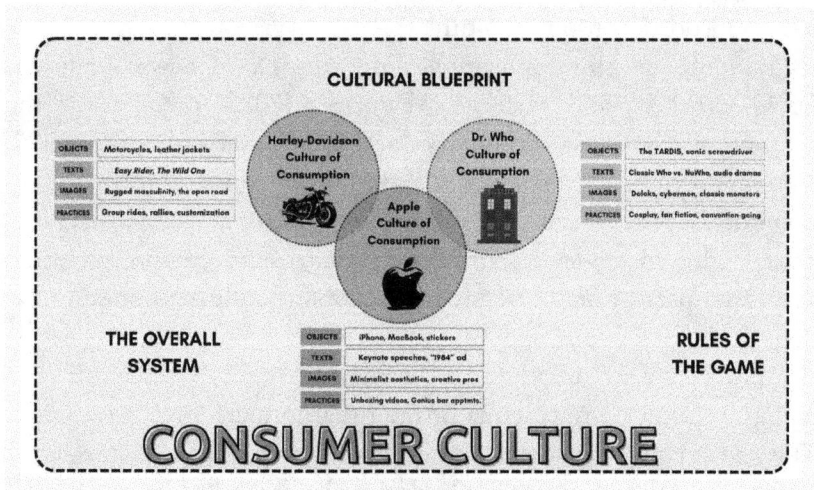

Figure 8.1: Consumer Culture and Specific Cultures of Consumption

As the figure shows, consumer culture can be understood as the broad, encompassing environment—the "cultural blueprint" that contains the general rules, norms, and symbolic resources available in a given society. Within this larger system exist numerous distinct cultures of consumption, represented here by the inner circles. Each one, whether centered on a brand like Harley-Davidson, a media property like Doctor Who, or a technology ecosystem like Apple, is defined by its own particular and interconnected system of commercially produced images, texts, and objects. The framework allows us to see how different groups of people draw upon these specific systems to build their identities and make collective sense of their world. The overlapping nature of the circles signifies that individuals are not confined to a single culture; rather, they move between them, assembling their identities from the diverse resources that the broader consumer culture makes available. This model provides a clear way to conceptualize both the structural power of the macro-level system and the dynamic, creative agency of groups as they forge their own unique cultural worlds within it.

The crucial distinction lies in the unit of analysis. *Consumer culture* describes the entire gameboard and its rulebook. The *cultures of consumption* concept describes the specific plays being made by different groups using particular sets of pieces. We can better understand heterogeneity and disjuncture by focusing on the specific system of commercial resources used by a group. For example, Harley-Davidson riders and Tesla drivers both operate within the broader American consumer culture, but they participate in vastly different cultures of consumption. They draw upon distinct sets of objects (the vehicles), texts (owner's manuals, marketing materials, specialized magazines), and images (advertisements, films) to build different meanings, identities, and communities—sometimes in overlapping ways but often in ways that might conflict with one another. Fandoms are a prime example of this process in action: the Marvel Cinematic Universe and the DC Extended Universe are two distinct cultures of consumption, each with its own specific canon of texts, objects, and fan practices, existing competitively within the larger consumer culture of superhero entertainment but often consumed in ways that overlap by groups that might be highly inclusive or could be strongly antagonistic towards the other.

This lens helps us resolve the old tension between structure and agency in a more nuanced way. It fully acknowledges that consumers operate within a system of commercially produced resources (the structure). However, it emphasizes their active and creative work in selecting,

combining, and reinterpreting those resources to build their own meaningful worlds (the agency). This moves beyond the outdated "media
dupes" argument not by simply asserting that consumers have power,
but by showing the mechanism through which that power is exercised:
the ongoing, dynamic construction of a culture of consumption. The
meanings consumers place on market-based objects are not fixed but are
constantly negotiated in particular social situations and relationships.
From this perspective, consumers and the cultures they create constitute
a self-supporting system, where people are not merely living against the
backdrop of consumer culture but are continuously using its resources
to actively build the essence of how they perceive, interpret, and act in
the world.

Global Scapes and Local Cultures of Consumption

The anthropologist Arjun Appadurai (1990) calls the streaming
global flow of images, ideologies, finances, peoples, and technologies
globalization's "scapes," and his concept is a powerful reminder of the
uncontained and dynamic nature of culture today. A densely woven
network of global connections penetrates even the most local of
cultures. Fans and consumers navigate, negotiate, and engage with a
world where commercial narratives are interwoven with the filament
threads of social and personal identities, local and regional meanings,
technological intermediations, and global trends.

Appadurai's vibrantly fluidic conceptual apparatus affords us a
powerful way to understand how fandoms operate as consumer collectives embedded within these disjunctive global flows. If we need
concrete proof that Apparadurai's concepts are more than merely
abstract forces or academic theories, we only need to look around us.
These scapes are the conduits that deliver the rich and colorful rainbow
of commercially produced images, texts, and objects that surround us.
They are the channels from which emerge the raw materials we use to
build our specific, local cultures of consumption. The mediascape
delivers the blockbuster film, the technoscape provides the Reddit
forum to discuss it, the financescape funds its production, and the
ideoscape infuses it with values. A culture of consumption, then, is the

particular way a group of fans assembles these elements from the various global scapes to make collective sense of their world and orient their lives. The scapes provide the raw materials, but the culture of consumption is the unique architecture that the people in a specific collective build with them.

Assembling Fandom: Ethnoscapes and Mediascapes

Each scape offers a distinct yet interconnected lens for analyzing consumer culture's powerful forces. Ethnoscapes, the landscapes of moving people, highlight the fluid and deterritorialized identities of fans whose allegiances transcend geographic boundaries. Consider the worldwide phenomenon of K-pop fandom, a topic explored in **Fandom as Agent of Globalization** and elsewhere across the series. Millions of fans in ethnoscapes far removed from South Korea engage deeply with the cultural products of Korean pop stars, creating localized cultures of consumption while maintaining digital connections to the culture of origin.

Suweon Kim's (2023) study of K-pop fandom in South Africa reveals how a distinct culture of consumption is formed at the intersection of global flows and local realities. South African fans use the texts (music videos) and images (idol aesthetics) flowing through the global mediascape to construct a unique community grounded in a "highbrow empathy" and South-South solidarity. Nevertheless, their culture of consumption is also defined by what it lacks. The frustration arising from local barriers—the inability to access key commercial objects like merchandise and concert tickets—creates a sense of "hollowness" and highlights the inequalities of global consumption, demonstrating how a culture of consumption is shaped by both connection and constraint.

Mediascapes—the rushing tide of trademarked images, stories, and symbols—are particularly essential, as they constitute the narrative and imagistic flows that feed fan imagination. Media conglomerates like Disney or Netflix are architects of vast, intentionally designed cultures of consumption. Transmedia franchises like Star Wars or the Marvel Cinematic Universe are sprawling, interconnected systems of images, texts, and objects designed to foster deep and continuous engagement.

These narratives are cultural wellsprings that fans draw upon for their own creative purposes. As fans produce and share their own creations— new game rules, fan fiction, art, and analysis—they actively contribute new texts and images to their specific culture of consumption, amplifying and, at times, subverting the mediascape's original flow.

The Infrastructures of Passion: Techno-, Finance-, and Ideoscapes

Technoscapes, the global flows of technology, provide the crucial infrastructure that empowers and enables these fan collectives. Platforms like YouTube, Facebook, and Reddit, alongside a vast range of specialized fan sites and forums, provide the digital backbone for fans to identify one another, connect, communicate, and collaborate. Shaped by algorithms, policies, and user cultures, these platforms play a key role, influencing how connections are made and which narratives are amplified. The specific affordances of each platform mediate how fans can interact with the core texts and objects of their fandom, giving rise to diverse practices within a single culture of consumption. Harry Potter fandom, for example, operates across multiple technoscapes; the intense debates about the creator's ethics on X (formerly Twitter), the creation of new fictional texts on fan fiction archives like AO3 or Wattpad, and the performance of "New Age hybrid incantations" on TikTok are all distinct practices, hosted on different platforms, that draw their meaning from the same overarching culture of consumption.

Financescapes, the flows of investment capital, constitute the economic engine that determines which commercial images, texts, and objects are produced and circulated in the first place, thereby defining the boundaries of a potential culture of consumption. The tricky economics of entertainment production, licensing deals, and global distribution are underwritten by these flows. Sports team franchises or global properties like Doctor Who are supported by global consumer markets that purchase everything from tickets to apparel and from toys to branded household goods. The failure to properly merchandise *Toy Story* figures during the film's initial release, as *Marketing Week* (1996) estimated, allegedly cost Disney and Mattel as much as $300 million in lost revenue because it failed to supply the burgeoning culture of consumption with the tangible objects its members craved. Even more troubling would be the losses the company faced as a result of their consistent failure to market toys associated with its female protagonists, including Ray in Star Wars, Black Widow in the MCU, or Judy Hopps in *Zootopia*, based on the misperception that girls did not play with action figures. Conversely, the activities of fandoms themselves—creating content, organizing conventions, and participating in crowd-funding—add economic heft to franchises, allowing the collective to directly intervene in the financescape to fund the creation of new objects and texts for their culture. A key example of such a collaboration is classic or original Star Trek fans' funding of the *Axanar* film, which we discuss in **Fandom as Co-Creation**.

Finally, ideoscapes, global flows of ideologies, manifest in the ways fan collectives engage with the values embedded in their chosen brands and narratives. Fandoms often become powerful sites for the contestation and negotiation of broader sociopolitical issues. In their study of Taylor Swift's Indonesian fans, Nadzira Zafina and Annapurna Sinha (2024) demonstrate how the ideological "text" of a celebrity brand can resonate globally. Swift's public advocacy for gender equality, LGBTQ+ rights, and personal resilience is particularly impactful for her Indonesian fans, who operate within a more conservative local context. They use the progressive ideology embedded in Swift's commercial persona as a resource, empowering them to navigate and potentially challenge the societal norms they encounter. Their resistant approach illustrates how a culture of consumption can transcend the category of leisure activity and become a primary vehicle through which ideologies flow across the globe, to be interpreted, adapted, and given new meaning by specific fan communities.

Thus, Appadurai's conceptual categories help us to see fandoms not as isolated cultural phenomena but as complex, multi-layered collectives deeply embedded in the ongoing flows of globalization. The scapes provide the global raw materials, but it is through the active, creative, and often contentious work of specific individuals and groups working in local contexts that these materials are assembled into living, breathing cultures of consumption. It is in this dynamic process of assembly that global flows become local meanings and commercial objects become personal totems. It is through the creation of cultures of consumption out of global flows that fandoms reveal themselves as powerful engines of cultural production in a globalized world.

Beyond Resistance: Navigating Commercial and Brand Cultures

Our exploration of global scapes and local meanings requires us to move beyond simplistic models of consumer behavior. The notion that fan practices represent a form of pure resistance against a monolithic commercial culture, for instance, seems increasingly quaint and nostalgic. As this chapter's examples illustrate, fans and consumers operate squarely within the interconnected systems of global capitalism, not outside of them. This reality does not negate their agency, but it does demand a more nuanced and ambivalent perspective on their engagement with the marketplace.

The scholar Sarah Banet-Weiser (2013), in an interview with Henry, powerfully articulates this need for ambivalence. She argues against framing popular culture within a simple binary of "either authentic or commercial... real politics or corporate appropriation" (n.p.). Instead, she proposes thinking in terms of "brand cultures," which she sees as the "nuanced, multi-layered context for identity formation" in our time. For Banet-Weiser, brand cultures emerge from the "deeply interrelated discourses and practices of capitalism, history, culture, technology, and individual identity formation." Because they are a form of culture, they are inherently unstable and contested. Her perspective pushes us to analyze why certain lifestyles or politics are successfully incorporated into brand culture while others, which are not so easily commodified, are left out.

This concept of brand culture works in perfect harmony with our chapter's primary analytical lens. Banet-Weiser's "brand cultures" are a vivid example of what we are calling cultures of consumption. Her framework reinforces our own: these are specific, interconnected systems of commercial images, texts, and objects that become sites for cultural practice and identity work. Adopting this perspective allows us to embrace and amplify her call for ambivalence. It shifts our focus from judging fan engagement as either "resistant" or "co-opted" and instead prompts us to analyze how diverse groups—like the women Harley riders, the bilingual Hispanic communities, or the various sects of Whovians—creatively use, contest, and remake the meanings of the commercial resources available to them.

The Consumer as Cultural Assembler in a Globalized World

Banet-Weiser's more nuanced understanding allows us to see the consumer not merely as an individual actor but as a cultural agent who actively assembles their identity and social world from the resources around them. Consumers and consumption itself are social to the core. Families, peer groups, and broader online collectives all influence consumption choices, but the connection runs deeper. It is certainly true to say that consumers build relationships with products, brands, and media content. Susan Fournier's work on brands relationships (Fournier, 1998), which we discuss in **Defining Fandom**, is perhaps the most developed exposition of this truth. But it is equally true to say that consumers relate to one another through products, brands, and media content, forming networks crackling with the collective effervescence of shared meaning. Acts like wearing a concert t-shirt or posting in a fan group about roller skating serve as personal expressions of individual taste and behavior. But they also are potent social signals that create and reinforce the interlinking of group and individual identities.

This social engagement is also inherently productive. The traditional dichotomy of production as value-creating and consumption as value-destroying is defunct. The productivity of the marketplace both occurs within and contributes to specific cultures of consumption. From organizing fantasy sports leagues and watch parties to customizing purchased items and creating online commentary, consumers actively produce new meanings, symbols, and even material objects from the commercial products of the market, but they do so within the bounds of their chosen cultures of consumption. They create fan fiction for the Doctor Who culture or build intricate family trees within the Ancestry culture. Terms such as "prosumers" (Toffler, 1980) and "produsers" (Bruns, 2013), discussed more fully in **Fandom as Participatory Culture**, highlight how the energy of consumption extends the social and cultural life of the original work, amplifying its meanings and contributing to its ongoing value. Where would the Sherlock Holmes and Beatles franchises be without the perpetual and intergenerational life their fans consistently breathe into them?

Indonesian fans of Taylor Swift, for example, provide us with a nuanced example of the reception of a supposedly homogenizing Western media product. They are active assemblers, taking the ideological "texts" of Swift's advocacy and personal resilience from the global ideoscape and mediascape and weaving them into their own local lives to navigate more conservative societal norms (Zafina and Sinha, 2024). That process of selective incorporation affirms the arguments of scholars like Fiske (1989) and Hall (2006), who contend that consumers transform mass culture into popular culture when personal and collective meaning are assigned through everyday practices. Living in a globalized world, consumers have a plethora of cultural resources, enabling them to express their individuality with a custom mix of local, national, and global influences.

The frameworks developed throughout this book provide us with tools to better understand how this assembly takes place. Thinking about key elements of size, intimacy, structure, and officialness will help us to move beyond a general claim that consumption is social into one where we can read its various dimensions and link their differences to meanings, identities, rituals, and behaviors. They will allow us to analyze the specific forms that collective life takes. Consumers are social beings who navigate these social structures, making choices that both shape and are shaped by the specific character of the collectives they inhabit.

Finally, this act of assembly is a site of power and emotion. Earlier economic theories that framed consumer choice as a rational calculation of cost and benefit miss the intense role played by the frothy mix of collective, cultural, and emotional factors that compose everyday life. Consumers choose products not only for their practical functionality but also because they align with a deeply felt identity, value, or aspiration. The depth of these feelings means that power dynamics are inevitably negotiated in this space. For instance, fandoms frequently contest the dominance of large media companies over the creation of images, texts, and objects that matter to them. They assert their own power by reinterpreting and reshaping those materials in ways that reflect their values and experiences—treating them, as Henry has said, like pliable and moldable Silly Putty (Jenkins, 1992).

The Enduring Power of Collective World-Building

By situating consumers as cultural assemblers, we arrive at a more dynamic and powerful understanding of the relationship between global forces and local lives. The lens of cultures of consumption allows us to move beyond seeing globalization as a simple homogenizing force. Instead, we can appreciate the immense creativity and diversity at play. It allows us to see how the global flows of Appadurai's scapes provide a vast ingredient list of commercial images, texts, and objects, but it is specific groups of people—from Whovians debating canon to women claiming their space in the Harley-Davidson world—who select from that list, find their recipes, and cook up their own deliciously unique cultural meals. Fandoms, when viewed in this light, look less like the audiences of mass culture products and more like sparkling workplaces where cultural meaning is energetically disassembled, melted down, and recast.

This process of assembling a world from the resources of the marketplace, however, creates a fascinating and often uneasy internal tension within these collectives. In almost every example, we see a negotiation between the communal, gift-giving ethos that binds the group together and the intrinsic market-oriented logic of the commercial resources they use. This productive friction, this blurring of the line between a community of passion and a market of consumers, is a defining feature of contemporary collective life. In the chapter that follows, we will expand on this consequential tension, exploring the myriad ways that collectives navigate the uneasy merger of communal and market-oriented interactions in contexts as diverse as a fan magazine and a community that conducts digitally mediated treasure hunts.

CHAPTER 9
CANARIES IN THE GEMEINSCHAFT

The prior chapter developed and applied the cultures of consumption notion, synthesizing consumer research with insights from fan studies to explore how fandoms contribute to the broader consumer culture landscape, examining the intersectionality of identities within these subcultures, and looking at global flows of cultural products and power dynamics at work in consumer culture. All of these elements are situated in a social realm in which this cultural activity takes place through interacting in various ways with commercial producers and the images, objects, and texts they provide. These interactions of markets and communities can be very fulfilling. They can also be fraught. In this chapter, we examine them directly and explore some ways that markets and communities interact and overlap, albeit with some uneasiness, in consumer collectives.

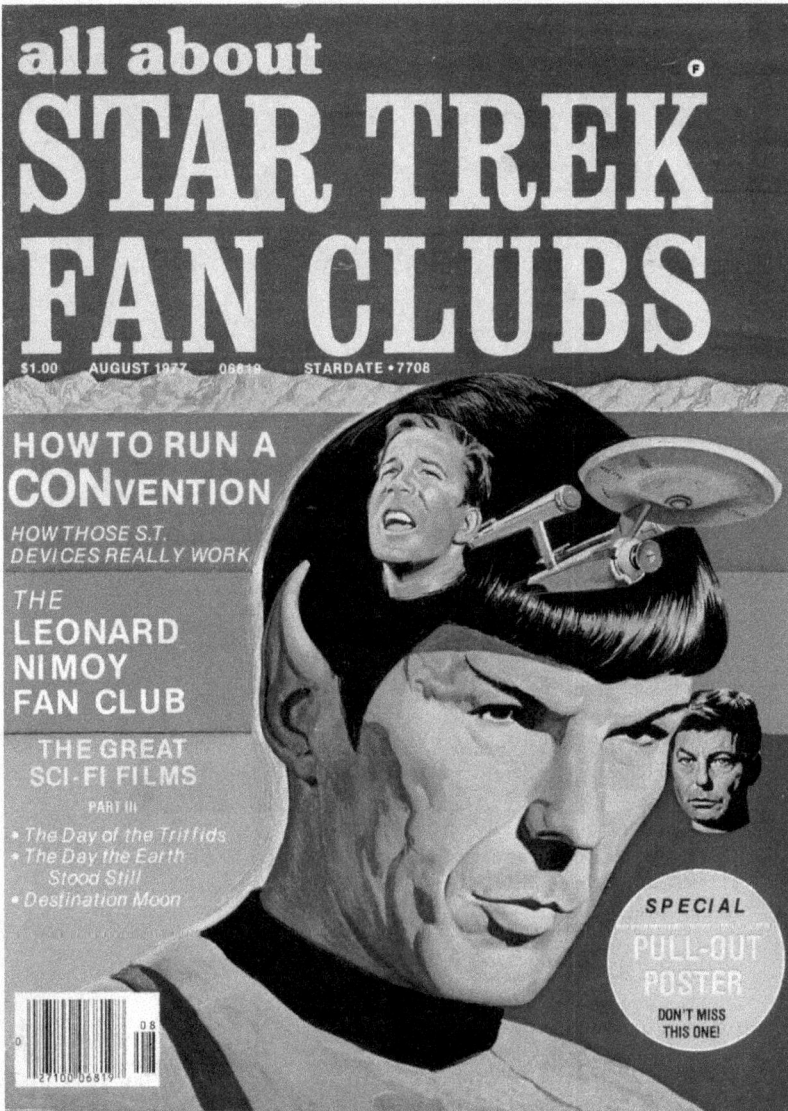

Figure 9.1: *All About Star Trek Fan Clubs* magazine. Issue #2 cover, circa 1977.

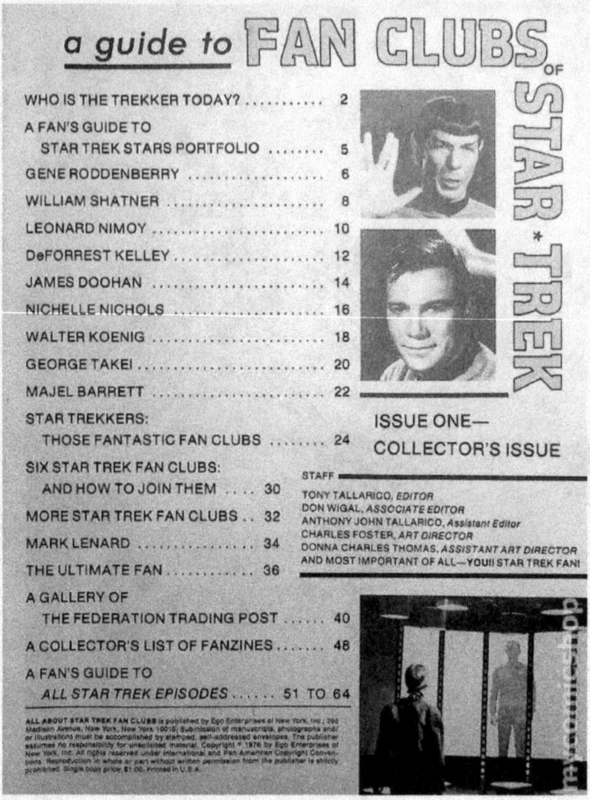

a guide to FAN CLUBS OF STAR*TREK

ISSUE ONE—
COLLECTOR'S ISSUE

STAFF

TONY TALLARICO, *EDITOR*
DON WIGAL, *ASSOCIATE EDITOR*
ANTHONY JOHN TALLARICO, *Assistant Editor*
CHARLES FOSTER, *ART DIRECTOR*
DONNA CHARLES THOMAS, *ASSISTANT ART DIRECTOR*
AND MOST IMPORTANT OF ALL—YOU!! STAR TREK FAN!

ALL ABOUT STAR TREK FAN CLUBS is published by Ego Enterprises of New York, Inc.; 295 Madison Avenue, New York, New York 10016. Submission of manuscripts, photographs and/or illustrations must be accompanied by stamped, self-addressed envelopes. The publisher assumes no responsibility for unsolicited material. Single copy price: $1.00. Printed in U.S.A.

Figure 9.2: ***All About Star Trek Fan Clubs magazine.*** **Issue #1 table of contents, circa 1976.**

All About Star Trek Fan Clubs

We begin this chapter with an example from Rob's personal collection of memorabilia (Henry has a copy of it as well!). We had previously looked at some of Rob's Led Zeppelin reading material and his Jimmy Page action figure. The collectible we are now featuring is a magazine called *All About Star Trek Fan Clubs,* whose cover is pictured in Figure 9.1, and a sample table of contents is provided in Figure 9.2. We chose it because it exemplifies an intriguing and important aspect of consumer collectives, including fandom: the ability of these collectives to combine both economic value, as indicated both by the price tag on the maga-zine's cover and the fact that Rob bought it in his neighborhood conve-nience store, and the cultural values it possessed that derive from its interaction within a communal or gift economy.

The theory underlying this understanding goes back to Tönnies' influential book, which postulated a core division in social groups. The first form, Gemeinschaft, translates to community in English and has many of the same positive connotations. In Kozinets (2002, p. 21), Rob explained the communal ideal as "a group of people living in close prox-imity with mutual social relations characterized by caring and sharing," placing its origins within "the deep trust and interdependence of family relations," and linking it to Robert Putnam's (2000) theory of dwin-dling social capital and the need for a renewed *gemeinschaft*-like sense of belonging, civic engagement, and social contribution.

The second type of social group, *Gesellschaft*, is the dark sister in this theoretical story. The English word *society* only roughly captures the connotations of Gesellschaft. Gesellschaft describes a relational situa-tion opposite to that of familiar or familial relations. Where families are informal and help one another, societies are formal, contractual, and transactional. When people interact in a large marketplace, they are interacting with the roles and rules—the social logics—of a Gesellschaft: keeping a distance, getting the best deal, and making a profit. Gemein-schaft communities prioritize caring for and sharing with those within the group, whereas Gesellschaft markets emphasize transactions with outsiders where each player is trying to get a better deal at the other's expense. Both settings are characterized by their own power dynamics. However, the divergence in social logics appears to account for the historical spatial and temporal confinement of markets to specific locales, occasions, and roles. People and institutions have sought to maintain a clear separation between the more ruthless and exploitative social logics of the Gesellschaft market and communal social institu-tions like home and family.

With the advent of industrialization and later, post-industrializa-tion, market influences have increasingly permeated aspects of life tradi-tionally dedicated to communal relationships. Times, spaces, and roles once exclusive to community-oriented interactions now often accommodate market-driven activities. Theorists like Biggart (1989), Frenzen and Davis (1990), and Granovetter (1985) have argued that markets and communities—Gemeinschaft and Gesellschaft—are now interdependent and even embedded within one another. This encroachment of market logic into communal spheres has led to criticism that the foundational communal values of caring and sharing are being eroded, as market-oriented self-interest reshapes the nature and quality of communal relations, making the actualization of the caring and sharing communal ideal in modern societies ever more challenging.

Communities and Markets: Contrasting yet Interconnected

A substantial body of research on consumer collectives and fandoms has explored these interconnections. In Jenkins (1992), Henry observes that many media fan communities establish nonprofit trade relationships to create a sense of shared communal experience. In Kozinets (2001), Rob suggested that Star Trek fans' distinction between the commercial and the sacred reflects a broader cultural tension between consumer communities and markets. Henry and Rob, along with others too numerous to mention, tended to hold the fort, noting the differences and tensions between these two pervasive and historically important forms of social logic.

Conversely, another strand of research suggested that the relationships between communities and markets might be less problematic than they seemed. Studies on various communities, including river rafters (Arnould and Price 1993), Harley-Davidson subcultures (Schouten and McAlexander 1995), and Macintosh, Saab, and Bronco brand communities (Muñiz and O'Guinn 2001), show little tension between consumer communities and markets. As we noted above, Schouten and McAlexander suggest that marketers and subcultural communities could pursue a symbiotic relationship, implying benefits to both of them. Perhaps even more strongly, Muñiz and O'Guinn (2001) suggested that brands and communities had merged, a transformation they cast as generally positive.

A Commercial Artifact in a Communal World

Now, let's start to think about what went into the *All About Star Trek Fan Clubs* magazine and what else it tells us about how market and communal logics work. We can see how the magazine, despite being a widely distributed commercial product that was sold for profit, is deeply intertwined with the nonprofit, gift economy-driven elements of the *Star Trek* fan community. That interrelationship demonstrates some of the complexities inherent in many consumer collectives, which are hybrids where market and communal forces coexist and influence each other.

First, it is crucial to position this magazine in relation to the broader theoretical frameworks we have established. *Star Trek* fandom is a quintessential culture of consumption, as we have defined it—a vast, interconnected system of commercially produced images (the starship Enterprise, Spock's ears), texts (the episodes, films, and novels), and objects (phasers, uniforms, and model kits). This magazine, as a piece of merchandise, is undeniably one of those objects, produced by a media company whose goal is to profit from mass culture. By its very nature, popular culture depends on mass culture, and thus fandom is interrelated in its very DNA with the market logics of contemporary corporate capitalism.

However, the magazine occupies a fascinating, paradoxical space. Like fan fiction, its content and the core of its appeal are heavily reliant on the gift economy that fuels the fan community. It makes the legitimating claim that it is "made by fans for fans" (and there is no reason to doubt it, either). Although the eye-catching cover illustration features the trinity of *Classic Trek* characters and the iconic U.S.S. Enterprise, the magazine is not dedicated to Star Trek, per se. It is dedicated to *Star Trek* fan clubs—although, strangely, fans never graced any of the covers of its six-issue run. The *Fanlore* wiki describes its content as "a fusion of professional boosterism of Star Trek and its actors, and of fandom boosterism" (Fanlore, 2024). In this fusion, the magazine acts as a node, a physical artifact that channels the global flows that Arjun Appadurai (1990) describes. It circulates ideas about fan identity (the ideoscape), showcases fan art and stories (the mediascape), and provides the organizational know-how for fan-run conventions (the technoscape), all while being part of a commercial flow (the financescape).

From Individual Fanship to Collective Structure

The magazine's content reveals its role as a bridge, designed to guide what we might call the "fandom-curious" from individual engagement into deeper, more structured forms of collective life. In 1977, before the mass availability of the Internet, a fan's experience could be isolating. The magazine's articles serve as a direct intervention in the size and intimacy dynamics of the collective. The first major story mentioned on the cover, "how to run a convention," serves as a type of blueprint for transforming an unstructured gathering into a highly structured, self-governing event. It provides the tools for fans to scale up their activities from small, intimate groups into larger, more organized forms.

The second cover story, about a fan club dedicated to Leonard Nimoy, illustrates another key function: making specific fan collectives visible and accessible. By featuring this club and a fan painting of Mr. Spock, the magazine takes an unofficial, grassroots entity and grants it a form of official legitimacy by placing it within a professionally produced, commercial text. It serves as an advertisement for a specific subgroup within the larger fandom, offering a pathway for an individual fan to increase the intimacy of their involvement by joining a dedicated group. This process of highlighting and legitimizing unofficial fan activity is a primary way that the commercial marketplace identifies and engages with the energy of its most passionate consumers.

The final cover story, offering reviews of three "great sci-fi films," is particularly revealing. It acknowledges that fans are often "omnivorous" in their tastes and do not exist within a single, hermetically sealed culture of consumption. As we and numerous others have found, many *Star Trek* fans are not exclusively loyal to the show. This article functions to deliberately broaden the boundaries of the *Star Trek* culture of consumption, linking it to the wider universe of science fiction fandom, emphasizing the intersection of different cultural consumption circles, as we depict in Figure 7.1. The article on sci-fi films acts as another type of bridge—encouraging fans to explore the adjacent territories and demonstrating the fluid, overlapping nature of these cultural worlds.

Upon examining the table of contents, the mission to shape fan identity becomes even more evident. The lead story, "Who is the Trekker today?," is an explicit act of identity construction. By using and validating the (then-preferred) term "Trekker," the magazine tells its readers, 'Look, others might call you a Trekkie, but you are a Trekker. You can take your fandom seriously. We have worked these things out for you, and there is a community waiting for you.' Following the articles that profile the show's creators and actors, the magazine shifts its focus to the main topic: "Star Trekkers: Those Fantastic Fan Clubs." It features six specific fan clubs, offering instructions on how to join them. By profiling an "ultimate fan," listing collectible fanzines, and providing a thirteen-page "fan's guide" to all seventy-nine original episodes, the publication provides a comprehensive toolkit. It offers a prepackaged identity, a directory of collectives to join, and the cultural capital (episode knowledge) needed to participate, effectively serving as a primer for building a deeper, more structured, and more socially connected fan life.

Making It Official

We can usefully compare the *All About Star Trek Fan Clubs* magazine with another, much longer-lived publication, *Star Trek: The Official Fan Club* magazine, which was renamed *Star Trek Communicator* after its 99th issue. The most important word to note regarding the magazine's title is the term "official."

The magazine actually began as a fan publication created by Dan Madsen at the age of 18 as an outgrowth of the fan club he started. Madsen's publication found its way to Paramount, who asked him to license the publication—and, later, to make his fan club the "official" one.

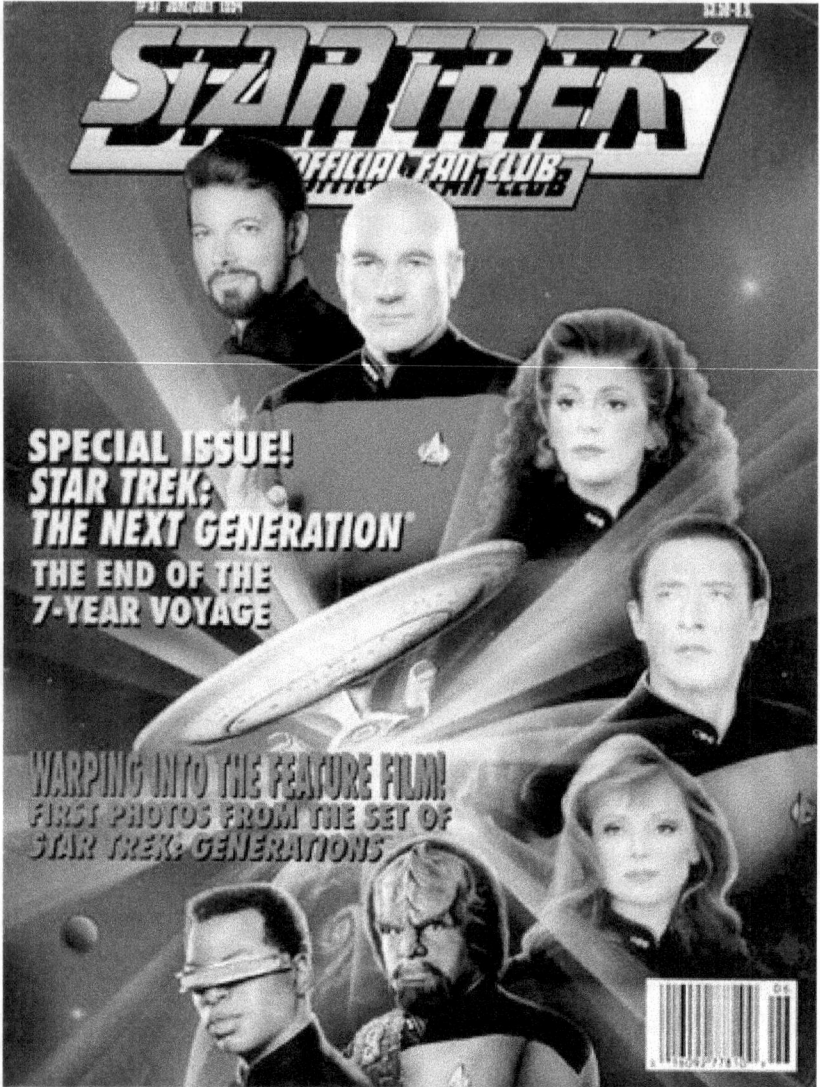

Figure 9.3: Star Trek Official Fan Club magazine. Issue #97 cover. Circa 1994

As the 1994 cover to issue # 97 featured in Figure 9.3 shows, the publication's focus is not actually about fan clubs per se, but the Star Trek franchise itself. The cover in the figure offers fans exclusive information such as "first photos from the set of *Star Trek: Generations*." But it does not offer them information about fandom and how it operates or how to identify oneself as a fan, although Dan Madsen—who is also a devoted Star Wars fan, fan organizer, and publisher—continued as publisher of the magazine until it was sold and stayed on until it was abandoned by its new owner.

Recall the distinction we made earlier between official and unofficial fan spaces and activities. Official publications are beholden to rights holders and as a consequence, they are policed to ensure that nothing occurs that might raise the risk of damaging the value of the franchise. Official organizations typically support affirmational forms of fandom (see **Defining Fandom**) but allow much less space for unauthorized and transformative fan activities. Zines, in the old days, might be sold under the table at a Creation con but other fan conventions center around fan works, which are openly displayed and celebrated. Fan authors have the opportunity to read excerpts from their works. Huge piles of new and vintage fanzines may be displayed on the dealer's tables rather than the kinds of authorized merchandise that are sold at, say, San Diego Comic-Con. The same fan may go to official and unofficial conventions but an experienced fan knows what to expect from each.

We can see from this analysis that the "All About" magazine, although it is a published market offering, serves the function of helping to educate and potentially build individual fanships into collective fandoms. It provides a socializing and enculturating platform for individual fans. It offers them DIY and how-to-type guides on things like starting a convention, broadening their tastes and knowledge, buying merchandise, and collecting fanzines. It caters to fans' sometimes eclectic tastes, such as featuring poetry written by *Classic Trek* star and fan favorite Nichelle Nichols, something that would not be likely to appear in the official magazine. The general fan community benefited from the presence of the "All About" magazine. The All About magazine's existence generates value for the fan community by facilitating connections, circulating knowledge, and providing a sense of shared identity. This value generation aligns with the communal aspects of a gift economy, where the focus is on mutual benefit and shared resources.

Datazine: Unofficial and Unbound

We might contrast both of these publications with *Datazine*, which, from 1980 to 1991, served as a key resource for—rather than about—the fan fiction community (see Figure 9.4).

Figure 9.4: Datazine zine. Issue # 43 cover. Published August/September 1986

Unlike the other two publications, which engaged to some degree with the commercial sphere, *Datazine* was totally unauthorized—by any official group, including the copyright holders. *Datazine* was closer to *Factsheet Five* which had been central to the larger zine movement

coming out of the underground press efforts of the 1960s counterculture. The magazine never sought nor needed a mass audience, as long as
it maintained the support of highly motivated readers who were themselves often also producing its content. Witness the fact that it makes
extensive use of fan slang and jargon: you have to be invested in the
community to understand what's being said. Put differently, *Datazine*
could be insular and exclusive. Unlike the commercial publications,
Datazine had no incentive to broaden the ranks of fandom. *Datazine*
was uninterested in formal fan clubs unless they had grassroots publications to offer. *Datazine* published notices from fan editors about their
publications, where you could order them, and how much they cost. In
one sense, these were advertisements, but the underlying logic was that
of a gift economy since, in most cases, the zines were sold at cost.

Henry found *Datazine* to be a key resource when he began his work
on *Textual Poachers* (Jenkins, 1992). The world Henry described in that
book was largely circumscribed by the contents of this publication in
ways he would only belatedly recognize. At that point, what had begun
as a female fandom around *Star Trek* was expanding to incorporate
more and more other fan objects, although mostly within the realm of
genre films and television series. Thus, a passion for *Star Trek* led to
interests in Star Wars, the original *Battlestar Galactica*, the British
Blake's 7, and so forth. But it also includes cop partner shows like
Starsky and Hutch or the British series, *The Professionals*. *Datazine* also
played important roles in identifying and codifying genres of fan fiction.

Kirk/Spock, understood as a very particular relationship, was
expanded there to the concept of slash, which could incorporate any
number of other same-sex partnerships from across the spectrum of
popular media. Some of the publications supported by *Datazine* were
multimedia publications where smaller and diverse fandoms worked
together. These zines might introduce readers to shows they had never
heard of before, but if readers followed particular writers and editors,
their range of fan objects might broaden. *Datazine* paved the way for
today's even more inclusive fan fiction archives like Archive of Our
Own (discussed in **Fandom as Participatory Culture**).

Datazine also provided other resources in support of fan creators, such as advice columns and, somewhat more controversially, reviews of fanzines. Fans had a heated debate about whether reviews were negative, especially in a public context, or whether they could be vital in nurturing the creative development of the fans involved. Were reviews— which often imply a consumer orientation ("should you read this story?")—consistent with the caring and sharing ethos of the fan gift economy?

The readers were assumed to be invested in building up the infrastructure of a fandom perceived to be a loosely affiliated network of people who both consumed and created fan works. In this realm, *Datazine*'s low production values were a badge of honor. *Datazine*, thus, has a different conception of how fandom was structured than publications that delimited themselves around Star Trek, sought to support the interests of formal fan clubs, and were primarily oriented around commercial efforts rather than grassroots publications. *Datazine* was very much a byproduct of a counterculture conception of DIY production as applied to the realm of fandom.

Datazine thus represents a fascinating and powerful form of consumer collective, one that can be understood through the frameworks we have developed. It stands as a prime example of a self-governing or grassroots commons formation—fiercely unofficial and valuing its unstructured, networked nature over any formal hierarchy. This structure directly influenced its relationship with size and intimacy. *Datazine* deliberately operated at the small-scale, high-intimacy end of the spectrum, in contrast to the commercially oriented magazines that sought to expand their audience using the market logic of the gesellschaft. Its use of insider jargon and its focus on a gift economy were cultural mechanisms used for maintaining a manageable size and cultivating deep, trusting bonds among a core group of highly dedicated participants. The zine acted as a gatekeeper, prioritizing the quality of connection among initiates over the quantity of a mass readership. In doing so, it became the connective tissue for a multitude of overlapping cultures of consumption. While the other magazines primarily focused on the singular Star Trek culture of consumption, *Datazine* curated a space where fans could fluidly move between the Star Trek, *Starsky and Hutch*, and *Blake's 7* cultures, among others. The unifying principle was not a single fan object, but a shared passion for a specific creative practice—the writing and circulation of fan fiction—which itself became a vibrant, meta-level culture of consumption, complete with its own distinct objects (the zines), texts (the stories), and social norms.

Gift Systems in Consumer Economies

Markus Giesler's (2006) article, "Consumer Gift Systems," offers a framework for understanding how digital consumer collectives can operate as powerful gift economies, moving beyond traditional market transactions. Giesler introduces the concept of a "consumer gift system," directly critiquing the simplistic, dyadic (one-to-one) models of gift-giving that had dominated prior research. Drawing on the classic anthropological work of Marcel Mauss, he argues that the peer-to-peer music-sharing on Napster demonstrated a complex "system of social solidarity" characterized by three key features: "social distinctions, the norm of reciprocity, and rituals and symbolisms" (p. 283). This systemic view provides a compelling model for understanding the inner workings of many fandoms.

The power of Giesler's analysis lies in the details. Napster users created the first feature, social distinctions, as a way to define their community against the commercial music industry. The ethos was "sharing music" as a gift versus "paying for it" as a commodity (p. 285), creating a clear boundary between insiders who participated in the gift system and outsiders who did not. This mirrors how many fandoms create their identity by distinguishing their passionate engagement from that of casual viewers or the commercial interests of producers. Furthermore, Giesler describes the platform's structure as polyadic and rhizomatic; a single music file could be received from multiple users simultaneously, creating a weblike, many-to-many flow of exchange. His description is a perfect analogy for how fan knowledge, theories, and creative works circulate online—not as simple one-to-one gifts, but as part of a sprawling, interconnected network.

A strong norm of reciprocity held the system together. Giesler details how Napster users expected community members to give back, either by keeping their downloaded files available for others (internal multiplicity) or, even better, by uploading new and rare music into the system (external multiplicity). Those who violated this norm by downloading without sharing were said to be "leeching," a powerful term of communal sanction (p. 287). The sanctions parallel the strong social norms within many fandoms, where there is often an expectation to contribute—by creating fanworks, participating in discussions, or organizing events—rather than simply consuming content passively. Both systems are built on an ethos of circulation and a shared responsibility to maintain the vitality of the collective.

Finally, Giesler details the rituals and symbolism that gave the Napster community its textures and hierarchies. Users built reputations and asserted identities through symbolic usernames (like "sgtpepper71" for a Beatles expert) and meticulously curated playlists that showcased their taste and dedication. More importantly, they engaged in what Giesler, citing Appadurai (1986), calls "tournaments of value," in which social standing in the community had to be earned. Users competed to provide the rarest tracks, the highest quality files, or the sheerest quantity of music, becoming known as respected authorities within the community. This model is a powerful lens for understanding status within fandoms, where deep knowledge of lore, ownership of rare merchandise (a specific object), or the creation of high-quality fan fiction (a new text) function as markers of distinction and dedication. Giesler's study thus reveals how a consumer collective built around a specific culture of consumption—in this case, digital music sharing—can develop its own rich social world, complete with a unique moral economy, status hierarchies, and powerful rituals that resist and repurpose the logics of the commercial market.

Community-Market Hybrids in the Geocaching Community

We can see many of the same themes of hybridization recurring among studies of other consumer collectives, such as in Daiane Scaraboto's study of the geocaching community. Geocaching is an outdoor recreational activity in which participants use a mobile phone or other Global Positioning System (GPS) receiver, along with other navigational techniques, to hide and seek containers, called geocaches or caches, at specific locations that could be anywhere in the world. The first known geocache was placed in 2000; by 2025, there were over 3.4 million active caches worldwide. Although the activity emerged from the grassroots innovations of numerous players, one company, Groundspeak, which is largely owned by a geocacher named Jeremy Irish, controls the technological infrastructure for this hobby and runs it as a profit-making company.

Scaraboto's research involved four years of in-person ethnographic participant observation at geocaching events and conducting structured netnographic research using digital immersion principles, as well as eleven interviews with members of this consumer collective. The resulting work explores the emergence and sustainability of geocaching and Groundspeak's hybrid economies as a type of collaborative network, focusing on the way that market-based and non-market-based logics intertwine in this context. It tells us that these networks are characterized by the coexistence of various exchange modes and respond to the tensions between their different economic logics through a continuous process of brokering, mediating, discussing, and reconfiguring exchange performances.

The Performance of Hybrid Economies

To understand the uneasy but productive merger of market and community logics, we can turn to performativity theory. Going beyond the idea that people simply "perform" roles, performativity, as elaborated in the work of philosophers like Judith Butler, suggests that our repeated actions, utterances, and social rituals are not simple expressions but creative acts that construct the social realities they appear to be describing. This theoretical lens is key to Daiane Scaraboto's (2015) analysis of how the geocaching community, through its members' actions, constantly performs its hybrid economy into existence. Her work reveals the fuzziness of the traditional boundary between what is market and what is community, showing us numerous places where the lines are blurred as grassroots participants find themselves in alliances with the for-profit actors upon which their interests depend.

According to Scaraboto, the ongoing participation of community members is vital to sustaining these hybrid economies, requiring constant effort to reconcile competing market and communal logics. She finds that "performativities of hybrid modes of exchange and the assembling and reassembling of sociotechnical agencements are constantly required... because the hybrid status of these economies is continually under threat of destabilization by the struggle between competing performativities of market and nonmarket modes of exchange" (p. 171). One of the key strategies participants use is the creation of what she calls "zones of indeterminacy"—spaces where the meanings of transactions are intentionally kept ambiguous, reducing the need for community-wide consensus on whether an action is a gift or a commodity.

Staging the "Digi-Gratis" in Festive Spaces

This dynamic of a hybrid economy finds a useful name in Paul Booth's concept of "digigratis." As he explains in an interview with Henry, this term describes "the mutually beneficial relationship between the gift and the market economies within contemporary media and culture... The 'Digi-Gratis' economy thrives because neither the gift nor the commodity economy outweighs the other. Instead, through mutual reciprocity, their mashup forms a third type of encounter" (Jenkins, 2010, n.p.). To understand the kind of space where this "Digi-Gratis" hybrid can thrive, we can turn to the foundational work of consumer researcher John Deighton. In his early and insightful analysis of consumption as experience, Deighton (1992) identified several types of dramatistic performance, but his category of "festive performance" is particularly relevant here. He defines it as an event that involves "active consumer participation in a built context created by deliberate staging" (p. 367).

This framework perfectly describes the hybrid spaces where communal and commercial logics meet. Fan-centric marketplaces like Etsy, creative funding platforms like Patreon, and fan writing sites like Wattpad are all contemporary festive performances. They are commercially "staged" platforms that provide a "built context" for "active consumer participation." It is within the container of the festive performance that the Digi-Gratis can exist. The very staging of the event as a "festival"—implying fun, participation, and communality—allows the commercial and gift-economy elements to coexist without a direct clash. It creates precisely the "zone of indeterminacy" that Scaraboto describes. Is a fan artist on Etsy a community member sharing a gift of their creativity or an entrepreneur running a business? Within the festive frame, they can be both simultaneously, allowing the uncomfortable coexistence of market and non-market logics to become a source of energy and vitality.

From Performance to Possession

This chapter has explored the complex and often contradictory ways that market forces and community logics merge in contemporary consumer collectives. We have seen how a commercial magazine can become a tool for building grassroots fan structures and how a digital platform designed for mass file-sharing can become the site of an intimate gift economy. Through the lenses of performativity and Deighton's concept of festive performance, we can appreciate these spaces not as simple brand communities or resistant subcultures, but as complex social worlds where the rules of commerce and community are constantly being negotiated. The examples in this chapter, from the Star Trek magazine to Napster and geocaching, exemplify this hybrid nature, as they abet both commercial interests and the cooperative ethos of fandom.

But if so much of modern consumption is about participating in these performances—many of which are fleeting and experiential—a crucial question arises: What happens after the performance is over? How do individuals create a sense of stable, enduring identity in a culture defined by ephemeral events? One powerful answer lies in the very materials of the performance itself. If all the world is a stage, then we should definitely be visiting the prop room, and this sentiment sets the stage for our next chapter, which will explore the relationship between collecting, materiality, and identity within consumer culture and fandom. We will show how activities such as collecting fan objects transcend mere acquisition or displays of materialism and, instead, serve indispensable processes of self-construction and meaning-making. Paradoxically, as we will see, collecting things can offer people a path for resisting the fleeting nature of consumer culture by affording them a way to create personal, familial, and communal narratives that endure, often by resisting commodification through the sacralization of certain objects.

CHAPTER 10
THE COLLECTOR'S WORLD

A key area where the fanship and fandom experience intersects with the realm of consumer culture is in collecting. This is a practice driven by a deep psychological current, a desire that connects our modern condition to our earliest formative experiences. Thinkers in the psychoanalytic tradition, from Freud to his relative and marketing consultant Ernst Dichter, and their intellectual heir in consumer research, Sidney Levy, understood that consumption is rarely just about utility; it is about managing the anxieties and fulfilling the deep-seated needs of the self. Philip Cushman (1990) has argued that modern life often produces an "empty self," ceaselessly on the prowl for things to buy to give it a sense meaning and connection. Cushman would likely interpret the need to collect as a powerful way people in consumer society attempt to fill that unfillable void. The black hole at the center of consumer identity inexorably draws in as much as it can of the vast material resources of a mass merchandise-producing consumer culture.

Consumers' identities and cultural experiences are shaped and reshaped by their interactions with the conjoined objects, texts, and images of the culture of consumption, and they forge them into shape using their collections. Sometimes, the forging of self takes place individually. Sometimes, it takes place collectively. When it takes place individually, it often manifests through personal collections assembled from mass marketplace goods: a physical exhibition of one's choices in the demanding consumer context, allowing each of us to select from a massive inventory. When it takes place collectively, collections can build family ties or break them down. Although individual in its form, a collection can serve as a site of collective identity formation—as stamp and coin collectors, comic book collectors, and bracelet collectors can attest. As a personal collection, it can involve the pursuit of remembrance, status building, or immersive imaginative play, all essential to the production of subjectivity.

The memories, needs, hopes, and dreams embedded within people's collections of toys, merchandise, and collectibles are emblems of the self, markers of identity, and symbolic of the cultural capital that fans accumulate in their lifelong engagement with a media text" (Geraghty, 2014, p. 4) . As Jean Baudrillard (2005, p. 97) says, "What you really collect is always yourself," or, perhaps more precisely, aspects of yourself and your experiences, captured in material forms. But what aspect of yourself is available for capture? A Jimmy Page action figure? A platform-shared family tree? A first issue of the *Datazine* zine?

The act of collecting extends beyond the explanation that it is born of compulsion, like hoarding, or that it is a base expression of consumption. The Great Odyssean Russell Belk defines collecting as "the process of actively, selectively, and passionately acquiring and possessing things removed from ordinary use and perceived as part of a set of non-identical objects or experiences" (Belk, 2013, p. 67). Passion, activity, and selectivity are the keywords here. He carefully constructs this definition to spotlight the intentionality and emotional resonance of collecting and to distinguish it from both casual accumulation and hoarding. A key part of his definition is that collected objects are "removed from ordinary use." They are special, set apart—sacred, perhaps, as Belk suggests.

While this concept of sacralization through removal from the everyday is incredibly valuable, we would like to offer a slight "tune-up." Many of the most meaningful collections are, in fact, deeply integrated into the fabric of ordinary life. Kelly Tian and Russell Belk (2005) wrote about employees' workplace displays of items like their Pez collections, which are anything but set apart. Consider the common collections of t-shirts or coffee mugs; these are objects that are both part of a curated set and used in daily routines. For some, it is their shoes; for us, it is our books and old concert ticket stubs. Rob's action figures are out of their boxes, actively posed and re-posed for photographs. And what of art? It is the quintessential collectible that is explicitly meant to be "consumed" through daily display and enjoyment, a practice that goes back thousands of years from the busts of ancient Rome to public sites like Stonehenge. Collecting, then, is not always about setting things apart; it can also be about bringing the special meanings associated with the collectible into the everyday.

Material Autobiographies

Peering into the psychological motivations for collecting, Belk turns to the unfulfillable nature of desire that Philip Cushman (1990) called "the empty self." In the search for satisfaction that can fulfill this emptiness, the collector's collection offers real, albeit temporary, respite. Belk suggests that the collector's quest for a complete collection is a metaphor for their "quest for self-completion and happiness," both of which are ultimately impossible (Belk, 2013, p. 67). In this sense, collecting can express and lead to materialism, a devotion to finding happiness through possessions. It may well be that collecting channels the drive to bind time and capture special moments into the drive to purchase and own. But, in another sense, collecting is not only about having things but about constructing a coherent sense of self by arranging a diverse set of objects into a networked display of an externalized identity. As Susan M. Pearce (1995, p. 279) so eloquently puts it,

Collections are psychic ordering, of individuality, of public and private relationships, and of time and space. They live in the minds and hearts of their collectors, for whom they act as material autobiographies, chronicling the cycle of a life, from the first moment an object strikes a particular personal chord, to specialised accumulation, to constructing the dimensions of life, to a final measure of immortality.

This notion of the collection as a "material autobiography" resonates deeply with the duo-autobiographical style we employ throughout this book series. It is a process of externalizing and making sense of a life—or, in our case, two lives—through the curation of stories and examples. As we will see in greater detail at the end of this chapter, the family Christmas tree is perhaps the ultimate collaborative material autobiography, a physical chronicle of a family's shared tastes, travels, and passions, lovingly assembled one memory at a time.

This is certainly not to say that collecting cannot become problematic. In **Fandom as Audience,** we write about Dale Watts, the successful attorney who obsessively collected over 300,000 comic books while neglecting his family. We dispute labeling him a superfan, but he was doubtlessly a supercollector and someone suffering from mental illness. His story also demonstrates how collectors can lose themselves in their collections. Dale Watts is a cautionary tale for us all for, under the right conditions, our lust for material culture can overcome us.

Appraising Desire, Reclaiming Value

The deep, often passionate desire that drives collecting is not only about self-completion or status; it is also about the thrill of finding, creating, and negotiating value. The anthropological literature on materiality starts from the premise that, as objects enter our life world, we find them more or less meaningful. In *Spreadable Media*, Henry and his co-authors, Sam Ford and Joshua Green (2013), explore the various forms of appraisal fans and consumers perform across their everyday lives:

We use the term "appraisal" to describe the process by which people determine which forms of value and worth get ascribed to an object as it moves through different transactions... An appraisal performed in an archive or museum may be just as concerned with an artifact's historical, cultural, or symbolic value... as it is with the item's monetary value. (pp. 84-85)

Drawing on the writings of Lewis Hyde (1983), they make a generative distinction between value (economic exchange) and worth (personal or collective meaning). Appraisals among fans are driven by both. In "Cardboard Patriarchy," John Bloom (2002) discusses how baseball card collecting is driven by a desire to reclaim the "worth" of a nostalgic, presexual boyhood, a world of innocence and homosocial bonding. He insightfully notes that collecting requires a focus not just on the objects themselves but also on the social relations between collectors that are facilitated through their exchange. Bloom is attentive to the material consequences of this desire, including the conflicts with romantic partners over the time, money, and space these collections consume.

This fannish appraisal often focuses on residual elements of popular culture—old television shows, for example—that producers had shelved, believing they no longer held commercial value. When fans reclaimed them through collecting networks, savvy producers recognized that this fan-generated "worth" might signal a renewed market "value," leading them to reactivate and recirculate these properties.

Michael Thompson brilliantly theorizes this process in his book *Rubbish Theory: The Creation and Destruction of Value* (1979). Thompson distinguishes between the transient (whose value decreases over time), the durable (designed to last and gain value), and rubbish (which has no value). He stresses that these are not fixed categories; appraisals shift over time: "We are all familiar with the way despised Victorian objects have become sought-after antiques; with Bakelite ashtrays that have become collector's items; with old bangers transformed into vintage motor cars" (Thompson 1979, p. 9). The power to make these appraisals stick, Thompson argues, often resides with those at the top of the cultural hierarchy. Yet, he also notes that innovation and creativity arise in a "region of flexibility" between the transient and the durable. The leap from rubbish to durable is an "all-or-nothing transfer" that happens when an object emerges from obscurity and discards its "polluting properties" (Thompson 1979, p. 26). The He-Man minicomics (which Henry discusses later in this chapter) were initially part of the "rubbish" of toy packaging. However, they were preserved by fans, became collectibles, and, with their recent hardbound reissue, have made the leap to the status of a durable cultural artifact, their worth and value reappraised.

The Collector's World: The Social Life of Collections

While collections are often born from deep personal and psychological motivations, their meaning and power are ultimately realized within a social context. It is in the act of sharing, displaying, trading, and discussing that a private passion becomes a public identity and a personal archive becomes the basis for a community. This section shifts our focus from the collector's internal world to the social dynamics of collecting. It explores how collections function in contexts like fandoms, families, and friendships, crossing over into the realm of publics where the power dynamics of inclusion and exclusion are constantly at work.

Identity and Memory in Collections

Paradoxically, collectors engage in this pursuit not simply to partake in the spoils of consumer culture but to individuate and resist the passage of time. As Belk (1998) astutely notes, we might see collecting as the very opposite of consuming, then, because it involves conserving rather than using things up or disposing of them. When viewed in this light, the saving, capturing, and curating of collected object things may be a transcendent act that usurps the transient nature of consumer culture, asserts individual control over both time and identity, and, to echo Belk's intriguing claim, meets commodification processes with ones devoted to sacralization.

At the crossroads of public and private spheres, you will find fan collecting. Objects are private things that hold deeply personal meanings for individual collectors. But they also have brands, price guides, auctions, and websites, functioning as sources of value and meaning within larger fan economies. The communal side of this duality reflects Henry's description of fan culture as a "culture that is produced by fans and other amateurs for circulation through an underground economy and that draws much of its content from the commercial culture" (Jenkins, 2006, p. 325). As a look inside the frenetic activity inside a convention dealer room quickly reveals, the act of collecting brings people together into transactions. Collectors meet with other collectors to trade, certainly, but also to discuss, display the latest acquisitions, and tell stories about the ones that got away. The act of displaying one's collection connects people, becoming an aspect of participatory culture that can also be enacted online. Just as offline exhibition does, online display of a successful collection "brings the collector heightened status (within his or her collecting sphere) and feelings of pride and accomplishment" (Belk, 1995: 68) and so "we might understand the importance and continued popularity of physical sites such as the convention, cult shop and Megastore in relation to this very real need to show off in the digital domain" (Geraghty, 2014, p. 161) . Among the showiest of the showoffs, by necessity, are the many entrepreneurs whose carnie collectible tables at conventions are both evidence of their elite collector status and also significant sites of fan sociality.

Racial and Gendered Representations in Collecting Collectives

Once collections enter the social sphere to be shared and displayed, they inevitably become sites where broader cultural norms and power dynamics are performed, negotiated, and often reinforced. The act of forming a collective around a shared set of objects is simultaneously an act of drawing boundaries. These boundaries, which define who belongs and what behaviors are considered appropriate, are rarely neutral; they are frequently shaped by the often-unspoken assumptions of the dominant culture regarding gender, race, and social status.

No two collections are the same, and no two collectors are. To understand the powerful role collections play in modern life, we must link the act of collecting to the complex identity work of gender, social status, and cultural norms. Russell Belk and Melanie Wallendorf (2012,

p. 240) argue that "gender is expressed, shaped and marked through the process of collecting." They demonstrate just how deeply collecting is implicated in how people construct and perform identity. Their analysis of two institutionalized private collections—the "Mouse Cottage" filled with a woman's collection of mouse replicas and the "Fire Museum" housing her husband's collection of firefighting equipment—vividly illustrates this process. The Mouse Cottage is presented as a feminine space: diminutive, home-focused, playful, and even a bit chaotic in its cluttered display. The Fire Museum, in contrast, provides a quintessentially masculine display: gigantic, orderly, and serious, representing "powerful achievements of masculine control over nature" (p. 251). These collections, they argue, are carefully, if sometimes unconsciously, curated stages that make "visible the gender distinctions governing social life."

Just as Belk and Wallendorf's (2012) work reveals how collecting can reify and perform traditional gender roles, other research shows how these consumer collectives can also become sites where racial hierarchies are subtly, and sometimes overtly, reinforced. A powerful example is the netnographic study by Rebecca West and Bhoomi Thakore (2013) of an American Girl doll collecting forum. The American Girl brand is itself a complex culture of consumption, offering a wide array of commercially produced objects (the dolls) and texts (the accompanying historical books) that are used by a predominantly female collector base to engage with ideas of history, identity, and girlhood (see Diamond et al., 2009). Despite the diverse racial representation of the dolls, the forum's membership was overwhelmingly white (91% of respondents). West and Thakore found that this demographic imbalance created an exclusionary environment. For instance, moderators engaged in "friendship steering" (West and Thakore, 2013, p. 260) directing new Black members toward other Black members, a practice that, while perhaps well-intentioned, presumed that shared racial identity was the primary basis for connection, overriding all other fannish interests and reinforcing racial segregation within the collective.

Furthermore, when non-white members attempted to discuss the lack of racial diversity in the product line—specifically, the absence of an African-American "Girl of the Year" doll—they were often met with resistance from white members who found such conversations uncomfortable or divisive. This silencing of critical discussion effectively maintained the unmarked whiteness of this particular fan culture, leading many collectors of color to abandon the forum and form their own alternative and more inclusive online spaces. These visible and hidden conflicts demonstrate that consumer collectives are not utopian spaces free from the biases of the outside world. They are often microcosms of society where the seemingly innocent act of collecting becomes a venue for negation, negotiations, and silencing, and at times the painful reinforcement of social and racial norms. By analyzing these subtle practices, scholars add a critical, intersectional dimension to our understanding of how these collectives function.

From Commodity to Relic: The Sacralization of Fan Objects

A core process in collecting involves transforming a mundane object into something extraordinary. In his essay on collecting, Russ Belk explains that a central part of the activity is to grant objects a "non-utilitarian sacred status," removing them from ordinary use so they may be "treated as extraordinary" (Belk 1994, p. 317). Picture an old guitar with the word "Jimbo" carved into its back. This guitar, a Fender "no-caster," began its life as a mass-produced commodity, a tool for a working musician. For years, it languished in a Dallas recording studio. To a casual observer, it might still appear to be just an old, beat-up, but playable guitar. For fans, however, the object has been utterly transformed, for this was Stevie Ray Vaughan's first professional-level guitar.

This transformation from commodity to relic is achieved through narrative. As the historian Krzysztof Pomian (2012) argues, collected objects function as intermediaries, connecting the "visible" world of the object to the "invisible" world of meaning, history, and myth. The "Jimbo" guitar is no longer just an instrument built of wood and wire but becomes a sacred intermediary that connects the fan to the invisible history of Stevie Ray Vaughan's formative years. Its stories and its direct connection to the artist have sacralized it. It would be purchased not to practice upon or play (at least not often), but to hold onto and cherish as an object connected to a great musician who passed away in 1990, much too young, at the age of thirty-five.

Figure 10.1: Stevie Ray Vaugh's "Jimbo"-etched guitar, sold at auction in 2018; image generated by generative-AI (Gemini), Sept 2025; image (c) Robert V. Kozinets.

The sacred value of this singular, unique, guitar is then reflected, however imperfectly, in its market value. In a 2018 auction, the guitar sold for $250,000. An even more expensive example is the 1968 Fender Stratocaster played by Jimi Hendrix at Woodstock, which was purchased by Microsoft co-founder Paul Allen for a reported $2 million. Obviously, these prices do not merely reflect the value of that model of guitar but their status as sacred relics within the rock and roll culture of consumption. They are not just guitars, but famous guitars, collectibles.

The process of using the items of collection to connect between visible and invisible realms is not limited to celebrity artifacts but can be considered a fundamental activity for all collectors. According to a survey of 1,537 consumers, 61% of Americans are self-proclaimed collectors, with coins (collected by 17%), toys or dolls (12%), trading cards

(12%) and jewelry (12%) holding the status of most-collected items (Cook, 2022) . In each case, the collector engages in a similar kind of magic. They search for and select objects from the vast world of commodities. Then, through the power of their passion and knowledge, they elevate them, transforming the profane into the sacred and building a personal archive of meaningful objects from the pursuit.

The Power of Things: Materiality and Agency

To understand what collectors are truly building, we must first appreciate the power of the materials they use. Materiality plays a foundational role in shaping consumer collectives and fandoms, as objects form the tangible substrates upon which identities and cultural practices are enacted. In his book *Cult Collectors*, Lincoln Geraghty (2014) emphasizes the role of physical objects in anchoring fans to tangible experiences, even as their actions transpire within an increasingly digital world. The importance of physical material—of "stuff"—leads us to distinguish the concept of materialism—the belief that acquiring possessions is the key to happiness—from the notion of materiality. Materiality is a way of acknowledging and understanding the profound interrelationship between people and the qualities of objects, such as their texture, form, and functionality.

In his introduction to the materiality of consumer culture, Paul Mullins (2018) critiques traditional studies that reduce objects to mere symbols shaped by marketers. Instead, he advocates for a deeper engagement with their sensory, experiential, and historical dimensions. Mullins asserts that materiality is a process that unfolds over time, and he draws attention to the scholarship of Jane Bennett (2010, p. 6), who emphasizes the "thing power" of objects and their "curious ability" to "animate, to act, to produce effects dramatic and subtle." He also invokes Bruno Latour (1993, 2005), whose Actor-Network Theory reconceptualizes agency as a reciprocal relationship between human and nonhuman "actants." In this view, both humans and objects share a mutual subjectivity that extends beyond symbolic projection. Mullins also draws from Dick Hebdige's (1979) subculture studies, which demonstrate how working-class youth took commercial products like motor scooters and suits and turned them into assemblages loaded with new style and meaning. Materiality, then, encourages us to see how collecting can be framed in complex ways that reach beyond simple market determinism or resistance. As Mullins (2018, p. 363) writes, "Materiality underscores that things are part of an imagined and embodied human experience that is profoundly shaped by objects themselves."

Another relevant contribution is Benjamin Woo's (2014) article "A Pragmatics of Things: Materiality and Constraint in Fan Practices," which asserts that fandom is fundamentally anchored in material practices. Fans rely on physical objects—costumes, game pieces, memorabilia —not only to participate but also to signal their identities and connect with other fans. Woo's scholarship usefully highlights the practical challenges that accompany acquiring, maintaining, and disposing of fan-related items, often within the confines of domestic spaces. His research emphasizes that objects both enable and limit fan activities, serving as tools for participation while demanding labor and resources. Building on these foundations, Maria Christina Ferreira and Daiane Scaraboto's (2016) study of plastic shoes extends our understanding by exploring the "creative space" presented by physical goods. Inspired by psychoanalytic theories of object relations, they position materiality as a dynamic process that bridges our internal and external worlds. This resonates with the lived experience of fandoms, where objects serve as conduits for emotional expression, social connection, and identity work through the pursuit of play, a point Lincoln Geraghty (2014, p. 48) rightly locates in the many interstices of fanship and collecting, from playing with toy objects to playfully displaying rare memorabilia.

The Continuous Consumption Collectible Constellation (C4)

Having established the power of things, we can now ask: what are collectors building with them? To answer this, we must move from the macro-level "cultures of consumption" discussed in previous chapters to a more localized and personal level. We propose that individuals and small groups assemble their own unique worlds of meaning by curating specific objects, texts, and images. This idea builds upon the established marketing concept of the "product constellation," which Basil Englis and Michael Solomon (1996) defined as a cluster of complementary products, brands, and activities used by consumers to define, signal, and perform a social role.

We extend this concept to introduce what we call the Continuous Consumption Collectible Constellation, or C4. A C4 is the unique, dynamic, and personally curated assemblage of objects, texts, and images that an individual, dyad, or family selects from multiple product constellations and wider cultures of consumption over time. It is *continuous* because it is an ongoing, lifelong project of identity construction. It is based in *consumption*, built from the resources of the marketplace. It is *collectible*, involving the passionate selection and sacralization of specific items. And it is a *constellation*, a cluster of meaningful things that, when viewed together, forms a map of the self. As William James (1890, pp. 291-292), the American psychologist who laid the foundations for modern conceptions of self, wrote:

> a man's Self is the sum total of all that he CAN call his, not only his body and his psychic powers, but his clothes and his house, his wife and children, his ancestors and friends, his reputation and works, his lands, and yacht and bank-account. All these things give him the same emotions. If they wax and prosper, he feels triumphant; if they dwindle and die away, he feels cast down—not necessarily in the same degree for each thing, but in much the same way for all.

Russell Belk (1988) extended James' core notion that our possessions are key elements of our identities, and collections (as prized possessions) are a prime way that people expand themselves. The fact that they extend themselves into these fannish constellations shows how central the transmutation of mass culture into popular culture—and finally into individual meaning—is in our society, a process driven by both psychology and sociology.

Constellations in Practice: Case Studies in Material Meaning-Making

These Continuous Consumption Collectible Constellations are the product of the tangible, lived realities of how people use shopping and acquiring to make sense of their lives through stuff. The rich case studies that follow are not just stories, but ethnographic evidence of the C4 concept in action. They are detailed portraits of how these personal constellations are built, curated, displayed, and performed, revealing the intricate craft of assembling a material self.

He-Man Comics: What Our Parents Did Not Toss Makes Us Stronger

Henry here. Consider the case of Mattel's *He-Man and the Masters of the Universe* franchise, introduced on the market in the early 1980s. Each new action figure was released with a mini-comic, which was part of the toy's marketing and packaging. These comics are now understood as a key element in the transmedia storytelling (see **Fandom as Audience**), creating a backstory for each character and showing how they fit within the franchise's larger mythology (Jenkins, 2010). The focus of the mini-comics ranged from primary figures, such as Skeletor or Beast-Man, to novelty figures, such as Stinkor ("The Stench of Evil"), as they tapped influences ranging from classical mythology to Conan the Barbarian and Marvel Comics.

Peggy Charren, an outspoken advocate for tighter regulation of the relations between marketing and children's programming, famously described *He-Man* and other syndicated programs of the era as "half-hour commercials," implying that they had no intrinsic interest as stories except as a means to get children to buy more toys. From Charren's perspective, these narratives were worthless. Children of that generation, however, thought otherwise. Many of today's transmedia producers cite *He-Man* and Star Wars as early influences. I recall gathering all of the comics from my son Charlie's collection and rubber-banding them together. I was fascinated with the broad range of stories that my son constructed using these action figures, often mixing and matching characters—such as Pee-Wee Herman—who belonged to other popular series. Far from blocking creativity, the toys gave him license to question and rewrite what he saw on television, acting as an authoring platform from which new narratives emerged.

Charen may be right that the toys were inseparable from the stories, but from my perspective, the toys became vehicles for creating new stories that better expressed the child's own identity, as when I observed my son use his He-Man figures to rehearse strategies for a bully he was encountering at school. Charen's critique underestimated the expressive potential of these toys and their meaningfulness to children. As a father during that period, I have vivid memories of the intense pain of stepping barefoot on some molded piece of plastic when I was called into my son's bedroom at night. I'd pick up the plastic shield, sword, or pickaxe and "grumble, grumble snarl Teela." My son, a stickler for details, would correct me, "No, Dad, that belongs to Sorceress." These details mattered. The accessories were extensions of the characters, artifacts of their stories, and signs of their capacities for action. *He-Man* was teaching this generation to think not just about individual stories but about the process of world-building. Part of the pleasure of collecting these toys was to demonstrate mastery over the lore of these worlds.

Through the years, Mattel had observed the ongoing interest of adult collectors. Action figures—sold for a few bucks each in the 1980s—now fetch several hundred dollars on eBay. Many collectors have sought to acquire complete sets, much as baseball card collectors sought to reclaim everything their parents tossed. Fan artists are doing detailed renderings of their childhood collections, while model builders create more elaborate figures and environments. Both circulate these images via social media. Mattel has made several attempts to revive the franchise, understanding these adult collectors as an important secondary market. In 2024, Dark Horse Comics reissued a complete hardbound collection of the original minicomics. Contrary to what Charen assumed, the stories still maintain interest almost forty years later, and they continue to live (and make profit for Mattel) thanks to the active collecting and advocacy of their most hardcore fans. What had begun as rubbish (literally packing materials) had gained prestige through the years, becoming a durable, in Thompson's terms.

Playing With and Displaying Collections

Both here. In an autoethnographic essay exploring how she displays her own collection of Marvel Cinematic Universe-themed action figures, Tara Lomax (2024) seeks to reclaim the concept of "play," which is embedded but often lost within the term "display." She sees collecting as the first step in a larger process, one that rests on holding onto the potential for dynamic action that action figures allow. She was inspired by the work of Katriina Heljakka and J. Tuomas Harviainen (2019), who explain that, "contrary to common belief, adults, besides collecting, also engage in both manipulative and imaginative play with contemporary character toys... in multifaceted ways that involve multiplatform play scapes" (p. 354). Lomax (2024) writes:

> To display an action figure collection can be a form of artistic expression akin to hanging a painting on a wall ... .While the goal is to admire the aesthetic presentation..., the process requires physical interaction with the material design of the toy's articulation that also constitutes a form of play... As an expression of play, my approach to action figure display is shaped by a fundamental commitment to preserve the perception of action in the action figure form. (n.p.)

Lomax's photography and her ongoing analysis of the creative choices involved make a strong case for seeing display as an important mode of fan expression and a key practice in the craft of building a personal constellation.

Studying "Stuff"

British anthropologist Daniel Miller (2013) studies the investments people make in the "stuff" of our everyday lives—our "belongings" and "longings." While acknowledging the materialistic values of our culture, he is more interested in seeing our "stuff" as the focus for meaning making and memory management. He sees collecting as a form of everyday curation through which we shape our environments. Stuff is difficult to study, Miller suggests, because these relationships often take place behind closed doors: "Families are created in bedrooms and sometimes divorced there. Memories and aspirations are laid out in photographs and furniture. Yet, peering into the wardrobe, you may be accused of voyeurism" (Miller 2013, p. 109).

Miller's book, *The Comfort of Things* (2008), takes us inside thirty households on the same London street, using ordinary objects to document material culture at work. His approach is descriptive and narrative; he constructs portraits of people and their stuff. There is an order to things:

> They put up ornaments; they laid down carpets... Some things may be gifts or objects retained from the past, but they have decided to live with them, to place them in lines or higgledy-piggledy... These things are not a random collection. They have been gradually accumulated as an expression of the person or household. (Miller, 2008, p. 2)

A Cosmology of Things

For Miller, people's relationship to these everyday objects might best be described as a cosmology or an aesthetic. People are making meaning of themselves and their lives via what they accumulate and display:

> The aesthetic form that has been located in these portraits is not simply a repetitive system of order; it is above all a configuration of human values, feelings, and experiences. They form the basis on which people judge the world and themselves. It is this order that gives them their confidence to legitimate, condemn and appraise. These are orders constructed out of relationships, and emotions and feelings run especially deep in relationships. (Miller 2008, 296)

Similarly, Anna McCarthy (2001) conducted an ethnographic study of the ways people place familiar objects in and around their television sets—such as knickknacks or family portraits—to create personal shrines to their media consumption: "The TV set is a kind of semiotic magnet in social space, a place to put stickers, posters, plastic flowers, real flowers, and written signs that communicate something about the space to others" (p. 128).

One recent book by Sunanina Maira and Elisabeth Soep, *Youth-scapes: The Popular, The National, The Global*, (Maira and Soep, 2011) explored youthscapes, using them as windows to look at the socialization and enculturation processes impacting immigrant and minoritized youth. On the one hand, their most intimate spaces often contain objects they brought with them from their motherlands, sometimes family heirlooms or cultural symbols meant to express who they are and where they come from, sometimes objects grabbed quickly as they escaped from danger and risk and thus embodying the trauma of being a refugee.

On the other hand, these immigrant youth may also decorate their rooms with objects that signify their affiliation with Western popular culture. Such objects express their aspirations of belonging in this new world, of being part of a wider and more diverse youth culture. Alexandra Schneider (2011, pp. 144-145), for example, traces the range of material practices deployed by a Tamil foster child named Mani to express his affiliations and identifications with Hong Kong action star Jackie Chan:

> Over a period of roughly five years, his encounter with Jackie Chan led him to produce a series of texts of different types. His "initiation" into Chan's filmic world took place in the foster home, where he saw his first Chan movie on TV. His fandom started out with watching movies, and in a first phase, Mani developed classical fan activities such as clipping, collecting, and archiving newspaper articles and promotional materials in fan albums, creating collages from printed materials, making film lists, and imitating the star's poses in personal photographs. Later, Mani started making short movies of his own, such as Jackie Chan trailers and video clips....Using semi-professional digital video cameras and video editing software, Mani currently uses his spare time to produce so-called "Schlegli" films (which

roughly translates from Swiss German as "beat'em-up movies") in a style reminiscent of Jackie Chan's work.

Here, we see a progression from collecting pre-existing materials that reminded Mani of his entertainment experiences but gradually he began to produce his own media objects, including his own "beat'em-up movies" as he locates himself in relation to the imagined world he had seen in Chan's movies.

Christmas Trees as Fannish Displays

Henry here. One of Miller's households in *The Comfort of Things* (2008) displays an obsession with all things Christmas. He writes, "In the bay window is the most perfect Christmas tree... None [of the ornaments] is too large or gaudy, there is nothing plastic or vulgar" (p. 18). Miller is interested in how a "tasteful" performance of Christmas can become the center of one's identity. As I read the passage, I was inspired to think about what it might mean to celebrate Christmas as a member of a fandom, where many of the choices made are indeed "gaudy," "plastic," and "commercial." Christmas trees become vehicles for expressing a range of meanings, and today, we often customize them to reflect the personal mythologies we have constructed.

My brother, Russell, decorates his tree in Coca-Cola red and with ornaments that reflect a multi-decade campaign to associate the brand with Christmas (see Figure 10.2). For Russell, this is not just about a beloved brand but also a source of civic pride, since Atlanta, where we grew up, is Coca-Cola's corporate headquarters.

The ornaments on my family tree, pictured in Figure 10.3, are more eclectic, functioning as the intertwined portrait of our family as our tastes and interests evolved. When we first married, both my wife and I brought beloved ornaments from our own families. We made felt ornaments for our first few Christmases. When our son was little, his love for spooky things led to a plastic coffin candy container, now holding a Tony the Tiger toy, becoming a cherished heirloom. His stained-glass He-Man characters also remain.

I collect plastic animals from zoos I visit. We have ornaments from our travels around the world. We have a wooden Russian Orthodox cross from my grandfather, carved when I was obsessed with Leo Tolstoy. We have a stone hand-carved by an Inuit artisan to commemorate the Raven Festival from *Northern Exposure*. Characters from Doctor Seuss, Winnie the Pooh, and the Wizard of Oz represent childhood favorites.

Our fandoms are a recurring theme: Disney, Marvel Comics, *Good Omens*, *Game of Thrones*, *Doctor Who*, and *Downton Abbey*, among many others. A 1950s ray gun is generic; the tech from Star Trek is highly particular. The Varsity, a beloved Atlanta hotdog stand, suggests I share my brother's civic pride. Unpacking and placing the ornaments becomes an occasion for memory-making and storytelling. The ornaments are carefully curated to convey things that mattered to us across the span of our lives.

Edward, one of my boyhood friends, has two or more trees each year, each a portrait of his evolving tastes, often including icons from cinema and pop culture, from Star Trek to Marilyn Monroe. As someone involved with the arts, he is drawn towards vivid colors and a more flamboyant presentation (see Figure 10.4). While each of these trees may reflect individualistic ways to display fannish identities, they also reflect the expanding market for distinctive decorations, so that, as Miller might suggest, our trees become mirrors of our own consumption practices.

Figure 10.2: Henry's brother themes his Christmas tree around Coca-Cola-related ornaments. Photograph © Cynthia Jenkins. Used by permission.

Figure 10.3: Ornaments from the Jenkins family Christmas tree, which suggest the eclectic mix of stories (both personal and collective) a family of fans accumulates across a lifetime together. Photograph © Cynthia Jenkins. Used by permission.

Figure 10.4: Henry's boyhood friend Edward's Christmas tree decorations incorporate the peace symbol and the Gay Liberation rainbow flag. Photograph © Edward McNalley. Used by permission

Figure 10.5: The Kozinets Family Tree in Los Angeles, California. Photograph © Robert V. Kozinets. Used by permission.

Rob here. I could not resist adding a photograph of our Christmas family tree (see Figure 10.5). If you care to peep closely, you may indeed find a Star Trek Spock figure accompanied by an Eddie Van Halen painted guitar, mirror balls, Monsters Inc. and other Disney figures, and many other fannish touches hanging alongside numerous perfect shiny balls, handmade styrofoam balls we made with our neighbor, Patty, old handmade crafts from Austrian villages and small towns in the forest, local images of Santa in a Hawaiian shirt and shorts, and sparkly octopi and jellyfish. Because my wife and I only began living together when we began our life in Los Angeles, the story our tree tells is one of a combined life of forests, mountains and beach life, fandoms, food, music, and cats. It seems pretty obvious that these trees function as active, living archives.

The annual ritual of putting those decorations onto the Christmas tree is a key moment when, as Daniela Petrelli and Ann Light (2014, p. 162) describe it, "the present meets the past." It is memory work. Taking memories out of boxes, placing them onto a tree, and lighting them up: it is to pay respect, homage even, to your past selves and to the past itself. And the material memory metaphor continues as, each year, new ornaments are added to the old. The collection becomes an ongoing material assemblage. It displays a physical record of the family's evolving journey that is territorialized onto the temporal space of the holiday. The unboxing becomes an occasion to "reflect and reminisce about special moments" (Petrelli and Light 2014, p. 162), as each object is handled and its story is retold, reinforcing the family's unique narrative.

Lest the tree decorating be cast as overly jolly, Cele Otnes and her colleagues conducted in-depth interviews with twenty-six consumers about their Christmas tree rituals. They found that decorating was the result of a powerful negotiation that occurs within the family. Households face down, negotiate, and must repeatedly resolve a key conflict between "aesthetics vs. tradition." The "perfect" tree described by Miller, with its unified silver and gold baubles, represents a victory for a singular, impersonal aesthetic. In contrast, the fannish trees we have described, with their chaotic mix of handmade heirlooms, plastic pop culture icons, and travel souvenirs, demonstrate a deliberate choice to prioritize the family's unique history and personal stories (tradition) over any single, coherent design scheme. Within this ritual, the commercial objects are stripped of their purely market-based meaning and reinscribed with the intimate, sacred meaning of a specific memory—a trip taken, a movie loved, a private joke. This process reveals how a seemingly simple holiday decoration becomes a complex site for cultural work, where a family actively performs and solidifies its collective identity by curating and displaying the material artifacts of its shared life.

Towards an (Im)material Culture

Both here. Our exploration of collecting has thus far centered on tangible things—plastic action figures, cardboard comics, vinyl records. But what happens to the Continuous Consumption Collectible Constellation when the objects themselves dematerialize? Imagine a future, not far from our present, where the most prized collectibles exist only as lines of code. You could purchase a deed to a digital apartment in the Baxter Building, down the street from the Fantastic Four, or own a virtual plot of land in the Shire. Any fictional universe you dream of can be manufactured and merchandised, not just as physical toys, but as unique, ownable digital assets. This is the world of NFTs (non-fungible tokens) and other digital collectibles, a new frontier that both extends and radically challenges our understanding of what it means to collect.

This shift pushes us to reconsider the boundaries of our own concepts. The very idea of a personal culture of consumption is predicated on assembling a world from the images, texts, and objects provided by the marketplace. In the digital realm, these three categories can collapse into one. An NFT of a superhero's first appearance is simultaneously the image, the text (as it can contain the comic), and the object itself, verified by the blockchain. This development forces us to confront the nature of possession itself. The digital object cannot be held, displayed on a physical shelf, or accidentally stepped on in the middle of the night. Its existence is verified not by physical presence but by a record on a blockchain. As research on digital collecting practices shows, this (im)materiality creates significant challenges for the traditional pleasures of curation and exhibition that are so central to the collector's craft. It can be difficult to impose a meaningful personal order on digital files that are often managed by software, and even more difficult to create the kinds of socially visible displays that generate status and connection.

Yet, despite these challenges, lively fan communities have formed around these digital objects. Allison Sinnott and Kyrie Zhou's (2023, p. 2) study of the Bored Ape Yacht Club (BAYC) NFT collection, for example, found that ownership of a digital Ape included benefits such as "expressing their personality and identity, being granted exclusive access to social opportunities and online/offline events" as well as "enjoying the welcoming and supportive community atmosphere." Owning the right NFT becomes a status symbol that grants entry into a collective, much like owning the right piece of memorabilia grants status at a fan convention. Bryan White, Aniket Mahanti and Kaldrum Passi (2022) conducted a large-scale study of the OpenSea marketplace that sells most of the NFTs available. They found that the market was dominated by a small number of "heavy-hitters" and that "the top 20% of collections accounted for an impressive 97.4% of all transactions" (p. 492). Despite their finding of an imbalance, they still find numerous "closely connected communities of buyers and sellers who tend to operate within a specific category of NFT" (p. 495).

This turn towards digital collectibles such as NFTs also suggests that we might more closely consider and research the ordinary, daily collections we all make—of bookmarked websites, curated playlists, or saved hyperlinks—as explicit acts of acquisition. In this new, (im)material world, we can see some of the core tensions of collecting being played out in their most extreme and revealing forms. Those tensions include things like comparing something's subjective personal worth and its supposedly objective market value, or thinking about which elements of a tangible collection are valuable versus what exists merely in the imaginary realm: a topic we take up in the next chapter as we plunge into the topic of narrativity.

Material Substrates

To fully understand how these personal cultures of consumption are crafted, we must appreciate the nature of the materials themselves. The choice to engage with physical or digital objects brings with it a distinct set of experiences, constraints, and possibilities. If we consider fandom to be a stage, we need to think of the tangible "stuff" of fandom as consisting of more than the sets or props; it most certainly is not a passive backdrop. These commercial things come laden with relationships and connections. Each of them actively participates in the ongoing creation of meaning in consumers' lives, shaping how collectors experience their passion and build their worlds.

The anthropologist Daniel Miller has also contributed to our understanding of fan and consumer culture through large-scale research initiatives that explore the meanings that become attached to new media platforms and devices as they are absorbed into diverse cultures around the world. Comparative work on smartphone use in, among other locations, Brazil, Ireland, Israel, Japan, China, and Uganda led to a focus on metaphors of "crafting" to refer to the bottom-up practices through which users made the expensive and alien device into a resource for reflecting on their everyday lives:

The purchase of a smartphone handset is just the beginning of several transformative processes that result in the specific smartphones we encounter in fieldwork. It seems appropriate to respect such processes by regarding them as examples of artisanal craftsmanship. After all, crafting does not mean people are totally free to do what they like with smartphones, or with their lives. Artisans too are constrained by the material properties of the substance with which they work. They have to chip away certain elements carefully and add or mould others, according to the malleability and nature of those materials. But, unlike an artwork, the crafting of smartphones is always relative to context and usage. It is not a question of creating something autonomous. The aim of this crafting is rather to create alignment with everyday life. (Miller et al., 2021, pp. 135-136)

Another of his studies (Miller and Sinanan, 2017) compares the family snapshots and selfies taken by smartphone users in the United Kingdom and Trinidad as a way to understand the construction of childhood and kinship in the two countries. While Brits often used photographs to authenticate the "natural" child, the Trinidadians often manipulated images or constructed collages, which were more apt to acknowledge the process by which the child is absorbed into the culture around them. Here, again, we see models for how we might look at fan photography, for example, as a means for expressing personal fantasies and seeking belonging.

Will Straw (2007, p. 4) argues that the rise of digital networks has enabled many more exchanges amongst fans and collectors as material objects are displayed and sold across a range of different sites:

A significant effect of the Internet, we would argue, is precisely this reinvigoration of early forms of material culture. It is not simply that the Internet, as a new medium, refashions the past within the languages of the present, so that vestiges of the past may be kept alive. [. . .] In fact, the Internet has strengthened the cultural weight of the past, increasing its intelligibility and accessibility. On the Internet, the past is produced as a field of ever greater coherence, through the gathering together of disparate artifacts into sets or collections and through the commentary and annotation that cluster around such agglomerations, made possible in part by high-capacity storage mechanisms.

The smartphone, as Miller shows, is a material substance that is crafted into a personal tool for living. For collectors, as Straw argues, the internet is a key element that enhances the value and accessibility of *other* material objects. In both cases, the technology is not a replacement for the physical world but a tool that people use to move through and make meaning within it.

From Objects of Desire to Storied Worlds

This chapter has explored the multifaceted relationship between collecting, materiality, and identity within consumer culture and fandom. We find that collecting transcends mere acquisition and consumption and is a process of self-construction, memory-making, and meaning-making, where objects become imbued with personal and cultural significance. These processes offer fans a way to resist the ephemerality of consumer culture and create enduring narratives. Collections function as "material autobiographies" (Pearce, 1995) that chronicle the collector's life and passions. The collectors' acts of preservation and curation allow them to assert control over time and identity, transforming the transient nature of consumer goods into lasting markers of selfhood.

However, collecting is not solely an individualistic pursuit. It also fosters social connections and fuels participatory culture. Collectors gather at conventions, in online forums, and through trading networks to display, discuss, and exchange objects, creating meaningful relationships where shared passions are expressed and reinforced. These interactions highlight the communal dimension of collecting, as objects become mediators of sociality and catalysts for identity work within fan communities. This social dimension is inseparable from broader societal narratives. Collecting practices can reflect and reinforce existing social hierarchies and cultural norms, as seen in West and Thakore's (2013) study of the American Girl doll collecting forum, where racialized assumptions and exclusionary practices marginalized non-white participants. Their powerful example demonstrates how collecting intersects with and reproduces power dynamics, driving home the importance of critical engagement with the social and cultural contexts that shape these practices.

Moving beyond the social dimensions of collecting, this chapter has also explored the concept of materiality, emphasizing the agency of objects and their role in shaping human experiences and identities. Drawing on Jane Bennett (2010) and Bruno Latour (1993, 2005), we argue for a more nuanced understanding of materiality, one that recognizes the "thing power" of objects and their capacity to "animate, to act, to produce effects" (Bennett, 2010, p. 6). We challenge traditional views that reduce objects to mere symbols. Instead, we believe that future research will productively engage with the sensory, experiential, and historical dimensions of the physical stuff of consumer culture.

Materiality, then, is not simply a property of objects. Instead, it is a dynamic process of co-creation between humans and non-humans that unfolds through embodied interactions and shared practices. Woo's (2014) study of fan practices further illuminates the role of materiality, highlighting the practical challenges and constraints associated with acquiring, maintaining, and disposing of fan objects. Building on these theoretical foundations, we contend that materiality plays a central role in the expression and negotiation of identity within consumer collectives and fandoms. Objects serve as mediators of sociality, bearers of cultural meaning, and catalysts for playful exploration and transformation. By recognizing the memorializing, playful, and relational aspects of materiality, we can begin to more fully unpack the potentiating and co-constitutive nature of physical things.

Our exploration of materiality owes a lot to the work of Daniel Miller (2008, 2013), who examines the "stuff" of everyday life and its role in shaping our sense of self and belonging. His ethnographic studies, such as *The Comfort of Things*, offer valuable insights into how individuals curate their environments and construct meaning through their belongings. Miller's work resonates with McCarthy's (2001) study of television sets as "semiotic magnets," where objects placed around the TV become expressions of personal identity and media consumption practices. Similarly, Maira and Soep's (2011) research on youthscapes reveals how material objects can reflect the complex processes of socialization and enculturation, particularly for immigrant and minoritized youth. Schneider's (2011) study of a Tamil foster child's engagement with Jackie Chan further illustrates how material practices, from collecting memorabilia to creating fan films, can mediate identity formation and cultural affiliation. Drawing on these diverse perspectives, we have proposed that the act of collecting, intertwined with the concept of materiality, offers a rich lens through which we can gain a greater understanding of contemporary consumer collectives and fandoms. It is in the creation of what we have termed the Continuous Consumption Collectible Constellation—the C4—that individuals and families assemble their own personal cultures of consumption from the vast resources of the global marketplace.

This deep dive into materiality and the crafting of personal worlds sets the stage for our next chapter. We have seen how objects become imbued with meaning, but they do not speak for themselves. Their significance is almost always carried by stories. Because brands function as complex storytellers that resonate with consumers on both individual and collective levels, we can better comprehend the intersection of consumer cultures and fandoms by turning our focus to narrative. The next chapter explores the relationship between brands, narratives, and consumer collectives. It begins by defining contemporary brands as multifaceted entities that go beyond simple identifiers to embody values, aspirations, and cultural narratives. Brands have evolved to become sophisticated symbolic tools performing valuable cultural functions.

CHAPTER 11
IMAGINARIA

I f our discussion of collecting in the prior chapter emphasized a set of material practices through which everyday "stuff" may serve as the basis for manufacturing meaning, then this chapter reverses the coordinates. We will explore ways in which the rich, imaginative worlds offered by media and brands inspire the very material practices of collecting and curation that define so many consumer collectives. It is the power of the imagined world that confers the material object its value; it is the desire to visit, learn more about, spend time in, or even inhabit that world, to bring that world into their own world, to surround themselves with objects, images, and texts from that world, that drives the collector's passion. To understand this powerful drive, we must first build a framework for the way these imaginary elements move between commercial producers and individual and collective consumers.

In an essay on the 1942 movie *Casablanca* as a cult object, Umberto Eco (1985, p. 3) explains that for a work to attract such a following, "it must provide a completely furnished world. So that its fans can quote characters and episodes as if they were part of the beliefs of a sect, a private world of their own, a world about which one can play puzzle games and trivia contests, and whose adepts recognize each other through a common competence."

Eco is stressing the ways that a fictional world for a fan operates as a shared fantasy—to be intersubjective, it has to be consistent and know-able—and at the same time, it assumes the status of something like a real place, which we can learn more and more about. The physical objects fans collect help provide a material grounding to that imagined world as if we could touch it and hold its elements in our hands. They are the furniture sustaining Eco's "completely furnished" world. They can also be the sources of information—what did the helmets or weapons look like, say, in the Japanese medieval world depicted on the 2024 Hulu series *Shogun*. But we also find ourselves collecting information in a less material way, assembling "Making of" books or "Concordances" that allow us access to the information we need to fully master and "furnish" those realms. Today, we may bookmark hundreds of webpages, both commercial and fan-made, that document aspects of these imaginary worlds.

The need to do a "little homework" either to fully appreciate the source material or to extend it through fan fiction writing gives way to more and more scanning through the archive, acquiring knowledge but also objects that embody that knowledge. We need to know. We want things to fit, to be consistent. We want new stories that build on the old and fill in gaps in our mental model. This process, at once material and immaterial, is one of the major drivers of fandom.

Welcome to The Imaginarium

Eco's "completely furnished world" is what we will call the imaginarium: the rich, narratively dense, and psychologically resonant space that fans and consumers collectively inhabit. The imaginarium is the destination. It is the invisible realm of meaning, mythology, and shared fantasy that is the true object of a fan's desire. This specific, furnished world is made possible by a broader social and sociological concept, the *imaginary*. We can think of an imaginary as a shared set of values, institutions, laws, and symbols common to a particular social group. A national imaginary, for example, is the collection of stories, myths, and symbols that allows millions of strangers to feel they are part of a single nation. In our context, we can talk about a "consumer imaginary"—the general belief in the power of goods to shape identity—or a "fandom imaginary," the shared understanding that it is possible and meaningful to form a deep, passionate connection with a piece of mass culture. The imaginary is the background condition that makes a certain kind of collective life feel possible and coherent. The imaginary is also the condition that allows for the creation of multiple, distinct *imaginaria*, for example, the Metallica imaginarium, the Minecraft imaginarium, the Marvel imaginarium, the Apple imaginarium, and so on. Not all brands will have imaginaria sophisticated or intriguing enough to attract passionate consumers.

Because brands function as complex storytellers that resonate with consumers on both individual and collective levels, we can better comprehend the intersection of consumer cultures and fandoms by turning our focus to narrative. This chapter thus explores the relationship between brands, narratives, and this collective imaginarium. This last point brings us to a final crucial set of distinctions. The culture of consumption, as we have defined it, is the broader, organic, and all-encompassing ecosystem of meaning that surrounds a commercial entity. The imaginarium, in all its official and unofficial glory, occupies this territory. It is the entire ecosystem of meaning that surrounds a commercial entity. It includes not only the officially produced images, texts, and objects, but also all of the fan-created works, the decades of community history, the conflicting interpretations, the "rubbish" that gets reappraised, and the unsanctioned social practices. The Star Wars culture of consumption, for instance, includes not just the films and

Disney+ shows, but also the (dreaded) Holiday Special, the fan fiction on AO3, the debates on Reddit, the local fan clubs, the academic analyses, and the childhood memories of playing with the original toys. It is a vast, messy, and often contradictory social and symbolic field.

To access the imaginarium, consumers and fans often travel through more structured pathways. This is where the concept of the consumption world becomes vital. A consumption world is defined as a more curated and delineated subset of the larger culture of consumption. A consumption world is thus a specific, interconnected web of activity and cultural production—often designed and managed by the brand owner—that serves as an official portal into the imaginarium. The "Wizarding World of Harry Potter" at Universal Studios is an example of a consumption world that provides a specific, managed experience of the much larger, more chaotic culture of consumption that is Harry Potter fandom. A consumption world leads us in, like a portal, to an imaginary world containing the narrative complexity and fullness we will explore through the remainder of this chapter. The consumption world is the vehicle; the imaginarium is the destination.

Brands as diverse as Volkswagen, Warhammer, Apple, LEGO, and Prada spin engaging stories that create these powerful imaginariums and the consumption worlds that lead to them. The "Four As" framework—Arcadia, Allegory, Aura, and Antinomy—specifies the key components of the brand narratives that furnish these worlds, offering consumers the escapism, symbolic depth, authenticity, and intriguing contradictions we associate with complex media properties. An appreciation of this labyrinthine complexity allows us to see how brands build these consumption worlds. The concept of consumption worlds, as the portal to the imaginarium, thus provides a bridge between theories of branding, fan studies, and the broader concept of cultures of consumption. Through consumption worlds, we gain a more comprehensive understanding of the multifaceted and narratively driven mechanics at play in consumer collectives.

Brands and Narratives

From the Prada luxury brand to Harley Davidson, from Apple and Warhammer to EPCOT, the world of consumer collectives we have been exploring through this book and this series is chock full of brands. In Chapter 7, we investigated brand communities but we never specifically defined exactly what a brand is. So, what is a brand? We can think of a brand as a complex, multidimensional phenomenon that transcends simple identifiers like names, logos, or symbols. Brands today operate as strategic symbolic tools that are embedded within the cultural and economic fabric of society, mediating relationships between producers, consumers, and other stakeholders (Maurya and Mishra, 2012). Brands are a type of value system that aligns functional, emotional, and social benefits with cultural narratives and consumer identities; they reflect the quality or utility of a product or service, certainly. But they go beyond that into the ethos, imaginations, and aspirations of their audiences and consumers.

Rob often asks his MBA students, "Who creates a brand?" It's a bit of a trick question, because the obvious (and wrong) answer is that companies or managers do. But brands are always co-created (more on that in **Fandom as Co-creation**). Customers' impressions of the brand, their experiences with it, their sense of who typically uses it, the status of the brand and its users, the places it is associated with, its moral character: all of this and more become the set of impressions that constitute the brand.

This is the great irony of branding: the brand is co-created by the impressions of its users and consumers, but the trademark is owned by its producer. We see the consequences of that core branding tension throughout this book series in many ways. What constitutes the brand at any given moment involves a series of interactions between users, roles, images, personalities, and other types of relationships. These relationships evolve through continuous engagement and reinterpretation by the brand's various stakeholders. Moreover, the cultural power of a brand lies in its ability to condense, negotiate, or even symbolically resolve some of the complex social narratives and values of the day into accessible and resonant forms. For example, it is relatively straightforward to read culturally relevant (and humorous) discourses about the demands of contemporary masculinity into advertising depictions such as the spectacularly successful reboot of a venerable maritime-themed deodorant in which ex-NFL player Isaiah Mustafa played the role of the Perfect Man, the man your man could smell like: The Old Spice Guy (Kluch, 2015).

Similarly, one can interpret discourses about the complex tension around female body image and its media representation tension from promotional work around the Dove brand and its Dove Real Beauty campaign which rode a cresting cultural wave and seemingly helped define the body acceptance movement (Johnston and Taylor, 2008). These culturally resonant contemporary and gendered depictions are narrative functions. We find parallel narrative functions in other brands and can see how they operate in the consumer collectives they gather, including in the fandoms that surround popular culture brands like sports teams, musicians, and social media celebrities.

Brand Narrativity

Narrativity refers to the quality of a narrative or a story-like structure in any kind of communicative text, whether it is written, spoken, visual, or multimedia. It involves the presence of elements that make something a story, such as characters, a plot, a setting, and a conflict, which work together to construct a meaningful whole. An appreciation for what we might term brand narrativity is a recognition that they engage audiences by structuring information in a way that is compelling and memorable, often evoking emotional responses or offering insights into human experiences and values.

The psychologist Jerome Bruner (1987) proposed that our lives are best understood as narratives that we continually construct and reconstruct throughout our lifetimes as we tell them to ourselves and to others. Human thought, in Bruner's view, is not merely about logical thought and the processing of information, but about the consumption and creation of stories that we meld into a sense of self and through which we both perceive and produce our experiences. Drawing on philosophers like Paul Ricoeur, who emphasized the importance of narratives to our sense of lived time, Bruner argues that people are constantly world-making through stories and discusses how cultural and individual narratives are intertwined. Although culture provides individuals with a repertoire of narrative models, these individual stories in turn contribute to the culture in a process perfectly parallel to the process whereby consumers co-create the meanings of brands. This mutual influence underscores the importance of narratives in personal identity, cultural continuity, and contemporary branding.

Furnishing the Imaginarium: The Four As of Brand Narrativity

Figure 11.1: The Four As of Brand Narrativity. Original creation. Image © 2025 Robert V. Kozinets.

Having established our conceptual toolkit—the distinction between the vast culture of consumption, the curated consumption world, and the deeply desired imaginarium—we can now turn to a series of case studies. These examples will illustrate precisely how brands use the power of narrative to build the consumption worlds that serve as the tangible, commercially produced portals to the fan's imaginarium. We will see how stories, characters, and mythologies become the very architecture of these imagined spaces, providing fans with the rich materials they need to build their own worlds of meaning.

Arcadia

In their analysis of brand narrativity, Brown, Kozinets, and Sherry (2003) highlight the indispensable role of stories in shaping consumer collectives and fandoms. They theorize that the "Four As"—Arcadia, Allegory, Aura, and Antinomy—act as the key components of brand narratives that interact with consumer collectives. Figure 11.1 illustrates these components. They are the primary narrative tools brands use to build their consumption worlds and invite consumers into the imaginarium. The first and perhaps most foundational of these is Arcadia, which refers to a location, often a magical, positive, special, or perhaps past and nostalgic or a futuristic and utopian place, that brand narratives construct. The Arcadian location is not merely a setting; it is the very substance of the imaginarium itself, the details of the completely furnished world that offers consumers an escape from the mundane into a desired or idealized state.

Echoing the collector's impulse to remove an object from ordinary use and thereby sacralize it, the Arcadian narrative sets the entire imaginarium apart from the profane world of everyday life. The consumption world, then, becomes a portal, a bridge between the visible, material world of the consumer and the invisible, sacred world of Arcadia. For example, Star Wars offers fans a chance to engage with the saga's depiction of a galaxy far, far away, not just as a setting but as a notional space where moral clarity and heroism prevail. This sense of Arcadia unites fans in a shared aspiration for and belief in these idealized values, in some sense sacralizing the fanship, fandom, and related consumption.

Allegory

Allegory, another cornerstone of the theory, imbues narratives with symbolic depth, enabling consumers to collectively explore moral and philosophical themes. The tale of the Prada brand, for example, portrays the blending of tradition with radical modernity and reflects the resistant and quasi-political engagement with shifts in power, gender, and aesthetics. Its story is rooted in meticulous craftsmanship and elite exclusivity and serves as a symbol of timeless luxury, yet its evolution under Miuccia Prada transforms this heritage into a narrative of disruption and innovation. This narrative mirrors broader cultural themes: the overturning of patriarchal norms, boundary-breaking creativity, and the ongoing dialogue between heritage and modernity. Through its allegory, Prada embodies the idea that tradition is not static but a foundation for reinvention. The brand's minimalist aesthetic critiques and reshapes the ostentation often associated with high fashion, creating a new language of understated elegance that speaks to shifting consumer desires for authenticity and subtlety. As an allegory, Prada's evolution parallels the modern individual's search for identity—rooted in history yet also striving for novel, yet acceptable, forms of expression.

Aura

The concept of Aura is adapted from Walter Benjamin's (1936/1969) masterpiece, *The Work of Art in the Age of Mechanical Reproduction*. In Benjamin's theory, aura is the essence of a work of original artwork and the powerful sense of authenticity that it exudes. Because consumers' search for authenticity is a mainstay of contemporary marketing communications and branding is focused on identity and uniqueness, the aura of a brand can be conceptualized as its DNA—its unique, legitimate, established, and credible character. We can think of the uniqueness of the Harley-Davidson brand here.

Founded in a small wooden shed in Milwaukee, Wisconsin, in 1903 by William S. Harley and Arthur Davidson, Harley-Davidson began as a small operation producing simple and sturdy motorcycles designed for practical transportation. Over time, the company's products evolved into powerful machines synonymous with performance and individuality, renowned for their distinctive V-twin engines, iconic exhaust notes, teardrop-shaped gas tanks, and bold, proudly American logo. The company has fiercely defended its brand identity through careful branding strategies and legal protections. For example, Harley-Davidson has trademarked its engine sounds and logos and actively combats counterfeit products, ensuring that only genuine Harley-Davidson motorcycles carry the brand's heritage and prestige.

Similarly, the grimdark and morally ambiguous atmospherics of the story worlds, role-playing complexity, and form factors of the Warhammer games are what make this brand utterly unique in the world of storytelling and play. The term "grimdark," drawn from the tagline of Warhammer 40,000—"In the grim darkness of the far future, there is only war"—encapsulates the franchise's dread-drenched and dystopian tone, where every faction exists in a state of moral compromise and unending conflict. Partially inspired by Frank Herbert's *Dune*, its bleak future universe challenges traditional hero-versus-villain dichotomies and invites players to intellectually and emotionally engage with a tangled web of sophisticated political ideologies and power struggles.

What sets Warhammer apart further from other games is its emphasis on DIY painting and customization of miniatures. Players must artfully bring their gameplay and armies to life with their own eyes and hands through meticulous painting, assembly, and even terrain-building. The complexity of gameplay, with its intricate rules and strategic depth, further intensifies the brand's aura by demanding intellectual engagement and inviting players to develop mastery. Warhammer's multifaceted mechanics and evolving narratives require dedication, collaboration, and imagination, creating a community of highly invested players who uphold the brand's authenticity. The result is a brand with a dark and sophisticated aura that is as much about storytelling and craftsmanship as it is about competitive play.

Antinomy

Finally, Antinomy encapsulates the contradictions, ambiguities, and irresolvable paradoxes within narratives that generate engagement. The paradoxical soul at the heart of brand narratives creates what Greek philosophers called *aporia*: a state of puzzlement or doubt arising from seemingly irresolvable contradiction, often used in philosophy and rhetoric to provoke deeper inquiry or critical reflection. The Apple brand, as explored by Belk and Tumbat (2005), provides numerous examples of antinomies that foster both a communal and paradoxical allure. For example, Apple juxtaposes countercultural, anti-corporate imagery with its status as the world's second largest global corporation. Apple's iconic advertising campaigns, such as the *1984* Ridley Scott-directed "Big Brother" commercial and the later "Mac vs. PC" series, frame the multinational technology corporation as a revolutionary force disrupting conformity and authoritarianism. By positioning the Apple brand as a liberatory symbol of individuality, youth, hipness, and creativity, Apple established itself as the antithesis of corporate monotony and rigidity. Brand fans embrace Apple's storytelling, which positioned the brand as a visionary force opposing "evil empires" like Microsoft. Yet the interplay of contradictions—large versus small, artisanal versus industrial, rebellious versus corporate, simple versus sophisticated—created an enigmatic brand identity that would captivate and bind its consumer collective for decades.

Imaginarium Case Study: Quisp

The Quisp cereal brand provided its consumer collective with a rich allegory of rivalry, eccentricity, rebirth, and cultural mythology. Revived by two platforms—YouTube and eBay—Quisp's collective culture benefited by the accessibility of old advertising on YouTube and the ability of fans to sell boxes of the cereal on eBay. First, fans of the cereal brand were able to relive the old advertising narratives of the Quisp character. Quisp, a zany, UFO-piloting alien from Planet Q, wanted to bring his "quazy energy cereal" to the people of Earth. The character was created by Jay Ward Studios, the studio that generated *The Rocky and Bullwinkle Show* and was renowned for its quirky animation style and oddball appeal. Daws Butler, best known for his work for the animation studio and production company Hanna-Barbera, provided voices for many Quaker Oats products of this era, including Cap'n Crunch and Quisp. Here, we might think of the value associated with Quisp not simply in terms of the investments made by an appreciative brand community but also as building on active fan interests in the cult animator Jay Ward and voice actor Butler. There is a whole fandom dedicated to collecting and appreciating these cartoons and their imaginarium, along with their associated products, advertising, and other work available for hire. The Quisp ads combined the graphics of *The Rocky and Bullwinkle Show* with the voice of Huckleberry Hound, catnip for the generation that grew up with these cartoons.

Quisp, along with Quake, had been introduced on the market in 1966, both made of essentially the same sugar-coated formula Quaker Oats also uses for Cap'n Crunch, yet with significantly different brand narratives. Quisp was associated with speed, quick-wittedness, and space, Quake with honesty, hard work, and physical strength. These distinctions allowed the two brands to appeal to the subjectivity of different consumers and to meet their needs for certain "magical properties."

Henry tells this story:

I was obsessed with Qusip, while my brother, Russell, only wanted Quake. Our poor mother needed to keep boxes of both in the cupboard even though they were essentially the same cereal. We both believed that our cereal would strengthen the properties associated with the character. And the result is hard to deny. I am a quick thinking university professor and my more muscular brother spent much of his working life installing boilers in factories. It is hard to know though whether I preferred Quisp purely because it aligned with my emerging self-image at the time or if it helped to reinforce certain properties I was beginning to value and thus shaped my sense of myself. Either way brands are magic and brand preferences help to make us who we are.

Given this story, what do we make of the fact that Quisp, not Quake, is the cereal that internet nerds want to revive? And what does this do to the binary between Quisp and Quake that was part of the original branding? Justice for Quake!

Enter the Quisp Influencer

There is a rich imaginarium still associated with the cereal brand icon almost 60 years after its introduction, now shared online. With a little help from ChatGPT4.0, Rob even tried his hand at generating some spooky new fan art that combines the funny little propeller-headed alien with his own fascination with horror and genres (see Figure 11.2). Like a zombie extraterrestrial, Quisp lives!

Figure 11.2 New Quisp Fan Art. Created by Robert V. Kozinets with ChatGPT4.0 and other media. Image © 2025 Robert V. Kozinets.

What seems to have turned the Quisp cereal brand into a digital pop culture icon were the efforts of several devoted Quisp fans online acting in a role that we would now easily catalog as that of an influencer. Chief among them was Jim Leff, a journalist and entrepreneur who co-founded the popular cuisine site *Chowhound*. Jim's posts about Quisp cereal and his shared communications with Quaker Oats, which owned and continued to produce and distribute the cereal in a very limited way, were just as tantalizing as the advertising narratives, perhaps more so. He wrote about how, despite occasionally locating a box or two of the cereal, he began to suspect that Quisp was no longer for sale. However, he never fully abandoned hope of finding his childhood favorite. He called it "his breakfast Rosebud" (Leff, 2001, n.p.).

Leff talks about how he would travel to new cities and would comb through supermarket aisles "looking—hope against hope—for his treasured Quisp, jaw quivering in dejection when, as always, he'd fail to find it." Eventually he gave up his search. But then, one day, while he was surfing the Internet, Jim discovered many other people shared his hankering for Quisp and, moreover, that it was still available for sale, but only in three American cities. The power of the Internet meets the nostalgic longings of fandom! Jim then went on special trips to purchase Quisp. He made what he called a pilgrimage, whereupon he would buy cases of it and bring them home. Then, he would serve Quisp cereal on fine bone china with the best organic milk at a black-tie dinner party attended by his most devoted Quisp friends.

Here, the sheer weirdness of Quisp's alien charm is matched by Jim Leff's own weird charm. Through this intertwining narrative, the refusal of the brand to ever fully relinquish the shelves leads to Jim Leff's story about his own refusal to accept that Quisp is actually gone. It is a tale of personal and brand persistence and the overcoming of time and challenge. Like Rosebud, the childhood sled in Orson Welles' 1941 classic *Citizen Kane* that represented the simplicity, love, and comfort of childhood nostalgia, the elusive Quisp cereal represented a deeply held and special place as a childhood cereal of dreams.

James Bond, The VW Beetle, and Cosplay

Consumer researchers have increasingly taken to positioning entertainment franchises as "brands" and then studying them for wider insights into general brand management. Tony Bennett and Janet Woollacott's *Bond and Beyond: The Political Aesthetics of England's Greatest Secret Agent* (1987) is a foundational work in cultural studies, offering a cogent analysis of the James Bond phenomenon. The book examines the political and aesthetic dimensions of the Bond films and novels, exploring how they reflect and shape broader cultural anxieties and aspirations. It is widely considered a classic for its pioneering application of semiotic and ideological analysis to a key popular culture franchise. They demonstrate how the packaging of the franchise—the posters, the book covers, and the album covers—reframed the same characters and stories for different generations of audiences.

Three decades later, Chloe Preece, Finola Kerrigan, and Daragh O'Reilly (2018) used the same franchise, James Bond, to study brand longevity. Their research emphasizes the combination of continuity and change in the brand's management. They found that the James Bond films integrate consistent motifs, such as the powerful musical theme, the personalities and names of supporting characters like M and Q, and the titular character's archetypal and charming heroism. With these timeless elements, the James Bond films incorporate timely cultural references. They keep the film's theme music fresh by signing singers who are popular at the time, as shown recently in themes by Adele or Billie Eilish. The franchise is constantly introducing new stars, new geopolitical villains, new gender dynamics, and innovative types of plots. Considering the franchise as a brand, we learn how the complexity of its evolving narrative structure combines continuity and change, ensuring that it retains its core identity while remaining relevant in changing times.

The Volkswagen Beetle is driven by another compelling brand allegory. Originally conceived as a utilitarian vehicle for the masses under politically charged circumstances (World War II Germany), the Beetle underwent a remarkable transformation into a countercultural icon in the 1960s, symbolizing individuality and rebellion against corporate conformity. Its retro revival in the late 1990s further reinforced its status as a cultural artifact, blending nostalgia with modernity to attract a new generation of consumers. The VW Beetle's enduring appeal lies in its ability to straddle dichotomies—functional yet iconic, nostalgic yet contemporary—as its design and story resonate with a collective longing for simplicity and authenticity in a world of increasing complexity.

Through the brand narrativity lens of the Four As, we can see how brands like Apple, Harley-Davidson, Volkswagen Beetle, Quisp, and Star Wars function as alluring cultural symbols. The stories attached to the objects and the objects attached to the stories create a combined material and narrative assemblage that invites individual consumers into fanship and inspires them to form collectives. We can see these same narrative forces at work in an article by Usva Inei (formerly Anastasia) Seregina and Henri Weijo (2017) that examines the cosplay consumer collective. Cosplay at conventions serves as an Arcadian ideal, where participants reconstruct idealized scenarios from their fanships. The allegorical dimensions are evident as cosplayers embody iconic characters and weave their interpretations. The brand Aura is palpable in the meticulous craftsmanship and authenticity that cosplayers bring to their costumes. And Antinomy emerges as participants navigate contradictions between the commercial and the personal, such as the tensions between monetizing cosplay and preserving it as a leisure activity (Seregina and Weijo 2017, p. 153).

Fandom as Postmodern Identity Work

In related work on identity, Usva Seregina and John W. Schouten (2017) investigate how individuals from Finland, particularly those feeling a sense of identity ambiguity due to a perceived lack of cultural, social, and symbolic capital, use fandom as a tool to gain status, belonging, and ultimately, a clearer sense of identity. Their study provides the perfect ground for exploring one of the most profound functions of the concepts we have developed in this chapter. It helps us demystify exactly how the magical-seeming alteration of identities by narratives actually happens. It is not magic but a psychological process of syncretic merging. This process happens through the operations of the Four As and the effects that living with these narrative components have on the way consumers and fans construct their own narratives of self. Mass culture provides the necessary tools and elements for individuals to perform their important identity work.

Seregina and Schouten's study, which uses French sociologist Pierre Bourdieu's (1984) theories of cultural capital, also aligns with Jerome Bruner's (1987) theories on narrativity. Pierre Bourdieu (1984) described cultural capital as the non-financial social assets, like good taste, attractiveness, education, manners, and a sense of style, that promote social mobility beyond economic means. Bourdieu considered that certain types of knowledge, skills, relationships, and objects are valued, recognized, and rewarded within specific social or professional settings, or "fields," as he called them. According to his theory, these elements, known as field-specific capital, are unique to their respective fields and are not generally transferable.

Seregina and Schouten were interested in understanding whether participating in fandom or accumulating fandom-specific capital could help people build a more generalized type of cultural capital that would help them in broader social interactions. They studied Finnish citizens who were involved in specific brand and entertainment fandoms like Apple, World of Warcraft, Jersey Shore, or the Chicago Bulls. They found that these fandoms served as narrative frameworks that allowed these individuals to construct and reconstruct their identities. By participating in these cultures of consumption and becoming familiar with their specific imaginaria, these individuals gained cultural capital. In their study, they describe how the identity of one of their participants, Michael, was affected by his Harry Potter fandom.

Michael had been able, through his Harry Potter fandom, to construct an identity that was more creative and confident than his former or "real one." He eventually began asserting that creativity and confidence in aspects of his everyday life. He took up new hobbies, such as dancing and theater, which he finds to be "extremely cool," but which he had previously been "too shy" to engage in. Eventually, he was able to manifest a creative identity in his more generalized life context, building friendships and asserting himself through his new identity by finding, in his everyday life, similar types of sources of creativity he had within fandom. In effect, he had decontextualized the more creative and confident identity with its self-representation and associated behaviors from

Harry Potter and recontextualized it within the realms of dance and theater where fandom was not a prerequisite for acceptance or status (Seregina and Schouten, 2017, pp. 121-2).

Contrary to Bourdieu's predictions that these types of cultural capital were field-specific, they found that the identity-related narrative practices they learned in fandom were transferable to other social contexts in Finland, such as meeting people and work. Seregina and Schouten related their findings to the fragmentation of modern identities, or what they call "postmodern identity," a state in which "identity construction becomes a continuous individual project" in which the "resources for building identity and status are commoditized" and yet "identity or status in themselves cannot be bought" (p. 108). Their findings echo Bruner's suggestions that narratives are essential tools in identity negotiation. Transcending their development in fandoms, fans were leveraging their abilities with structured narrative frameworks to craft, assert, and understand their identities in relation to broader cultural stories. This finding indicates that dexterity with the narratives that furnish an imaginarium may confer useful skills for broader social functioning and personal development.

Ambiguous Brands

Fandom-like consumer collectives also emerge around "ambiguous brands" like the Titanic (Brown, McDonagh, and Shultz, 2013). The Titanic narrative embodies a panoply of myths, from hubristic ambition and technological marvel to tragic downfall. Its layered and ambiguous narrative sustains an enduring engagement with generations of diverse audiences, from maritime enthusiasts to fans of James Cameron's cinematic rendition to the active participants on the r/Titanic subreddit who engage with the ship, its passengers, the wreck, maritime history, the museum, and much more. We explore some of these topics more fully in **Locations of Fandom.**

The Titanic brand narrative's paradoxical quality as the "unsinkable" ship that sank constructs an aura of fascination that invites collective reflection. The Titanic narrative invites reinterpretation and personalization, allowing consumers to construct meaning that resonates with their individual or collective contexts. The authors emphasize Titanic's status as an open and ostensible "'writerly' text, which is amenable to all sorts of idiosyncratic, individualized readings (Barthes 1990)" (Brown et al. 2013, p. 599). Further, they find that the figure of the steamship is a rich centerpiece of the imaginarium containing "something for everyone, whether they're mystics, moralists, metallurgists, memorabilia collectors, maritime enthusiasts, manipulators of political, social, and cultural agendas for ideological/commercial purposes, or—in our own case—myth-minded analysts of textual ambiguity" (pp. 599-600).

Over a century of newspaper articles, music-making, films, literature, exhibitions, and memorabilia have enriched the Titanic culture of consumption. These elements provide access to various types of consumption-related interests, practices, and productions that connect to different social groups, such as the many fandoms discussed in this book. The complexity and multifacetedness of mass culture productions—with marketplace offerings related to their performers, athletes, and artists; stories of their history; recordings of associated music; duplicate versions of uniforms or costumes; intertextual references; and so on —provide a panoply of seeds from which many types of focused formations may grow. These different marketplace elements become like the "starters" of sourdough yeast, the living cultures used to ferment dough. Just as sourdough starters are nurtured, shared, and passed between bakers, creating a community of practice that connects individuals through the preservation of unique microbial ecosystems, so too are the fandom's various unique cultural elements shared as start packs for community formation.

A Star Wars fan participates in the overall fandom but is also part of a broader science fiction consumption world. Within that world, there are active Star Wars LEGO groups, collectives dedicated to Star Wars books, and collectors of Princess Leia figurines. Each of these can be recognized as resulting from engagement with the Star Wars culture of consumption that drew them in. The antagonistic news media loves to construct Star Wars and Star Trek fans as warring groups, but this model suggests they overlap in some ways. Both Henry and Rob consider themselves passionate fans of both franchises. Imaginaria are not just about the gathering of people around products but about the invitation to co-construct realities. Fans move fluidly between consumption worlds, remixing and hybridizing them. Consumption worlds like the various Star Wars themes rides and attractions at Disney theme parks are an invitation to enter the wider mass culture-related playgrounds—the imaginaria. Grounded in narratively rich products and services, they span multilayered new forms and spawn new social fields. The idea of consumption worlds provides a more grounded, location-centered bridge between theories of branding, the broader culture of consumption, and fan studies' worldbuilding.

Linking Through Narratives

In Chapter 6, we explored Bernard Cova's (1997) concept of linking value. This chapter has argued that it is the narrativity of brands and products that generates this powerful linking value. The chapter began by characterizing contemporary brands as complex symbolic tools incorporated into cultures of consumption worlds that link to collective imaginarium. Due to space constraints, this book is unable to dive deeply into the literary and psychological theories that underscore our understanding of narrativity. Nevertheless, our thinking on the matter is informed by works as diverse as Roland Barthes' (1966), *Introduction to the Structural Analysis of Narratives*, Vladimir Propp's (1968) *Morphology of the Folktale*, and Jerome Bruner's (1991) *The Narrative Construction of Reality*, among other key works.

Brands as diverse as Warhammer, Titanic, and Prada tell a myriad of fascinating stories. As developed through a deep examination of brand narratives like those for Quisp cereal and the Volkswagen Beetle, the "Four As" framework—Arcadia, Allegory, Aura, and Antinomy— defines the fundamental components that make these stories so compelling. Furthermore, the concept of ambiguous brands that thrive on narrative complexity asserts that multi-layered mythological worlds allow consumers to explore and participate within them in various ways. An appreciation for this labyrinthine intricacy leads us back to our concept of "consumption worlds" as the interconnected webs of locations, objects, and activities focused on mass culture offerings. With consumption worlds, brands become featured in place as lived experiential nodes connecting diverse cultural practices and communities to focus them on fandom. Star Trek conventions and Comic-Cons serve as such nodes, providing not only a catalyst but a location for the enactment of various fan-related activities, including collecting, gaming, writing and sharing fan fiction, cosplay, and so on. Imaginaria and consumption worlds serve as conceptual bridges between branding, the broader culture of consumption, and fan studies theories, providing a comprehensive understanding of the narratively driven cultural mechanics at work in consumer collectives.

CHAPTER 12
THE FANDOM LENS

There is more to consumers and their collectives than meets the eye. We have travelled in this book from the personal passions embodied in a single action figure to the global flows that shape our collective lives. We have merged the intellectual lanes of consumer culture research with fan studies, and in doing so, something new seems to have emerged: an integrated model for understanding collective life in contemporary times. This final chapter will bring these conceptual elements together, introducing and explaining how they work as a model before demonstrating how to apply them. We will illustrate how the conceptual toolkit developed across these pages can provide a new lens for scholars, managers, and fans to understand and work with a wide range of contemporary social, political, and cultural phenomena. Our goal is to demonstrate the usefulness of this framework by applying it to new domains, moving from the particularities of fandom to the broader worlds that our new understanding of fandom helps illuminate.

For readers joining us here, and as a recap for those who have been with us all along, our framework is built upon a nested system of concepts that moves from the vast and global to the intimate and personal.

This model, illustrated in Figure 12.1, provides an integrated way to understand the complex interrelationship between culture, commerce, community, and the self. Each of the elements in the model is explained in detail when it first appears earlier in the book. Reflecting the complexity of cultural life, many of the collective elements of the model are themselves networks, and they are nested within one another in the framework. We could thus call this a Nested Fandom Collective model (NFC model). The model is dynamic and includes collectives that are linked by various types of flow. To simplify things, we can also simply call it the Fandom Lens.

At the broadest, macro-level, we begin with the chaotic and disjunctive global flows of images, technologies, and ideologies that Arjun Appadurai (1990) calls "scapes": mediascapes, technoscapes, ideoscapes, finanscapes, and ethnoscapes. These scapes are the raw cultural material of our interconnected world, but they are not unstructured. They are organized and given coherence by an overarching consumer culture—the societal "cultural blueprint" (Arnould et al., 2023, p. 2) that provides the general rules and shared meanings for how we interact with the marketplace. Consumer culture is a tool for sense-making, offering "a system of meanings, values, ideals, and norms that influence consumers' perceptions of what is cool or outdated, attractive or unattractive, desirable or undesirable." It provides scripts for appropriate behavior but does not act as a unified system. "Instead, it operates as a diverse repertoire of meaning systems," and those include things like subcultures, fandoms, and other forms of consumer collectives.

From this large cultural field, more specific territories emerge at the meso level, which focuses on intermediate-sized groups or structures such as communities, organizations, or institutions.

GLOBAL SCAPES

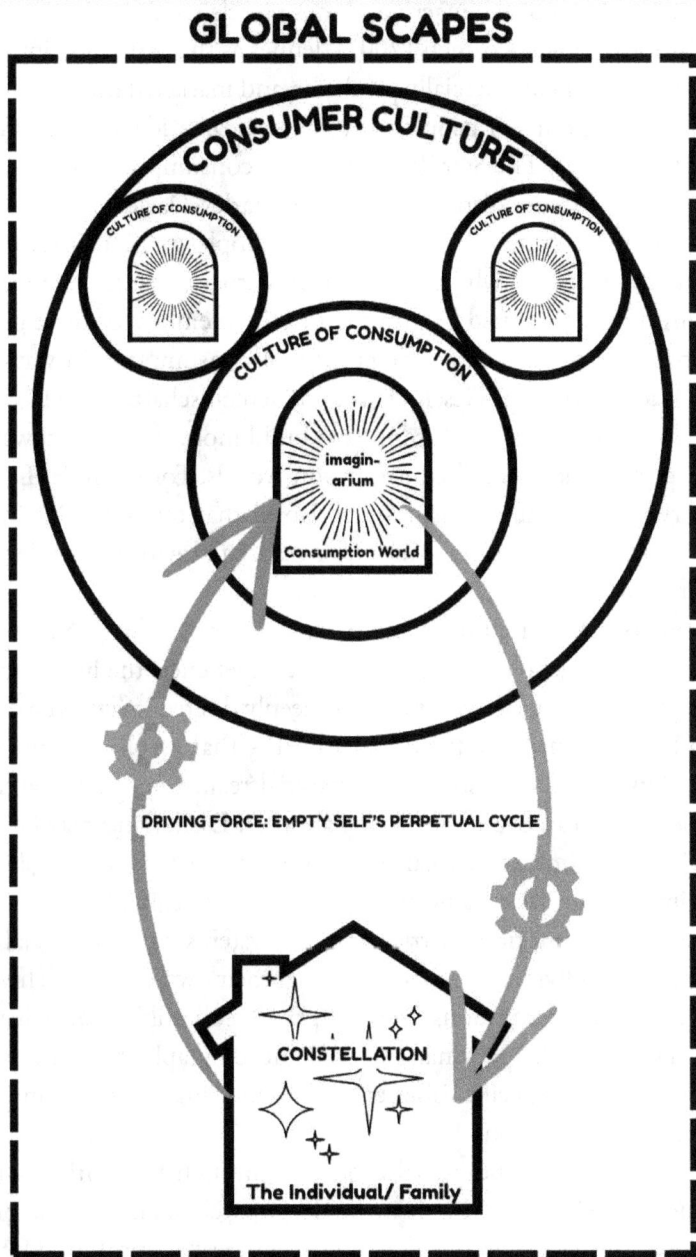

CONSUMER CULTURE

CULTURE OF CONSUMPTION

CULTURE OF CONSUMPTION

CULTURE OF CONSUMPTION

imagin-
arium

Consumption World

DRIVING FORCE: EMPTY SELF'S PERPETUAL CYCLE

CONSTELLATION

The Individual/ Family

Figure 12.1: The Fandom Lens

At the boundaries of the macro and meso levels are distinct cultures of consumption, which Kozinets (2001) defines as the particular, interconnected systems of commercially produced and marketed images, objects, and texts that groups of people use to express their identities and make sense of their lives. The Star Trek culture of consumption, for example, is a specific system, distinct from the Harley-Davidson culture of consumption or the one associated with Apple or Marvel (although there are intersections where these cultures cross over). Each culture of consumption can be used by groups, and the members of these groups relate to one another and to the culture of consumption in ways that relate to conceptions of Gesellschaft and Gemeinschaft. As well, within these broader cultures, producers often build more curated pathways or official portals that we call consumption worlds. For example, Disneyland serves as a specific consumption world that offers a guided entry point into the culture of consumption associated with Disney fandom or theme parks.

These pathways lead to an important object of a fan's desire, at the micro-level of psychological and collective experience: the imaginarium. This is the shared, narratively rich, and deeply desired imagined world—Eco's (1985) "completely furnished world"—that a collective inhabits. Like a ghost world coexisting with material reality, imaginaria and real world locations can overlap with one another. Disneyland may be a key part of a fans' imaginaria, existing simultaneously as a real place in Anaheim, California and a notional one in fans' imaginations. From the culture of consumption, particularly its systems of commercial and other objects, individuals and families craft their own unique archives of meaning: their continuous consumption collectible constellations (C4s). The C4 is the personal, material autobiography that one assembles by selecting specific objects, texts, and images from multiple cultures of consumption.

What powers an individual's journey through this entire system? Cushman (1990) claims that it is the deep, psychological engine of the empty self, the condition of modern life that creates a profound hunger for meaning and connection, satisfied by temporary pleasures and distractions. This hunger is perpetually fueled by the marketplace's "magic show" (Belk et al. 2024, p. 26), its perpetual, cyclic process of enchantment and disenchantment, where the initial thrill of a new engagement fades over time, creating a new desire that prompts the next quest for a meaningful connection. It is this complete, multi-layered framework—taking us from the global scape to the personal collection, driven by the enduring search to fill the self with meaningful texts, images, and objects—that we propose as a powerful, portable analytical tool.

The Fandom Model in Action: Three Applications

Having established our conceptual framework, we now turn to a series of powerful applications. The goal here is to demonstrate the utility and reach of the Fandom Lens, showing how it can illuminate complex phenomena far beyond the traditional boundaries of media fandom. We will explore how the dynamics of passionate consumer collectives, organized around commercially produced cultures of consumption and the imaginaria they offer, are at play in the crucial arenas of politics, organizational life, and even science and health.

The Power of Fandom and the Fandom of Power

"I created maybe the greatest brand." –President Donald J. Trump, January 11, 2018

Perhaps nowhere is the convergence of consumption, branding, and collective passion more evident and consequential than in contemporary politics. Our application of the Fan Lens demonstrates that this phenomenon is not a historical or social aberration but is, instead, a predictable outcome of our contemporary condition. It is fueled by the inner starvation of the empty self, the same gnawing hunger for meaning and connection that drives individuals to seek out powerful narratives and strong collective identities through ceaseless shopping, consumption, medical treatments, and therapy (Cushman 1990).

Political movements, just like fandoms, offer a potent remedy, providing access to what Belk et al. (2024, p. 26) term an unending "magic show" of perpetual enchantment and disenchantment, where the emotional highs of rallies and online victories offer a temporary but powerful sense of belonging that must be continually renewed. Scholarly work has increasingly recognized that modern political enthusiasm is often best understood as a form of media fandom, driven by what Cornel Sandvoss (2013) calls the "affective bond between citizens and politicians as fans and fan objects" (p. 252). This perspective suggests that in a complex and often confusing post-truth world, the emotional attachments and identity affirmations offered by fandom can become more compelling than empirical reality or detailed policy positions. The political movement surrounding Donald J. Trump serves as a master class in this phenomenon, representing the apotheosis of a brand-driven consumer collective.

To understand this remarkable phenomenon of Trump fandom, we must first recognize that it was built not in the machinations of Washington D.C., but within the global scapes of media, ideological, technological, ethnic, and commercial flows. We can view his entire career as the construction of a specific culture of consumption around his persona. The technoscapes of Twitter and social media, the global ethnoscapes of refugees and immigration, the financescapes of stock market investments and branded real estate, the ideoscape of ascendant neoliberal and right-wing thought, and the mediascape of cable news, reality television, professional wrestling, extremist talk radio, and podcasting all contributed to building a powerful system of commercially produced images, objects, and texts that converged with his political aspirations. As extensive research has shown, the 2016 election was not the beginning of the Trump brand; it was its ultimate product launch. Decades of branding everything from casinos to steaks had created a powerful and remarkably consistent culture of consumption built on core signifiers of wealth, power, and anti-establishment success (Cosgrove, 2022). Unlike previous politicians whose brands were tied to a party, Trump's brand was entirely personal: the brand is Trump, and Trump is the brand.

This pre-existing culture of consumption provided the architecture for a powerful political consumption world. The rallies are no traditional speeches but fan conventions, ritual gatherings designed to produce collective effervescence. Studying a Trump rally, Stephen

Reichler and Alexander Haslam (2016, n.p.) described it as "an identity festival that embodied a politics of hope." His social media feeds, particularly within the technoscape of Twitter, allowed him to bypass traditional media and perform a kind of "digital intimacy," making millions of followers feel as though he was speaking directly to them (Schill and Hendricks, 2017). This carefully managed world serves as a portal to a potent imaginarium, a new city upon a hill: the Arcadian promise of "Make America Great Again." It is a nostalgic and mythic space where America is restored to a perceived former glory and the fan-citizen is returned to a position of cultural centrality, a promise that speaks directly to a deep-seated and gnawing sense of what Pettigrew (2017), in his psychological analysis of Trump followers, terms "relative deprivation," a sense that they expected to possess and consume more relative to what "other 'less deserving' groups have acquired" (p. 111). The narrative is a powerful Allegory, casting Trump, with his unique and consistent brand Aura of gold, bombast, largeness, and winning, in the role of what Andrea Schneiker (2019, p. 210) calls the "superhero anti-politician celebrity," a singular hero doing battle against a corrupt cabal of villains. Trump's ambiguity as a political brand that combines the identities of businessman/billionaire and entertainer allows him to "create a brand persona that is convincing and credible despite consisting of contradictory elements" (p. 220).

As Joel Crombez and Steven Panageotou (2020, p. 38) write, in his governing style, Trump's political actions "most closely align with the logic of the personal brand. . . in which things like ideological narrative and material presences are fully malleable and plastic means that only have value in the atemporal present." Thus, like corporations, the modern state under Trump "abandons its role as the long-term strategist of society" (p. 39), prioritizes short-term planning that prioritizes immediate profit, and disengages itself "from the concerns of the future."

Within this culture of consumption, material objects become sacred artifacts. The baseball cap is a piece of merchandise for sale but is also a key component of a supporter's personal collectible constellation (C4). The red MAGA hat functions in precisely the same way a sports jersey does: it is a piece of fan merchandise that makes one's affiliation visible, identifies fellow fans in public, and antagonizes rivals. This single politically and emotionally charged item is supplemented by a vast array of other collectibles, from Trump-themed art and action figures to digital currency, all of which allow supporters to materially manifest their participation in the culture of consumption.

Figure 12.2: Trump-themed T-shirts for Sale in Hermosa Beach, California. Photograph © 2025 Robert Kozinets, taken August 3, 2025.

Merchandise utilizes popular and over-the-top aesthetics. This aesthetic, as well as insider language and imagery, is on display in many t-shirt and memorabilia stores around the United States. Figure 12.2 presents a wall display of Trump-themed t-shirts that Rob encountered at the time he was writing this section. Along with FGB and "Let's Go Brandon," some of the t-shirts have popular culture references to entertainment franchises like The Terminator and feature Trump in army battle dress, riding a Ford-style super pickup truck, and brandishing a rocket launcher. Displayed above tourist-themed and Teenage Mutant Ninja Turtles hoodies, the t-shirts fit the category of kitsch because of their mass appeal to popular taste rather their aspersions of artistic merit or intellectual depth.

Trump's forays into NFTs utilize similarly kitschy aesthetics. Some of the Trump digital trading cards depict him as a superhero in a skintight costume with a "T" on his chest and a flag cape, or even as a laser-shooting superhero. This aligns with a broader empowerment fantasy narrative, presenting him as a strong, almost godlike figure capable of overcoming obstacles. Beyond superheroes, the NFTs also show him in various other heroic or aspirational roles, such as an astronaut, a racecar driver, or a sheriff. These digital collectibles have also been bundled with perks like pieces of his suits worn during debates, adding a "relic" aspect to the fandom. This approach mirrors a profit-seeking visual culture that is, as Dorothy Barenscott (2024) analyzes, suspicious of established art and draws upon pop art sensibilities. Using laden imagery depicting Trump as a powerful superhero, the NFTs, t-shirts, digital trading cards, and Trump's over-the-top sneakers seem custom-made to appeal to fan sensibilities (Dubois, 2025). The Never Surrender high-tops, for instance, have a bright gold finish, a large "T" emblazoned on the side, and the U.S. flag stitched around the collar. Other versions include white "POTUS" shoes and red "T-Wave" shoes, often featuring gold accents. The overall design is described in its marketing as "bold, gold, and tough, just like President Trump," aiming to be a "rally cry in shoe form" for his supporters.

This participation is also highly creative. Supporters act as textual poachers (Booth et al. 2018), taking Trump's often contradictory or incoherent statements and weaving them into a larger, more mythic narrative of national salvation. At its most extreme, this productive activity can manifest in forms like the QAnon conspiracy (see **Fandom as Public**), which functions as a participatory Alternate Reality Game where followers become researchers decoding clues, and the January 6th insurrection, which can be analyzed as a form of political live-action role-play (LARP) (Petersen et al., 2023).

It is crucial to note that the Fandom Lens is an analytical tool, not a partisan critique. A similar analysis can be applied across the political spectrum, as research on the political fandom of Alexandria Ocasio-Cortez demonstrates (Rodriguez and Goretti, 2022). Her supporters also participate in a distinct culture of consumption, one built around an imaginarium of hope, resistance, and social progress that are staked to very different social actions and attitudes towards issues such as diversity, equity, and inclusion. Her consumption world is comprised of different platforms, like grassroots fundraising sites and a savvy social media presence, and is accompanied by its own material culture, where items like red lipstick and gold hoop earrings become powerful symbols of identity and defiance, key objects within a supporter's personal C4. And she can extend her influence outward to engage with other political figures through endorsements or fan objects. She did both when she recorded a YouTube video with Elizabeth Warren when the two discussed their conflicted responses as feminists and fans to the female characters in *Game of Thrones*.

Our framework elevates and extends extant thought by providing a specific, integrated toolkit for the analysis of contemporary politics. Although the mastery of celebrity and branding in contemporary politics is a recurrent theme in the aforementioned scholarship, our lens moves beyond these labels to explain the precise motivations and mechanisms that create such potent affective bonds. The concept of the imaginarium, for instance, assigns a name to the powerful, shared psychic space—often termed a "post-truth reality"—where the narratives and myths co-created within the collective can feel more authoritative than any external source. We can see the same empty self at work that seeks to be filled up by the products of consumer culture and then analyze the consumption world of rallies, merchandise, and social media as a curated portal that provides access to this imaginarium. The narrative tools of the Four As allow us to dissect how this world is furnished, revealing the Arcadian promise of a restored past, the Aura of a golden celebrity superhero anti-politician politician billionaire, the Antimony of the Radical Left, Enemies of the State, and the Immigrant Hordes, and the Allegorical casting of a leader in a heroic role.

Ultimately, this approach provides a comprehensive, multidimensional, and systematic understanding of political mobilization in the 21st century. It allows us to see the iconic red cap not simply as a piece of merchandise but as a sacred object in a supporter's C4, a tangible piece of the culture of consumption that functions as a weighty identity marker and marker of belonging. The Fandom Lens reveals the deep entanglement of contemporary politics with the mechanics of narrative, the power of material culture, and the engaged and enraged passions of fandoms. It is a toolkit that allows us to see these political movements not as historical anomalies but as powerful consumer collectives operating according to a cultural logic that is central to our times.

The Fandom of Work and the Work of Fandom

Our Fandom Lens is not limited to the analysis of external consumer groups; it also provides a powerful framework for understanding the internal dynamics of organizations themselves. It can help us reframe institutions as symbolically saturated consumption worlds embedded within larger cultures of consumption that function effectively as foci of fandom for their employees. Appadurai's (1990) five scapes provide the raw cultural material from which both fandoms and organizations draw. For instance, the global prestige of technology brands like Apple or Google depends on their position within overlapping mediascapes (global branding and visibility), technoscapes (infrastructure and product design), and ideoscapes (narratives of innovation, disruption, and individual empowerment). This book's conceptual framework, which traces nested levels from global flows to individual consumption constellations, finds rich application in the structures and affective dynamics of contemporary organizational life.

Beyond fostering simple brand loyalty among employees, certain companies—and the visionary leaders who guide them—succeed in cultivating an internal fandom. This form of organizational culture transcends the laborious reality where employees are merely workers exchanging labor for a wage. Ennobled and upraised by their passionate participation, workers in this new reality share a sacred mission and are bound together by a deep, affective connection to the company, its leaders, and its ideals. At the heart of many of these organizational fandoms is a figure who functions as a primary "fan object": the charismatic leader. Drawing on Max Weber's foundational concept of charismatic authority, we can see how these leaders command devotion not because of tradition or formal rules, but because their brand narratives ascribe to them an Aura glowing with extraordinary qualities.

In the Apple TV series, *Severance*, the figure of the charismatic corporate founder—exemplified by Kier Eagan—serves as a quasi-messianic presence whose mythologized persona and everlasting Aura orchestrate a regime of affective and epistemic control. Revered through rituals, iconography, and corporate catechism, Eagan's character reflects the sacralization of leadership endemic to certain corporate cultures, where founders become posthumous embodiments of institutional ideology. The performative sanctification surrounding the mythos of the leader sustains the firm's internal social order and legitimates extreme disciplinary practices. It also serves a critical function for viewers, inviting us to reflect on how charisma and narrative mythos function to mask structural violence within contemporary organizations.

As Ken Parry and Steve Kempster (2014) demonstrate, charismatic leadership is not merely an intrinsic trait but a relational narrative—a "gift from followers" that is co-produced through emotionally charged metaphors and follower identifications (p. 23). Followers often construct charismatic leaders through familial or romantic tropes, investing them with mythic meaning and emotional resonance. In the Apple imaginarium, Steve Jobs does not simply exist as a historical figure; he operates as a symbolic presence, a founder-hero whose Aura is continually reinscribed in employee and consumer narratives alike. Building on this insight, Ken Parry and his colleagues (2019) explore how charismatic leadership becomes embedded in the emotional structure of belonging. They assert that charisma functions less through love or fear and more through a durable "sense of community" that binds individuals together in a collective narrative arc (p. 400). Within the organizational imaginarium, leaders serve as mythic anchors, orienting identity and action around an emotionally saturated storyline. This dynamic mirrors fan devotion to narrative protagonists or franchise worldbuilders, other individuals who animate a collective symbolic space that participants enter and co-create.

This is not to say that organizational fandom is only about individual leaders. Often, the organization or the brand itself is the icon. A powerful founder figure like Steve Jobs becomes a central part of the Apple brand's legend, but the brand's Aura both includes and transcends Jobs' charismatic mythos. The leader's story becomes a key narrative that furnishes and stabilizes the imaginarium, but it is the brand's broader culture of consumption that employees inhabit. These cultures of consumption constitute the mid-range symbolic universes that connect people through shared rituals, vocabularies, and values. For, as much as it produces devices and software, Apple has constructed a lifestyle mythology around sleek design, creative empowerment, and aesthetic minimalism (Belk and Tumbat, 2005), and its internal organizational culture mirrors this mythology and circulates it through employee practices. In this way, the company itself becomes a culture of consumption—one that structures not just external brand relationships but also internal identification and community.

Nested like galaxies of Russian dolls going macro to micro, outside to within, these networked cultures of consumption are nestled carefully into place by caring curators, linked to institutional superstructures held by the gravity of various consumption worlds. Silicon Valley workplaces like Google's Mountain View campus offer classic examples: landscaped campuses, themed cafeterias, in-house massage therapists, climbing walls, and company-sponsored social rituals turn the workplace into a curated world of belonging and immersive engagement. Facilitating entry into their imaginaria, organizations construct immersive internal consumption worlds from a curated set of perks, missions, and narratives. Organizational management scholars make a useful distinction between climate, which refers to employees' shared perceptions of formal and informal policies and practices, and the deeper concept of culture, which encompasses shared values, beliefs, and norms (Permarupan et al., 2013). The legendary campus perks of a company like Google—the free gourmet food, on-site laundry, and creative workspaces—are masterfully designed to create a positive and highly engaging organizational climate.

TikToktopias

But their function goes much, much deeper. These elements are the identity components required to complete just a small part of the mission of a much larger project to construct a utopian corporate culture. Appletopia, Amazontopia, Googletopia, Netflixtopia, FoxNewstopia, TikToktopia. Each one of them is a culture of consumption, a vast network of separate and managed cultures of consumption, with fully owned databases full of legal trademarks and copyrights on texts and images. Companies such as Amazon, Apple, Google, Meta, OpenAI, and others consist of groups of people who collectively create an environment where technology is perceived as a holistic living space that blurs the lines between work and private life as well as public and private spaces (Ström, 2019), continuously expanding in influence.

Silicon Valley's companies' grand mission statements, often centered on the future and world-changing ideals like "organizing the world's information," provide powerful Arcadian and Allegorical narratives that suck us into their brand narratives—and their employees live inside this grand mission statement consumption world, surrounded by it. The stark competitiveness, frequent antitrust prosecutions, and races to develop new technologies such as AI provide rich conflictual fodder for ongoing Antimony narratives. There are always vicious, wicked opponents working against them. Organizations' consumption worlds, in sync with the Four A narratives, blur the boundaries between labor and lifestyle. Employees find their identity not just in what they do, but in the narrative universe their mentality orbits.

Individuals construct collection constellations or C4s in their homes, their sacred inner sanctums and the most intimate level of our model. Even those without homes carry with them their belongings. In a corporate context, an employee might curate a workspace adorned with branded merchandise, internal awards, and symbols of team membership, forming layers of identity from the material cultures of their workplaces and external identities (Tian and Belk, 2005). Employees often wear the brand both figuratively and literally: hoodies, laptops, water bottles, and team rituals become part of a material autobiography. As Yukthamarani Permarupan and colleagues (2013) show, organizational climates that foster a strong sense of "work passion" enable these collections to emerge and stabilize. Such climates support a set of shared meanings, values, and symbols that help employees see their work as an extension of the self.

This entire multilevel structure is animated by the same rotating magic show that powers consumer culture: a cycle of enchantment, disenchantment, and re-enchantment. At the core of this cycle is the empty self, a psychological-cultural condition characterized by an existential hunger for meaning, recognition, and identity. As our model suggests, the organizational imaginarium and its nested worlds provide temporary fulfillments of this hunger by offering an institutionally sanctioned and collectively shared sense of belonging, symbolic completeness, and purpose. But these experiences inevitably fade. The branded leader is exposed, the workplace becomes routine, and the passion wanes. Disenchantment reinvigorates the pleasure- and distraction-seeking empty self. The desire for re-enchantment propels the next cycle: a new product, a new leader, a new corporate value initiative, or a new badge or collectible hoodie.

The Fandom Lens reveals that contemporary organizational life is not simply a system of production or control but a richly symbolic, narratively structured, and emotionally saturated environment that is akin in many ways to a fandom. By tracing the layers from global scapes to personal constellations and by accounting for the roles of charisma, passion, collection, and enchantment, we offer a theoretical model that can reorient organizational research and practice as well as government administration and regulation. What if society fully recognized human labor not as an object of administration but as the inhabiting of a rich imaginative world—a consumption world—by people searching for meaning, identity, and symbolic fulfillment?

The Health of Fandom and the Fandom of Health

This final application extends the Fandom Lens into the domains of science and medicine, revealing how fandom operates in arenas structured around expertise, authority, and bodily transformation. Fandoms here form not only around scientists, celebrity doctors, diets, and fitness

regimens, but also around medical products and platforms—from phar-
maceuticals to biohacking tools to wellness apps. These objects of devotion promise consumers more than just health, for they offer them
identities, belonging, and an opportunity for self-mastery. Such promise
is particularly potent within a cultural milieu shaped by the hedonistic
"empty self" of the denizens of late modern Western societies, who feel
an inner void and yearn to be filled through consumption and therapeutic intervention (Cushman, 1990). Propelled by the decline of traditional communal anchors and amplified by therapeutic discourses that
encourage individuals to look inward for meaning, empty selves turn to
the market for remedies to what ails them and to numb the pain of existential dread.

This situation is fertile ground for the perpetual cycles of desire,
disillusionment, and re-enchantment that characterize contemporary
consumer culture (Belk et al., 2021). Within the vast and prolific
cultures of consumption dedicated to health—which include everything
from fitness and dieting to legitimate medical treatments and illicit
"snake oil" remedies—the cycle begins with the promise of transformation. And, although Ozempic is not actually "snake oil," it was discovered through research on Gila monster venom, but is now produced
synthetically. Like any new pharmaceutical, diet plan, or charismatic
guru, Ozempic offers salvation from pain, aging, or perceived bodily
flaws. Currently, the Ozempic fandom is so strong, and demand for its
weight loss miracles so high, that supply has become extremely limited.
The situation is so dire that South Park's *The End of Obesity* special sati-
rized the craze. As a medical Ozempic user himself, Henry can attest to
the challenges of finding supply to deal with diabetes in body image-
obsessed Los Angeles (having doctors shift him to one or another
generic alternative trying to maintain consistent access).

However, as the initial enchantment fades and the limitations of the
product or regimen surface (as they inevitably do), consumers will experience disillusionment. But the market and its narrative agents will then
respond with new formulations, influencers, or ideologies to reignite the
cycle. This dynamic, where hope is perpetually sold, is not new; the relationship between questionable medical claims and advertising is as old as
the craft itself, a key part of the "fables of abundance" that Jackson Lears

(1995) described. Thus, the culture of consumption is not peripheral to medical science, but central to its practice, promotion, and experience.

Today, this culture offers new kinds of fan objects: celebrity doctors and medical influencers, or "medfluencers." The public is profoundly influenced by health advice flowing from the mediascapes, where recommendations for foods, vitamins, diets, and procedures are constantly manifesting the latest finanscapes. Established in the dawn of modern media, this phenomenon has been supercharged by the technoscape of social media, which has seen the rise of medical influencers who cultivate passionate "fanbases" (Ng et al., 2024, p. 231). Their motivations are diverse, ranging from a genuine desire to improve public health literacy to the more commercial aims of advertising products and boosting their personal reputation. The popularity of these figures also underscores a deep-seated societal desire for science to have a human face. As Lawrence Krauss (2015) observes, turning scientists into celebrities may increase public engagement with science but risks emphasizing personality over epistemic rigor. In the medical domain, this tension is acute: the enthusiastic following of charismatic figures may amplify messages that resonate emotionally or ideologically, regardless of their alignment with mainstream medical consensus. They become the charismatic storytellers for a particular vision of health.

This convergence of science, charisma, and media mirrors the broader phenomenon of celebrity scientists who, like Nobel laureates or high-profile media figures, are celebrated not merely for their scientific contributions but for their personality, relatability, and narrative fluency (Johnson et al., 2018). These figures are often constructed by the media through a logic of personality-led representation that transforms complex science into compelling personal stories, sometimes blurring boundaries between scientific authority and entertainment. In this respect, medfluencers and health gurus perform a similar cultural role, embodying the expert-yet-approachable hybrid who simplifies science, builds public trust, and drives consumption behaviors within wellness fandoms.

A current example is the exuberant fandom surrounding the use of a pharmaceutical brand like the semaglutide GLP-1 agonist Ozempic. The multinational Danish pharmaceutical company Novo Nordisk and the pharmaceutical industry have built a powerful consumption world around Ozempic that offers an enticing portal to the imaginarium of a transformed, healthier, and more socially desirable self. The imaginarium is built with the narrative tools of the Four As: the Arcadia of a life free from the burdens of weight or illness; the Allegory of taking control of one's own body through modern science; the Aura of Oprah Winfrey's status; and the Antinomy of a diabetes drug becoming a lifestyle phenomenon (Williams and Monier, 2024). Riding on the back of this narrative, the Ozempic culture of consumption offers texts that include the direct-to-consumer television ads and sponsored testimonials from influencers, images that include "before and after" photos that circulate on social media, and objects that include the injectable pen itself, a piece of medical technology that becomes a tool for personal transformation.

This macro-level culture of consumption is ultimately translated into the intimate space of the home. We can analyze the medicine cabinet as a personal C4, a Continuous Consumption Collectible Constellation curated from the vast offerings of medical science. It is a material autobiography of one's health journey, containing a collection of objects from different and sometimes conflicting health "fandoms": the vitamins recommended by one podcast host, the prescription medication from a trusted family doctor, the herbal remedy passed down through generations, and the over-the-counter brand one's parents always used. Each object is a node in a different story, and the collection as a whole represents the individual's unique and ongoing project of self-care.

The concept extends to the institutions of medicine. The consumption world of health is composed not only of hospitals but also of pharmacies, vitamin stores, massage clinics, and the many other fantasy locations of healing. We can treat the hospital or the wellness clinic as a complex consumption world—a deliberately staged environment designed to produce a specific kind of experience, a "festive performance" of healing where architecture, uniforms, and professional scripts all work together to create an aura of safety and expertise. By applying the Fandom Lens, we see that our relationship transcends the logical and rational. It is consumerist at its core, branded and brand-centric, a profoundly narrative-driven quest for a better self, shaped by the same dynamics of passion, identity, and collective meaning-making that we also see in media fandom.

Implications

When we opened this book, we started with a defense of studying consumers not as exploited dupes, but as creative and passionate agents who build meaningful worlds from the raw materials provided by consumer culture, usually within a budget, and often to their consider-able satisfaction. That is, consumer culture does seem to offer people, ourselves included, a lot of pleasure. It seems silly, then, not to study it. We have journeyed from the personal altar of a Little Jimmy action figure to the global flows that shape our political lives, looked into the modern manifestation of Gemeinschaft and Gesellschaft, considered in great detail the drives and practices of collectors of many kinds, devel-oping a nested and networked framework called the Nested Fandom Collective model (NFC model), also colloquially known as the Fandom Lens along the way. In this final section, we draw out the explicit impli-cations of the Fandom Lens or Nested Fandom Collectives and Flows model, offering our integrated toolkit as something that can change the way scholars think, the way public relations and marketing brand managers manage brands, and the way fans do fandom.

New Heuristics for Connectable Worldbuilding

This book is, ultimately, about worldbuilding. Whether it takes place through genetic information shared on global platforms, enabling Rob to continually identify new family members around the world, or whether it is #Demthrones translating *Game of Thrones* for Black Twit-ter, whether it is Maradona through the generations, uniting everyone in Napoli, or whether it is Star Trek's *Official Fan Club* magazine reminding us of the uniqueness and fragility of community in the face of the modern marketplace, or whether it is the emergence of collective effervescence on Napster or in Silicon Valley workplaces, or the way *He-Man* figures or *American Girl* dolls anoint the connective tissues of particular collectives, we are talking about the construction of imaginary worlds that transform into spaces for habitation: imaginaria. The search for examples of these spaces encompasses much more than the traditional entertainment properties, including geocaching and its science fictional zones of indeterminacy, and Bullwinkle, Natasha, and Rocky zipping by in a flying saucer in Jay Ward's Quisp Cereal case study, in all its quirky richness.

This book presents, in its entirety, a new integrated and nested model through which to understand consumer collectives such as fandoms. The personal collection serves as a site of intimacy and satisfaction while facilitating contact with the culture of consumption. What drives it is a belief in narrative, a faith in the Four As of Arcadia (especially the utopian), Allegorical story, Walter Benjamin's Aura, and The Antimony of the conflict, even the enemy. What motivates it is an underlying hunger and a need for perpetual reamusement. What satisfies it, temporarily, is entry into a specialized consumption world that offers exciting experiences and tantalizing hints of the imaginaria. That consumption world could be contained in a comic book or a book, encapsulated in a movie or TV show, or experienced through an amusement park ride or an amusement park itself. What forms consumer culture are Appadurai's five scapes. Consumption worlds are fragmentable, fragmentary, and fragmenting, but some may have nearly permanent cores or tap into ancient drives and ideals.

When combined, the toolkit offers a shared language for analyzing passionate collectives, much of which was previously published but never before integrated in this manner. The application of this model awaits any discipline—not just political science and organization management, but also nursing, computer science, linguistics, and many more.

We will demonstrate its application to two academic fields here—education and geography—with a few quick thoughts about climate science. Consider whether a nested fandom viewpoint might offer a collective perspective on some of the paradoxical issues faced by educators. Can we say that "fandoms" often form around charismatic pedagogical theories or influential educational thinkers? Would it make sense to see these theories and their thinkers, as well as the "stars" and "influencers" of the educational instruments, as creating cultures of consumption complete with their own sacred texts, revered objects (e.g., specific curricula), and an imaginarium of the "ideal classroom"?

What about geography and tourism studies? Can a fandom lens help cultivate comprehension about how cities and regions raise a "fandom" through branding and the creation of a consumption world of tourist sites and local experiences? How can it be placed into a place so as to provide tantalizing access to the enchanting imaginarium of a place? Why not place climate science under the lens and look at its contending narratives and the varying consumption worlds upon which it impinges and is impinged—a struggle of narratives, imaginaria, consumption worlds, and access to consumption worlds and cultures of consumption, and perhaps a threat to them. The model coaxes us to look beyond surface-level affiliations and try to see the narrative, material, and psychological mechanics; the networked flows; and the managed systems that attract, collect, and bind these collectives together.

A New Toolkit for a New Era of Market Communication Practice

If you are a manager, this next question is for you. Do you still feel like "managing customers"? The stakes in this poker game just went up. The 7-part Swiss Army knife we just handed you, with each tool corresponding to C4, Cultures of Consumption, the Four As, Consumption Worlds, Scapes, Imaginaria, and the Empty Self/Enchantment cycle, could make a difference to how you do your marketing and branding in this fan-driven and digital age.

The framework in this book offers some fundamental changes in how we think about working with consumers. Psychographics and demographics as tools of market segmentation can be significantly boosted by thinking about how they link with the competing imaginaria that different consumer groups inhabit. Brand positioning transcends any functionality or feature list and instead becomes one hundred percent about crafting a powerful and resonant narrative built from the Four As. Brand storytelling lies at the very core of the model. And the model tells us that the key type of management leadership is the kind that can furnish a compelling consumption world for employees and customers alike.

Consequently, the managerial focus shifts from the tactical management of products to the strategic curation of these interconnected systems of meaning. The lifecycle of a product becomes secondary to the ongoing evolution of the consumption world it inhabits, demanding a level of narrative coherence across all touchpoints—from R&D to customer service interactions. Performance metrics must also evolve. Traditional KPIs like short-term ROI or market share, although still relevant for some purposes, are insufficient for enacting the type of narrative brand enterprise that contemporary businesses have become. They must be augmented by measures of community health, narrative resonance, and the brand's ability to facilitate the ongoing enchantment cycle. This requirement necessitates a move beyond the social quantitative dashboards of today toward qualitative and ethnographic approaches that map the contours of consumer imaginaria. In this model, the manager becomes a godlike figure, like the player of Sid Meier's Civilization or Spore, presiding over the evolution a brand's core stories as they evolve in concert with the ever-flowing scapes of a living, changing sociocultural environment.

This is where the true paradigm shift occurs, equipping the manager with a control deck previously unimaginable. The conceptual framework of the Fandom Lens becomes the operational logic for a new generation of technological tools. A sophisticated digital social dashboard becomes the central nervous system, enacting an ongoing netnography with the world. The manager is tasked with launching, tuning, and keeping up with transformations of business, product category, and brand imaginaria in real time, identifying which elements of a brand's Four A narrative are resonating or not, detecting the genesis of new fan-driven rituals, and collecting practices. This type of analysis is not market research as we know it. Management becomes a continuous and active act of observing, understanding, adjusting, and communicating in an organic narrative ecosystem, utilizing and constantly consulting the deep cultural intelligence required for authentic engagement.

Brand and product managers become next generation meaning managers, with an unprecedented creative arsenal at their fingertips.

Brainstorming and generative AI become the co-pilots in the narrative creation process. Fed with insights from the analytical dashboard, these tools can generate potential story extensions, product concepts, or social media artifacts that the system finds to be consonant with the brand's established Aura and Allegory. Yet AI by itself flies blind. The crucial work of synthesis, taste, and strategic direction remains an inherently human task. The brand manager's work becomes synthesized with that of a Hollywood showrunner and a social media community manager: a master curator who orchestrates a complex symphony of data analytics, AI-driven creation, online community orchestration, and human story-telling. Branding now means seeding narrative threads, empowering fan co-creation, and ensuring in an ongoing way that the consumption world remains relevant, enchanting, and meaningful.

Aca-Fan Reflexivity and the Question of Need

To be an aca-fan is not just to research fandom, nor merely to iden-tify with it. It is to look both inward and outward—to participate and to question, to love something deeply while also interrogating what that love means, where it comes from, and what it asks of you. This book has equipped fans, and especially aca-fans, with a conceptual toolkit that does exactly that. The Nested Fandom Collectives model shows us, even diagrammatically, how fandom operates at various levels of human scale, from the home to the store to the convention to the theme park, and similarly, it tells us how brands co-opt our passions. But perhaps more tellingly than any of this is the way it shines a light on the connective threads between the puppet arms of our personal attachments and the puppeteer hands of the larger architectures of meaning and power in which they are entangled.

We can use the fandom lens to decode our own enthusiasms. Why do we construct these intricate worlds of attachment, care, rivalry, and devotion? Why do we collect? What do we connect to? Part of the answer is joy. Fandom brings us pleasure. It is playful and communal and inventive in a way few other aspects of our lives are. But this book has also asked us to consider something deeper. Fandoms do more than entertain us. They offer identity when identity feels unstable. They offer belonging when institutions have withdrawn. They offer narrative when the world feels incoherent. They offer ritual and repetition in a secular time.

So the question the aca-fan must ask is not simply What do I love? but What need is being met by this love? Is it an echo of Cushman's "empty self"? Is our shopping merely a way of browsing for cheap substitute sources of meaning, identity, and emotional replenishment? Or perhaps it is legitimate and vital, an act of self-extension, a vital feeding of our imagination, a source of inspiration, a reaching outward toward others, toward play, and toward the fulfillment of **Fandom as Co-creation**? Our fandoms console us, inspire us, and give us things to focus on, talk about, post about, and think about, and they sometimes compensate for what's missing. But they also challenge us to become more than we are. They give us tools for worldbuilding.

The concept of the imaginarium reminds us that fandom is not there simply to fill up an empty self. Fandom populates a possible world with possible selves. Fans inhabit the identities and cultures and co-produce it. They assemble authentic-seeming towers of meaning, whole cities even, out of the fragments and cookie crumbs of commercial culture. They smelt Gesellschaft from Gemeinschaft and place bricks in the edifices of consumption worlds. They raise from the earth sacred geographies of meaning, significance, and affect.

This is the deeper function of the aca-fan: not just to defend fandom, but to reflect on it. Not just to celebrate the pleasures of consumption, but to ask what lies beneath them. It becomes an almost sacrosanct task to race across the waves raging between enchantment and need, between story and structure, and between identity and infrastructure. In this book, we take fandom and consumption seriously by considering them as a specific type of social configuration, a cultural system, an emotional economy, a social technology, and a lived philosophy. And so we close with more questions than answers. If this book has helped you to ask those questions, then it has completed its mission. The rest is up to you.

GLOSSARY

———

#BlackVanlife: A social media movement and community that highlights the experiences and challenges of Black individuals participating in vanlife culture, challenging the often white-centric narratives of this lifestyle.

#DemThrones: A hashtag and online community where Black fans of Game of Thrones reimagined the show's characters and narratives through a Black cultural lens.

Actor-Network Theory (ANT): A theoretical framework that views both humans and non-human objects as "actants" with agency, emphasizing the interconnectedness and relationships within networks.

Allegory: The use of symbolic narratives to explore deeper meanings and cultural values in branding; one of the Four As of brand narrativity.

Ambiguous Brands: Brands that cultivate complex and multilayered narratives, often embracing contradictions and inviting diverse interpretations.

Antinomy: The presence of contradictions and paradoxes within brand narratives that create intrigue and engagement; one of the Four As of brand narrativity.

Appraisal: The process of assessing the value and worth of a particular fan object, which can include monetary value, historical significance, or personal meaning.

Arcadia: The creation of an idealized or utopian world associated with the brand; one of the Four As of brand narrativity.

Ascribed Social Categories: Social groupings that individuals are born into or assigned, such as family, race, or social class.

Aura: [From Walter Benjamin (1936/1969)] The unique, authentic, and credible character of a brand, often associated with its history and origins; one of the Four As of brand narrativity.

Auto-netnography: A research method that combines autoethnography (the study of one's own experiences) with netnography (the study of online communities).

Blitzkrieg Ethnography: A term used to describe the rapid, multi-sited approach to ethnographic research employed during the Consumer Behavior Odyssey.

Brand Community: A specialized, non-geographically bound community, based on a structured set of social relations among admirers of a brand.

Brand Desire Spiral: A concept that describes how brands engage consumers in progressively deeper levels of engagement and desire through multiple touchpoints and experiences.

Branded Freedom Consumer Collective: An unstructured but official group that operates within a brand-provided framework but maintains informal interactions, such as the LEGO Ideas community.

Brand Narrativity: The storytelling qualities of a brand, including its history, values, and identity, that create a compelling and engaging narrative for consumers.

Burning Man: an annual countercultural event transpiring in Nevada's Gerlach dry lake bed, Black Rock City.

Collective Effervescence: A feeling of excitement and unity experienced by individuals within a group, often during shared rituals or experiences.

Collecting: The active, selective, and passionate acquisition and possession of objects removed from ordinary use and perceived as part of a set.

Consciousness of Kind: A sense of shared identity and belonging among members of a community, recognizing themselves as part of a distinct group.

Consumer: An individual who acquires or uses resources from a market-based system of images, texts, services, and objects not only to satisfy a range of needs, but also to make sense of their environment and to orient their experience and life

Consumer Behavior Odyssey: A research project led by Russell Belk in the 1980s that involved ethnographic fieldwork across the United States to study consumer culture.

Consumer Collective: A social group formed around a shared interest in a consumption activity, brand, product, or mass culture phenomenon. Examples include fandoms, brand communities, and subcultures of consumption.

Consumer Culture: A dynamic network of material, economic, symbolic, and social relationships or connections that function both as a sense-making device (or worldview) and a cultural blueprint.

Consumer Emancipation: The process of freeing consumers from the manipulative or exploitative aspects of consumer culture, allowing them to make informed and autonomous choices.

Consumer Revolution: A period of significant change in consumption patterns, marked by increased availability and variety of goods, often driven by economic and technological advancements.

Consumer Tribe: A network of individuals linked by a shared passion for a consumption activity, often engaging in collective action and advocacy; a contested and likely outdated concept.

Consumption Collective: As used by Arnould, Arvidsson, and Eckhardt (2021), a term to describe networks of social relations that form around consumer goods, brands, and commercial symbols.

Consumption Ethnogenesis: A process in which consumption practices are altered by the actions of ethnogenesis.

Consumption Worlds: Expansive, social networks of activity and cultural production centered around specific mass culture offerings

Counter-storytelling: The act of challenging dominant narratives by sharing alternative perspectives and experiences, often by marginalized groups.

Cultural Capital: Non-financial social assets, such as knowledge, skills, and taste, that contribute to social mobility and status.

Culture of Consumption: A system of commercially produced images, texts, and objects that groups use to make sense of their world and orient their lives.

Disembedding Mechanisms: Social processes that lift social relations out of local contexts and restructure them across time and space.

DNA Testing: The analysis of genetic material to determine ancestry and familial relationships.

Dyad: A group of two people, often characterized by high intimacy and strong social bonds.

Elective Affinities: The idea that individuals are drawn to each other based on shared interests, values, and experiences, leading to the formation of social groups.

Emic and Etic Perspectives: Emic refers to understanding a culture from an insider's perspective, while etic refers to analyzing a culture from an outsider's perspective, often using theoretical frameworks and categories.

Ethnogenesis: The process by which a group of people comes to identify as a distinct ethnic group, often involving the construction of shared narratives and cultural practices.

Ethnography: A qualitative research method that involves immersing oneself in a particular culture or community to observe and understand their behaviors, beliefs, and practices.

Ethnoscapes: Global flows of people, including tourists, immigrants, and refugees, that contribute to the diversity and complexity of cultural landscapes.

Fan Object: The focus of a fandom's interest, which can be a media franchise (e.g., Star Wars, Harry Potter), a brand (e.g., Apple, Harley-Davidson), a celebrity, a sport, a hobby, or any other cultural object or activity.

Fandom: A dedicated and passionate collective of fans who share a common interest in a particular media franchise, brand, or cultural phenomenon; a specific type of consumer collective.

Fanship: The individual's connection to and engagement with a fan object.

Feminist Perspectives: Approaches that examine gender dynamics and challenge traditional power structures and representations of women.

Financescapes: Global flows of capital and financial resources that shape economic activity and global markets.

Four As of Brand Narrativity: A framework for analyzing brand narratives, consisting of Arcadia, Allegory, Aura, and Antinomy.

Friendship Steering: The practice of directing individuals towards others based on assumed shared identities, potentially leading to exclusion and marginalization.

Gemeinshaft: A type of social group characterized by close, personal relationships, shared values, and a strong sense of community, often associated with traditional, rural societies.

Gesellschaft: A type of social group characterized by impersonal, contractual relationships, individualism, and a focus on self-interest, often associated with modern, urban societies.

Genealogy: The study of family history and lineage.

Gendered Collecting: The influence of societal expectations and gender roles on the types of objects people collect and the meanings associated with them.

Global Flows: The movement of cultural products, ideas, and people across national borders in a globalized world.

Grimdark: A subgenre of fantasy and science fiction characterized by a bleak, dystopian setting and morally ambiguous characters; originally from descriptions of Warhammer.

Haplogroup: A genetic population group of people who share a common ancestor.

Harley Owners Group (H.O.G. ®): A brand-sponsored community for Harley-Davidson motorcycle enthusiasts.

Heritage Tourism: Travel motivated by a desire to connect with one's ancestral roots and cultural heritage.

Humanistic Methods: Research approaches that emphasize empathy, understanding, and the subjective experiences of individuals and groups.

Hybrid Economy: An economic system that combines elements of both market and gift economies, often found in consumer collectives and fandoms.

Imaginary: a shared set of values, institutions, laws, and symbols common to a particular social group

Imaginarium: rich, narratively-dense, and psychologically resonant spaces that fans and consumers collectively inhabit

Intimacy: The depth of emotional connection and closeness among members of a collective, shaped by shared experiences, trust, and vulnerability.

Linking Value: The ability of a product or service to create and sustain social bonds among consumers.

Loyal Customer: An individual who consistently purchases a specific brand or product, potentially due to habit, convenience, or satisfaction, but not necessarily with passionate enthusiasm.

Marketing and Consumer Research: Academic disciplines that study consumer behavior, motivations, and decision-making processes, as well as the strategies used by businesses to reach and engage consumers.

Material Autobiographies: The idea that collections can serve as a reflection of the collector's life, experiences, and identity.

Materialism: The belief that possessions are the key to happiness and fulfillment.

Materiality: The relationship between people and the material world, recognizing the agency of objects and their role in shaping human experiences.

Mediascapes: Global flows of images, narratives, and cultural symbols that shape our understanding of the world.

Melungeon: A historically marginalized group in the Appalachian region of the United States, often perceived as having mixed Native American, African, and European ancestry.

Moral Economy: The social norms and shared understandings that govern transactions and relationships in close social groups based on caring and sharing, and which are often based on notions of fairness, reciprocity, gifting, and community values.

Moral Responsibility: A sense of duty and obligation towards other members of a collective, often expressed through mutual support and assistance.

Narrativity: The quality of being narrative or story-like, involving elements such as characters, plot, setting, and conflict.

Netnography: A qualitative research method that adapts ethnographic techniques to the study of online groups, social media, and immersive technology experiences.

Official Collective: A group formally affiliated with or endorsed by a brand or organization, often providing access to resources and official channels but potentially limiting autonomy.

Official Fan Spaces: Spaces or activities officially sanctioned or endorsed by media producers or brands, often characterized by greater producer control and consequent limitations on fan creativity.

Oppositional Brand Loyalty: A process where community members strengthen their identity by defining themselves against competing brands or communities.

Participatory Culture: A culture where individuals actively participate in the creation and sharing of content, blurring the lines between producers and consumers.

Passionate Brand Enthusiast: A consumer who demonstrates fanlike qualities in their engagement with a brand, exhibiting strong enthusiasm and emotional connection.

Performativity: The idea that actions and utterances can shape social reality and create or reinforce social structures.

Praxiology: The study of human action and practice.

Produser: A term that emphasizes the blurring of lines between technology use and media production, highlighting the active role of consumers in shaping media and culture.

Prosumer: A consumer who also actively produces content and participates in the creation of cultural products and experiences.

Qualitative Methods: Research techniques that focus on exploring and understanding the meanings, experiences, and social contexts of individuals and groups, often through in-depth interviews, observations, and textual analysis.

Quantitative Methodologies: Research methods that focus on collecting and analyzing numerical data to identify patterns and relationships.

Reflexive Project of the Self: The ongoing process of self-construction and identity formation in relation to personal and collective narratives.

Regulated Affiliation Consumer Collective: A structured and official group with formalized rules and hierarchies, often providing access to resources but potentially limiting creative freedom, such as the Harley Owners Group.

Rubbish Theory: A framework for understanding how the value and meaning of objects change over time, moving between categories of rubbish, transient, and durable.

Scapes: (from Arjun Appadurai) five distinct, yet interconnected, dimensions of global cultural flow

Self-Governing Consumer Collective: A structured but unofficial group that operates with formalized rules and organization, such as a local running club.

Shared Rituals and Traditions: Common practices, customs, and celebrations that reinforce community bonds and express shared values.

Size: The number of participants in a collective, influencing the types of interactions and relationships possible within the group.

Structured Collective: A group with formalized rules, hierarchies, and organized activities, such as clubs or official fan organizations.

Stuff: material culture, including everyday objects and the meanings/memories they carry for us

Subculture of Consumption: A distinctive subgroup of society that self-selects on the basis of a shared commitment to a particular product class, brand, or consumption activity.

Symbiosis: A close and long-term relationship between two different organisms, often implying mutual benefit; in the consumer collective context, it refers to the relationship between marketers and consumer collectives such as subcultures of consumption.

Technoscapes: Global flows of technology and technological information that influence how we connect and communicate.

Thing Power: The agency and influence of objects in shaping human experiences and relationships.

Touchpoint: Any interaction a consumer has with a brand, product, or service, including advertising, social media, customer service, and product use.

Transmedia Storytelling: A narrative strategy where a story unfolds across multiple media platforms, creating a more immersive and participatory experience for audiences.

Triadic Structure of Consumer Collectives: A model that illustrates the interconnected relationships between individual consumers, fan objects, and collectives, with fandom acting as the connective force.

Unofficial Collective: A group that emerges organically from shared interests and passions, independent of formal affiliations, offering greater autonomy but potentially lacking resources.

Unofficial Fan Spaces: Spaces or activities created and organized by fans independently of official channels, often characterized by greater freedom and creativity.

Unstructured Collective: A group with fluid participation, informal interactions, and flexible organization, allowing for spontaneous engagement and individual expression.

Utility Maximization: A principle from economics that assumes consumers make rational choices to maximize their satisfaction (or "utility") from purchases.

Value vs. Worth: Value refers to the economics of exchange, including both exchange value and use value; worth refers to the meaningfulness of a transaction, including personal and collective forms of sentimental and symbolic associations

Virtual Communities of Consumption: Online collectives that form around shared consumption interests, such as brand enthusiasts, collectors, or hobbyists.

Youthscapes: The material and symbolic environments that shape the experiences and identities of young people.

Zones of Indeterminacy: Spaces where the meanings of transactions or exchanges are intentionally blurred, allowing for the coexistence of different economic logics.

EXERCISE

Deepening the Exploration of Consumer Collectives

Please note that, although they were designed for workshop or classroom facilitation, these exercises can also be completed individually or in any small group formation of your choice. They are reflective exercises intended to deepen your thinking about the topics in this book. You are welcome to customize them as you see fit.

Activity 1 Description: Choose one special object from your home, preferably one that is related to a fandom or passionate commitment of yours. Write about it. Describe the item and its importance to you. Find one or more like-minded others and present your object to them. Tell them the object's story. Relate how its story relates to your story. If they are willing, have them do the same exercise. Share your results. Think about how you can better understand your relationships with this object and what it represents. In what way does this object connect you to yourself? In what way does it connect you to other people? Discuss and consider these and other ideas relating to your relationship to this special object. You might broaden to consider other special objects as well.

Activity 2 Description: Consider one consumer collective or fandom you are personally involved in. Examples could include brands (Apple, Nike), franchises (Marvel, Harry Potter), hobbies (running, gaming), or communities (a local sports team, a favorite band's fan group).

For the collective, answer some or all of the following questions. These questions can be discussed in a group or class context as well.

    i. **Type of Collective:** Should this be classified as a subculture of consumption, a brand community, a culture of consumption, or another type? Why? How would you catalog it based on the different dimensions described in this book?

    ii. **Engagement:** How do you engage with this collective? For example, this could include attending events, following social media accounts, purchasing products, or engaging in discussions.

    iii. **Shared Values and Rituals:** What common values or rituals are present in the collective?

    iv. **Online vs. Offline Engagement:** How do virtual and physical spaces shape the collective experience?

    v. **Types of Membership:** Are these groups highly inclusive, or do they have barriers to entry (e.g., knowledge, resources, exclusivity)?

    vi. **Fandom Lens**: Can you see the various operations of the Fandom Lens (scapes, culture of consumption, consumption worlds, C4, etc.) at work within your fandom?

SOURCES

Althusser, Louis (2006/1970), *Lenin and Philosophy and Other Essays*. Aakar Books.

Appadurai, Arjun (1986), *The Social Life of Things: Commodities in Cultural Perspective*. University of Cambridge Press.

Appadurai, Arjun (1990), "Disjuncture and difference in the global economy," *Theory, Culture & Society*, 7, 295–310.

Ariely, Dan (2008), *Predictably Irrational*. New York: HarperCollins.

Arnould, Eric J., Adam Arvidsson, and Giana M. Eckhardt (2021), "Consumer collectives: A history and reflections on their future," *Journal of the Association for Consumer Research*, 6(4), 415-428.

Arnould, Eric J., Craig J. Thompson, David Crockett, and Michelle F. Weinberger, Eds. (2023), "Introduction," in Arnould, Eric J., Craig J. Thompson, David Crockett, and Michelle F. Weinberger, (Eds.), *Consumer Culture Theory, 2nd Edition* (pp. 1-12). SAGE.

Bacon-Smith, Camille (1992), *Enterprising Women: Television Fandom and the Creation of Popular Myth*. University of Pennsylvania Press.

Barenscott, Dorothy (2024), "Trumpism, NFTs, and the cultural politics of 21st-century kitsch." In Grant Hamming and Natalie E. Phillips (Eds.), *Interrogating the Visual Culture of Trumpism* (pp. 28-36). Routledge.

Barthes, Roland (1966), "Introduction to the structural analysis of narratives." In Jeppe Sinding Jensen (Ed.), *Myths and Mythologies* (pp. 290-307). Routledge.

Baym, Nancy K. (1993), "Interpreting soap operas and creating community: Inside a computer-mediated fan culture," *Journal of Folklore Research*, 30 (2/3), 143-176.

Belk, Russell W. (1975), "Situational variables and consumer behavior," *Journal of Consumer Research*, 2(3), 157-164.

Belk, Russell W. (1988), "Possessions and the extended self," *Journal of Consumer Research*, 15(2), 139-168.

Belk, Russell W., ed. (1991), *Highways and Buyways: Naturalistic Research from the Consumer Behavior Odyssey*, Provo, UT: Association for Consumer Research.

Belk, Russell W. (1998), "The Double Nature of Collecting: Materialism and Antimaterialism," *Etnofoor*, 11 (1), 7-20.

Belk, Russell W. (2013), *Collecting in a Consumer Society*. Routledge.

Belk, Russell W. (2014), "The labors of the Odysseans and the legacy of the Odyssey," *Journal of Historical Research in Marketing*, 6(3), 379-404.

Belk, Russell, and Gülnur Tumbat (2005), "The cult of Macintosh." *Consumption Markets & Culture*, 8(3), 205-217.

Belk, Russell W., and Melanie Wallendorf (2012), "Of mice and men: gender identity in collecting." In Susan M. Pearce (Ed.), *Interpreting Objects and Collections* (pp. 240-253). Routledge.

Benjamin, Walter (1936/1969), "The work of art in the age of mechanical reproduction." In Hannah Arendt (Ed.), Harry Zohn (trans.), *Illuminations* (pp. 218-222). Houghton Mifflin Harcourt.

Bennett, Jane (2010), *Vibrant Matter: A Political Ecology of Things*. Duke University Press.

Bennett, Tony and Janet Woollacott (1987), *Bond and Beyond: The Political Aesthetics of England's Greatest Secret Agent*. Macmillan Education.

Bensman, Joseph and Arthur J. Vidich (1995), "Race, ethnicity and new forms of urban community." In Philip Kasinitz (Ed.), *Metropolis: Center and Symbol of Our Times* (pp. 196- 203). New York University Press.

Biggart, Nicole Woolsey (1989), *Charismatic Capitalism: Direct Selling Organizations in America*. University of Chicago Press.

Bishop, Jeff, and Paul Hoggett (1986), *Organizing Around Enthusiasms: Patterns of Mutual Aid in Leisure*. Comedia.

Blackshaw, Tony (2010), *Leisure*. Routledge.

Bloom, John (2002), "Cardboard patriarchy: Adult baseball card collecting and the nostalgia for a presexual past." In Henry Jenkins (Ed.), *Hop on Pop: The Politics and Pleasures of Popular Culture* (pp. 66-87), Duke University Press.

Booth, Paul (2010), *Digital Fandom: New Media Studies*. Peter Lange.

Booth, Paul, Amber Davisson, Aaron Hess, and Ashley Hinck (2018), *Poaching Politics: Online Communication During the 2016 US Presidential Election*. Peter Lange.

Bourdieu, Pierre (1984), *Distinction: A Social Critique of the Judgement of Taste*. Harvard University Press.

Brandon C. Boatwright and Karen Freberg (2023), "Exploring the value of multi-modal corporate influencers: A case study of Peloton instructors' engagement, community building, and branding functions," *International Journal of Strategic Communication*, 17(2), 134-150.

Brown, Stephen, Robert V. Kozinets, and John F. Sherry, Jr. (2003), "Sell me the old, old story: Retromarketing management and the art of brand revival," *Journal of Customer Behavior*, 2 (June), 85-98.

Brown, Stephen, Pierre McDonagh, and Clifford J. Shultz (2013), "Titanic: Consuming the myths and meanings of an ambiguous brand," *Journal of Consumer Research*, 40(4), 595-614.

Bruner, Jerome (1987), "Life as narrative," *Social Research*, 54(1), 11-32.

Bruner, Jerome (1991), "The narrative construction of reality," *Critical Inquiry*, 18(1), 1-21.

Caldwell, Linda L. (2005), "Leisure and health: Why is leisure therapeutic?" *British Journal of Guidance & Counselling*, 33(1), 7–26.

Căpăţînă, Gabriela, and Florin Drăghescu (2015), "Success factors of new product launch: The case of iPhone launch," *International Journal of Economics and Finance*, 7(5), 61-70.

Chick, Garry (1998), "Leisure and culture: Issues for an anthropology of leisure," *Leisure Sciences*, 20(2), 111-133.

Clerc, Susan J. (1996),"DDEB, GATB, MPPB, and Ratboy: The X-Files' media fandom, online and off." In David Lavery, Angela Hague, and Marla Cartwright (Eds.), *Deny All Knowledge: Reading the X-files* (pp. 36-51). Syracuse University.

Clifford, James (1992), "Traveling cultures." In Lawrence Grossberg, Cary Nelson, and Paula Treichler (Eds.), *Cultural Studies* (pp. 96-116). Routledge.

Cook, Alex (2022). "Coins, toys and trading cards: 83% of collectors think their collection will pay off." *MagnifyMoney,* available at https://www.magnifymoney.com/news/collectors-survey/.

Cosgrove, Kenneth M. (2022), *Donald Trump and the Branding of the American Presidency,* Palgrave.

Cova, Bernard and Veronique Cova (2002), "Tribal marketing: The tribalisation of society and its impact on the conduct of marketing," *European Journal of Marketing,* 36(5/6), 595-620.

Cova, Bernard (1997), "Community and consumption: Towards a definition of the 'linking value' of product or services," *European Journal of Marketing,* 31(3/4), 297-316.

Cova, Bernard, and Franck Barès (2025), "Extricating the concept of linking value from its tribal gangue," *Marketing Theory,* 25(2), 167-175.

Crombez, Joel M., and Steven Panageotou (2020), "The United States of Trump Corp.: The 'not normal/new normal' governing style of a personal brand," *Fast Capitalism,* 17(1), 25-52.

Cushman, Philip (1990), "Why the self is empty: Toward a historically situated psychology" *American Psychologist,* 45(5), 599-611.

Dalli, Daniele (2021), "Consumers and consumption: From individual, to collective, and beyond," *Italian Journal of Marketing,* 1-4.

Davis, Erik (2005), *[Led Zeppelin IV].* Continuum.

De Castell, Suzanne, and Milena Droumeva (2022), "McLuhan meets convergence culture: Towards a new multimodal discourse," *MediaTropes,* 8(1), 1–14.

de Groot, Nina F., Britta C. van Beers, and Gerben Meynen (2021), "Commercial DNA tests and police investigations: A broad bioethical perspective," *Journal of Medical Ethics,* 47, 788-795.

Diamond, Nina, John F. Sherry Jr, Albert M. Muñiz Jr, Mary Ann McGrath, Robert V. Kozinets, and Stefania Borghini (2009), "American Girl and the brand gestalt: Closing the loop on sociocultural branding research," *Journal of Marketing,* 73(3), 118-134.

Dubois, Derek (2025), "Sneakerheads for Trump: Information flows in the online news media," *Online Information Review,* 49(3), 459–480.

Durkheim, Emile (1893/1933), *The Division of Labour in Society.* Macmillan.

Eco, Umberto (1985), "*Casablanca*: Cult movies and intertextual collage," *SubStance,* 14(2), 3-12.

Englis, Basil G. and Michael R. Solomon (1996), "Using consumption constellations to develop integrated communications strategies," *Journal of Business Research,* 37 (3), 183-191.

Epstein, Barbara (1991), *Political protest and Cultural Revolution: Nonviolent Direct Action in the 1970s and 1980s.* University of California Press.

Fanlore (2024), "*All About Star Trek Fan Clubs*" accessed on January 1, 2025, *Fanlore wiki.* Available at https://fanlore.org/wiki/All_About_Star_Trek_Fan_Clubs

Ferreira, Marcia Christina, and Daiane Scaraboto (2016), ""My plastic dreams": Towards an extended understanding of materiality and the shaping of consumer identities." *Journal of Business Research,* 69(1), 191-207.

Florini, Sarah (2019), "Enclaving and cultural resonance in Black *Game of Thrones* fandom," *Transformative Works and Cultures,* 29, accessed August 30, 2025, available at https://doi.org/10.3983/twc.2019.1498.

Firat, A. Fuat, and Alladi Venkatesh (1995), "Liberatory postmodernism and the reenchantment of consumption," *Journal of Consumer Research*, 22(3), 239-267.

Fiske, John (1989), *Understanding Popular Culture*. Routledge.

Fournier, Susan (1998), "Consumers and their brands: Developing relationship theory in consumer research," *Journal of Consumer Research*, 24(4), 343-373.

Fox, Kathryn Joan (1987), "Real punks and pretenders: The social organization of a counterculture," *Journal of Contemporary Ethnography*, 16 (October), 344-370.

Frederick, Christine (1929). *Selling Mrs. Consumer*. The Business Bourse.

Frenzen, Jonathan K., and Harry L. Davis (1990), "Purchasing behavior in embedded markets," *Journal of Consumer Research*, 17(1), 1-12.

Geertz, Clifford (1973). *The Interpretation of Cultures*. Basic Books.

Geraghty, Lincoln (2014). *Cult Collectors*. Routledge.

Giesler, Markus (2006), "Consumer gift systems," *Journal of Consumer Research*, 33(2), 283-290.

Godbey, Geoffrey (1999), *Leisure in Your Life: An Exploration*. Sagamore-Venture.

Goldie, John Gerard Scott (2016), "Connectivism: A knowledge learning theory for the digital age?" *Medical Teacher*, 38(10), 1064-1069.

Granovetter, Mark (1985), "Economic action and social structure: The problem of embeddedness," *American Journal of Sociology*, 91(3), 481-510.

Holbrook, Morris B., and Elizabeth Caldwell Hirschman (1993), *The Semiotics of Consumption: Interpreting Symbolic Consumer Behavior in Popular Culture and Works of Art*. Walter de Gruyter.

Hall, Stuart (1980), "Encoding/Decoding," In Stuart Hall et al. (Eds.), *Culture, Media, Language* (pp. 134–148). Hutchinson.

Hebdige, Dick (1979), *Subculture: The Meaning of Style*. Metheun.

Heljakka, Katriina and J. Tuomas Harviainen (2019), "From displays to dioramas to doll dramas: adult world building and world playing with toys." *American Journal of Play*, 11 (3), 351–378.

Hill, Jonathan D. (Ed.) (1996), *History, Power and Identity: Ethnogenesis in the Americas, 1492–1992*. University of Iowa Press.

Hills, Matt (2002), *Fan Cultures*. Routledge.

Hirschman, Elizabeth C. (1988), "The ideology of consumption: A structural-syntactical analysis of *Dallas* and *Dynasty*," *Journal of Consumer Research*, 15(3), 344-359.

Hirschman, Elizabeth C. (2010), "Evolutionary branding," *Psychology & Marketing*, 27(6), 568-583.

Hirschman, Elizabeth C., and Donald Panther-Yates (2007), "Suddenly Melungeon! Reconstructing consumer identity across the color line," in Russell W. Belk and John F. Sherry (Eds.), *Research in Consumer Behavior: Consumer Culture Theory*, (pp. 241-259). Emerald Group.

Hirschman, Elizabeth C., and Donald Panther-Yates (2008), "Peering inward for ethnic identity: Consumer interpretation of DNA test results," *Identity: An International Journal of Theory and Research*, 8(1), 47-66.

Hoggett, Paul and Bishop, Jeff (1986), *Organizing Around Enthusiasms: Mutual Aid in Leisure*. Comedia.

Holbrook, Morris B., and Mark W. Grayson (1986), "The semiology of cinematic consumption: Symbolic consumer behavior in *Out of Africa*." *Journal of Consumer Research*, 13(3), 374-381.

Holbrook, Morris B., and Elizabeth C. Hirschman (1982), "The experiential aspects of consumption: Consumer fantasies, feelings, and fun," *Journal of Consumer Research*, 9(2), 132-140.

Holbrook, Morris B., and Elizabeth Caldwell Hirschman (1993), *The Semiotics of Consumption: Interpreting Symbolic Consumer Behavior in Popular Culture and Works of Art.* Walter de Gruyter.

Hoole, Alice (2024), "This is my team... we've got this and we're not going to stand for any of this shit!': A queer anarchist do it yourself approach to football," *DIY, Alternative Cultures & Society*, 2(3), 243-256.

Hyde, Lewis (1983), *The Gift: Imagination and the Erotic Life of Property*. Vintage.

Iso-Ahola, Seppo E. (1980), *The Social Psychology of Leisure and Recreation*. Wm. C. Brown.

Jackson, Emma (2020), "Bowling together? Practices of belonging and becoming in a London ten-pin bowling league," *Sociology*, 54(3), 518-533.

James, William (1890), *The Principles of Psychology*, Volume 1. Henry Holt.

Jenkins, Henry (1988), "Star Trek rerun, reread, rewritten: Fan writing as textual poaching," *Critical Studies in Mass Communication*, 5 (2), 85-107.

Jenkins, Henry (1992), *Textual Poachers: Television Fans and Participatory Culture*. New York University.

Jenkins, Henry (1995), "'Do you enjoy making the rest of us feel stupid?': alt. tv. twinpeaks, the trickster author, and viewer mastery," in David Lavery (Ed.), *Full of Secrets: Critical Approaches to Twin Peaks* (pp. 51-69). Wayne State University.

Jenkins, Henry (2006), *Convergence Culture: Where Old and New Media Collide*. New York University.

Jenkins, Henry (2010), "Henry Jenkins and Camille Bacon-Smith at Gaylaxicon 1992," *Pop Junctions* (originally *Confessions of an Aca-Fan*), February 21, http://henryjenkins.org/blog/2010/02/gaylaxicon.html

Jenkins, Henry (2010), "He-Man and the masters of transmedia," Pop Junctions, May 20. http://henryjenkins.org/blog/2010/05/he-man_and_the_masters_of_tran.html

Jenkins, Henry (2010) "ARGs, fandom, and the digi-gratis economy: An interview with Paul Booth," *Pop Junctions*, August 13 http://henryjenkins.org/blog/2010/08/args_fandom_and_the_digi-grati.html

Jenkins, Henry (2013) "Thinking critically about brand cultures: An interview with Sarah Banet-Weiser," *Pop Junctions*, http://henryjenkins.org/blog/2013/04/thinking-critically-about-brand-cultures-an-interview-with-sarah-banet-weiser-part-one.html

Jenkins, Henry (2014), "Fandom studies as I see it," *Journal of Fandom Studies*, 2(2), 89-109.

Jenkins, Henry (2023), "How to Read *Uncle $crooge* After *How to Read Donald Duck*," *Participations*, 19 (3), 9-28.

Jenkins, Henry, Sam Ford and Joshua Green (2013), *Spreadable Media: Creating Meaning and Value in a Networked Culture*. New York University.

Johnson, David R., Elaine Howard Ecklund, Di Di, and Kirstin RW Matthews (2018), "Responding to Richard: Celebrity and (mis)representation of science," *Public Understanding of Science*, 27(5), 535-549.

Johnston, Josée, and Judith Taylor (2008), "Feminist consumerism and fat activists: A comparative study of grassroots activism and the Dove real beauty campaign," *Signs: Journal of Women in Culture and Society*, 33(4), 941-966.

Karababa, Eminegül, and Guliz Ger (2011), "Early modern Ottoman coffeehouse culture and the formation of the consumer subject," *Journal of Consumer Research*, 37 (5), 737–60.

Kennedy-Eden, Heather and Ulrike Gretzel (2021), "My heritage in my pocket: Mobile device and app use by genealogy tourists," *Journal of Information Technology & Tourism*, 23(3), 327–350.

Kennedy-Eden, Heather and Ulrike Gretzel (2022), "Personal heritage tourism," in Marina Novelli, Joseph M. Cheer, Claudia Dolezal, Adam Jones, and Claudio Milano (Eds.), *Handbook of Niche Tourism* (pp. 144-157). Edward Elgar.

Kim, Suweon (2023), "Almost South–South solidarity: The frustration of K-pop fans (but not true fans) in South Africa," *International Journal of Cultural Studies*, 26(5), 518-535.

Klein, Alan M. (1985), "Pumping iron," *Transaction; Social Science and Modern Society*, 22 (September/October), 68-75.

Klein, Alan M. (1986), "Pumping irony: Crisis and Contradiction in Bodybuilding," *Sociology of Sport Journal*, 3(June), 112- 133.

Kluch, Yannick (2015), "'The man your man should be like': Consumerism, patriarchy and the construction of twenty-first-century masculinities in 2010 and 2012 Old Spice campaigns," *Interactions: Studies in Communication & Culture*, 6(3), 361-377.

Kozinets, Robert V. (1997), "'I Want to Believe': A Netnography of The X-Philes' Subculture of Consumption," in Merrie Brucks and Deborah J. MacInnis (Eds.), *Advances in Consumer Research, Volume 24* (pp. 470-475). Association for Consumer Research.

Kozinets, Robert V. (1999), "E-tribalized marketing?: The strategic implications of virtual communities of consumption," *European Management Journal*, 17(3), 252-264.

Kozinets, Robert V. (2002), "Can consumers escape the market? Emancipatory illuminations from Burning Man," *Journal of Consumer Research*, 29(1), 20-38.

Kozinets, Robert V. and Mina Seraj-Aksit (2024), "Everyday activism: An AI-assisted netnography of a digital consumer movement," *Journal of Marketing Management*, 40 (3-4), 347-370.

Kozinets, Robert V. and Jay M. Handelman (1998), "Ensouling consumption: A netnographic exploration of the meaning of boycotting behavior." In Joseph Alba and Wesley Hutchinson (Eds.), *Advances in Consumer Research, Volume 25* (pp. 475-480), Association for Consumer Research.

Krauss, Lawrence M. (2015), "Scientists as celebrities: Bad for science or good for society?" *Bulletin of the Atomic Scientists*, 71(1), 26-32.

Latour, Bruno (1993), *We Have Never Been Modern*. Harvester Wheatsheaf.

Latour, Bruno (2005), *Reassembling the Social: An Introduction to Actor-Network-Theory*. Oxford University.

Lavin, Marilyn (1995), "Creating consumers in the 1930s: Irna Phillips and the radio soap opera," *Journal of Consumer Research*, 22(1), 75-89.

Lawson, Caitlin E. (2021), "Skin deep: Callout strategies, influencers, and racism in the online beauty community," *New Media & Society*, 23(3), 596-612.

Lears, Jackson (1995), *Fables of Abundance: A Cultural History of Advertising in America*. Basic Books.

Leff, Jim (2001), "Quisp!" *Chowhound*, May 22, accessed 19 November 2002, at https://www.chowhound.com/quisp.

Levy, Sidney J. (1966), "Stalking the amphisbaena," *Journal of Consumer Research*, 23(3), 163-176.

Levy, Sidney J. (1959), "Symbols for sale," *Harvard Business Review*, 37 (4), 117–124.

Lomax, Tara (2024), "Marvel on the shelf: The art and play of the action figure," *Pop Junctions* (previously *Confessions of an Acafan*), December 21 https://henryjenkins.org/blog/2024/12/20/marvel-on-a-shelf-the-art-and-play-of-action-figure-display.

Maffesoli, Michel (1996), *The Time of the Tribes: The Decline of Individualism in Mass Society*. SAGE.

Magrath, Rory (2021), "Gay male football fans' experiences: Authenticity, belonging and conditional acceptance," *Sociology*, 55(5), 978-994.

Maira, Sunaina, and Elisabeth Soep (2011), *Youthscapes: The Popular, The National, The Global*. University of Pennsylvania.

Marcus, George E. (1995), "Ethnography in/of the world system: The emergence of multi-sited ethnography." *Annual Review of Anthropology* 24(1), 95-117.

Marketing Week (1996), "The toy fiasco that cost Disney 50m," *Marketing Week* June 22. Accessed June 23, 2024. Available at https://shorturl.at/HqSHG.

Martin, Diane M., John W. Schouten, and James H. McAlexander (2006), "Claiming the throttle: multiple femininities in a hyper-masculine subculture," *Consumption, Markets and Culture*, 9(3), 171-205.

Matthews, Tara, Kerwell Liao, Anna Turner, Marianne Berkovich, Robert Reeder, and Sunny Consolvo (2016), "'She'll just grab any device that's closer': A study of everyday device & account sharing in households," In *Proceedings of the 2016 CHI Conference on Human Factors in Computing Systems*, pp. 5921-5932.

Maurya, Upendra Kumar, and Prahlad Mishra (2012), "What is a brand? A perspective on brand meaning," *European Journal of Business and Management*, 4(3), 122–133.

McCarthy, Anna (2001), *Ambient Television: Visual Culture and Public Space*, Duke University.

McCracken, Grant (1986), "Culture and consumption: A theoretical account of the structure and movement of the cultural meaning of consumer goods." *Journal of Consumer Research*, 13(1), 71-84.

McCracken, Grant David (1988), *Culture and Consumption: New Approaches to the Symbolic Character of Consumer Goods And activities*. Indiana University Press.

McKee, Alan (2004a), "How to tell the difference between production and consumption: A case study in *Doctor Who* fandom," In Sarah Gwenllian-Jones and Roberta M. Pearson (Eds.), *Cult Television* (pp. 167-186). University of Minnesota Press.

McKee, Alan (2004b), "Is *Doctor Who* political?" *European Journal of Cultural Studies*, 7(2), 201-217.

McLuhan, Marshall (1964). *Understanding Media: The Extensions of Man*. McGraw Hill.

Miller, Daniel (2008). *The Comfort of Things*. Polity.

Miller, Daniel (2013), *Stuff*. Polity.

Miller, Daniel, Laila Abed Rabho, Patrick Awondo, Maya de Vries, Marília Duque, Pauline Garvey, Laura Haapio-Kirk, Charlotte Hawkins, Alfonso Otaegui, Shireen Walton and Xinyuan Wang (2021), *The Global Smartphone: Beyond a Youth Technology*. University College London.

Miller, Daniel and Jolynna Sinanan (2017), *Visualizing Facebook: A Comparative Perspective*, University College London.

Mullins, Paul R. (2018), "The materiality of consumer culture." In Olga Kravets, Alladi Venkatesh, Steven Miles, and Pauline Maclaran (Eds.), *The SAGE Handbook of Consumer Culture* (pp. 351-364). Sage.

Muñiz, Albert M., Jr., and Thomas C. O'Guinn (2001), "Brand Community," *Journal of Consumer Research*, 27 (4), 412–432.

Ng, Isaac K. S., Christope Thong, Li Feng Tan, and Desmond B. Teo (2024), "The rise of medical influencers: The pros and the cons," *Journal of the Royal College of Physicians of Edinburgh*, 54(3), 231–235.

Otnes, Cele C., Elizabeth Crosby, Robert Kreuzbauer, and Jennifer Ho (2008), "Tinsel, trimmings, and tensions: Consumer negotiations of a focal Christmas artifact." In Angela Y. Lee and Dilip Soman (Eds.), *NA—Advances in Consumer Research Volume 35* (pp. 773), Association for Consumer Research.

Parham, Jason (2021), "A People's History of Black Twitter," *Wired*, July 15, https://www.wired.com/story/black-twitter-oral-history-part-i-coming-together/.

Parry, Ken, Michael Cohen, Sukanto Bhattacharya, Andrea North-Samardzic, and Gareth Edwards (2019), "Charismatic leadership: Beyond love and hate and toward a sense of belonging?" *Journal of Management & Organization*, 25(3), 398-413.

Parry, Ken, and Steve Kempster (2014), "Love and leadership: Constructing follower narrative identities of charismatic leadership," *Management Learning*, 45(1), 21-38.

Pearce, Susan, Ed. (1994), *Interpreting Objects and Collections*. Routledge.

Pearson, Anthony (1987), "The Grateful Dead phenomenon," *Youth and Society*, 18 (June), 418-432.

Peer, Gregory Edward (2014), *Who We Are: How Sub-Cultural Capital Intensifies Communication Conflict between Whovians, Nuvians, and Fandom-At-Large*. [Unpublished Master's thesis]. San Diego State University.

Permarupan, P. Yukthamarani, Roselina Ahmad Saufi, Raja Suzana Raja Kasim, and Bamini KPD Balakrishnan (2013), "The impact of organizational climate on employee's work passion and organizational commitment," *Procedia-Social and Behavioral Sciences*, 107, 88-95.

Petersen, Line Nybro, Carrie Lynn D. Reinhard, Anthony Dannar, and Natalie Le Clue (2024), "New territories for fan studies: The insurrection, QAnon, Donald Trump and fandom," *Convergence*, 30(1), 313-328.

Petrelli, Daniela, and Ann Light (2014), "Family rituals and the potential for interaction design: a study of Christmas," *ACM Transactions on Computer-Human Interaction (TOCHI)*, 21(3), 1-29.

Pettigrew, Thomas F. (2017), "Social psychological perspectives on Trump supporters," *Journal of Social and Political Psychology*, 5 (1), 107-116.

Pomian, Krzysztof (2012), "The collection: Between the visible and the invisible." In Susan M. Pearce (Ed.), *Interpreting Objects and Collections* (pp. 160-174), Routledge.

Preece, Chloe, Finola Kerrigan, and Daragh O'Reilly (2019), "License to assemble: Theorizing brand longevity," *Journal of Consumer Research*, 46(2), 330-350.

Price, Linda L., and Eric J. Arnould (1999), "Commercial friendships: Service provider–client relationships in context," *Journal of Marketing*, 63(4), 38-56.

Propp, Vladimir (1968), *Morphology of the Folktale*. University of Texas.

Putnam, Robert D. (2000), *Bowling Alone: The Collapse and Revival of American Community*. Simon and Schuster.

Radway, Janice (1986), "Reading is not eating: Mass-produced literature and the theoretical, methodological, and political consequences of a metaphor," *Book Research Quarterly*, 2 (3), 7-29.

Raekstad, Paul, and Sofa Saio Gradin (2020), *Prefigurative Politics: Building Tomorrow Today*. Polity Press.

Raminnia, Maryam (2022), "Territorialization and deterritorialization in contemporary poetry: A Deleuzian perspective," *Literary Theory and Criticism*, 7(1), 259-282.

Reichler, Stephen and S. Alexander Haslam (2016), "The politics of hope: Donald Trump as an entrepreneur of identity," *Scientific American*, November 19.

Rheingold, Howard (1993), *The Virtual Community: Homesteading on the Electronic Frontier*. MIT.

Rodriguez, Nathian Shae, and Nadia Goretti (2022), "From hoops to hope: Alexandria Ocasio-Cortez and political fandom on Twitter," *International Journal of Communication*, 16, 65-84.

Rogers, Everett (1962), *Diffusion of Innovations*. Free Press of Glencoe.

Rojek, Chris (1995), *Decentering Leisure: Rethinking Leisure Theory*. Sage.

Sandvoss, Cornel (2013), "Toward an understanding of political enthusiasm as media fandom: Blogging, fan productivity and affect in American politics," *Participations: Journal of Audience & Reception Studies*, 10(1), 252-296.

Saunders, Robert A. (2024), "Genealogical journeys, geographical imagination, and (popular) geopolitics in *Who Do You Think You Are?*" *Social & Cultural Geography*, 25(5), 698-717.

Scaraboto, Daiane (2015), "Selling, sharing, and everything in between: The hybrid economies of collaborative networks," *Journal of Consumer Research*, 42(1), 152-176.

Schill, Dan, and John Allen Hendricks (2017), *The Presidency and Social Media*. Routledge.

Schneiker, Andrea (2019), "Telling the story of the superhero and the anti-politician as president: Donald Trump's branding on Twitter," *Political Studies Review*, 17(3), 210-223.

Schouten, John W. and James H. McAlexander (1995), "Subcultures of consumption: An ethnography of the new bikers," *Journal of Consumer Research*, 22(1), 43-61.

Schneider, Alexandra (2011) "'Jackie Chan is nobody, and so am I': Juvenile fan culture and the construction of transnational male identity in the Tamil diaspora." In Maira, Sunaina and Elisabeth Soep (Eds.), *Youthscapes: The Popular, The National, The Global* (pp.137-154). University of Pennsylvania.

Seregina, Anastasia, and Henri A. Weijo (2017), "Play at any cost: How cosplayers produce and sustain their ludic communal consumption experiences," *Journal of Consumer Research*, 44(1), 139-159.

Seregina, Anastasia, and John W. Schouten (2017), "Resolving identity ambiguity through transcending fandom," *Consumption Markets & Culture,* 20(2), 107-130.

Sinnott, Allison and Kyrie Zhixuan Zhou (2023), "How NFT collectors experience online NFT communities: A case study of Bored Ape," *arXiv preprint*. arXiv:2309.09320.

Stebbins, Robert A., Ed. (2007), *Serious Leisure: A Perspective for Our Time*. Routledge.

Straw, Will (2007), "Embedded Memories" in Charles R. Acland (Ed.) *Residual Media* (pp. 3-15), University of Minnesota Press.

Ström, Timothy Erik (2019), "Into the glorious future: The utopia of cybernetic capitalism according to Google's ideologues." In Chris Hudson and Erin K. Wilson (Eds.), *Revisiting the Global Imaginary: Theories, Ideologies, Subjectivities: Essays in Honor of Manfred Steger* (pp. 105-121). Springer International.

Sunderland, Patricia L., and Rita M. Denny (2016), *Doing Anthropology in Consumer Research*. Routledge.

Thompson, E. P. (1971), "The moral economy of the English crowd in the eighteenth century," *Past & Present*, 50 (1), 76-136.

Thompson, Michael (1979), *Rubbish Theory: The Creation and Destruction of Value*, Oxford University Press.

Tian, Kelly, and Russell W. Belk (2005), "Extended self and possessions in the workplace," *Journal of Consumer Research*, 32(2), 297-310.

Trentmann, Frank (2016), *Empire of Things: How We Became a World of Consumers from the Fifteenth Century to the Twenty-First*. Penguin.

Tucker, William (1967), *Foundations for a Theory of Consumer Behavior*. Holt, Rinehart and Winston.

Veblen, Thorstein (1899), *The Theory of the Leisure Class: An Economic Study of Institutions*. Macmillan.

Villegas, Dino A., and Alejandra Marin Marin (2022), "Bilingual brand communities? Strategies for targeting Hispanics on social medium," *Journal of Product & Brand Management*, 31(4), 586-605.

van Dijck, Jose (2013), *The Culture of Connectivity: A Critical History of Social Media*. Oxford University.

Walpersberger, Tatjana, and Ulrike Gretzel (2024), "Illusion of inclusion: #BlackVanlife as counter-storytelling," *Tourism Geographies*, 26(1), 32-50.

West, Rebecca J., and Bhoomi K. Thakore (2013), "Racial exclusion in the online world," *Future Internet* 5(2), 251-267.

White, Bryan, Aniket Mahanti, and Kalpdrum Passi (2022), "Characterizing the OpenSea NFT marketplace." In Frédérique Laforest and Raphaël Troncy (Eds.), *Companion Proceedings of the ACM WWW 2022 Virtual Event* (pp. 488-496). Association for Computing Machinery.

Williams, Apryl, and Mel Monier (2024), "Oprah and Ozempic: a commentary on Oprah Winfrey's 'shame, blame and the weight loss revolution,'" *Critical Studies in Media Communication*, 41(3), 263-268.

Williams, Raymond (1989), "Culture is ordinary," in Raymond Williams (Ed.), *Resources of Hope: Culture, Democracy, Socialism* (p. 3-14). Verso.

Williams, Rosalind (1982), *Dream Worlds: Mass Consumption in Late Nineteenth Century France*. University of California.

Wilson, Pamela (1999), "Virtual kinship in a postmodern world." In Greg M. Smith (Ed.), *On a Silver Platter: CD-ROMs and the Promises of a New Technology*, (pp. 184-210), New York University.

Woo, Benjamin (2014), "A pragmatics of things: Materiality and constraint in fan practices," *Transformative Works and Cultures*, 16, accessed August 30, 2025, available at https://doi.org/10.3983/twc.2014.0495.

Zafina, Nadzira, and Annapurna Sinha (2024), "Celebrity-fan relationship: studying Taylor Swift and Indonesian Swifties' parasocial relationships on social media," *Media Asia*, 51(4), 533-547.

INDEX

———

A

Aca-fan, 2, 14

Aca-fan reflexivity, 225

Aca-nomads, 62

Actor-Network Theory, 161

Active leisure, 55

Active vs. passive consumer, 54-55

Adele, 196

Advertising, 50, 55, 58

Affiliation (Official vs. Unofficial dimension), 83, 90, 93

Affirmational fandom, 141

African American Vernacular English (AAVE), 41

Agency, 34, 123

Alexander (family informant), 23

Algorithmic collective, 47

All About Star Trek Fan Clubs (magazine), 134, 137, 141

Allegory (in brand narrativity), 185, 188, 190, 209, 216, 222

Allen, Paul, 160

Alphabet, 106

Althusser, Louis, 35

Amazon, 216

Ambiguous brands, 199

Ambivalence (towards brand community), 105

American Girl doll (collecting forum), 158-159, 180, 221

Ancestry (platform), 18-20, 23, 26, 30, 47, 130

AncestryDNA, 21

Anti-fans, 111

Antinomy (in brand narrativity), 185, 188, 191, 212, 216, 222

Anonymity/Pseudonymity, 86

AO3 (Archive of Our Own), 23, 126, 143, 184

Aporia, 192

Appadurai, Arjun, 124, 127, 131, 137, 146, 204, 222

Appalachia, 27-28

Apple / Appleheads / iFans, 3, 38, 88, 90, 99, 103-104, 115, 122-123, 184-186, 192, 197-198, 206, 213, 215-216

Appraisal (concept), 155

Arcadia (in brand narrativity), 185, 188-189, 209, 216, 222

Arnould, Eric, 44, 52, 60, 66-67, 89, 121

Z

www.ingramcontent.com/pod-product-compliance
Lightning Source LLC
Chambersburg PA
CBHW062048270326
41931CB00013B/2990